P9-CIV-151

WEAPONS OF
MASS
DISTORTION

WEAPONS OF MASS DISTORTION

The Coming Meltdown of
the Liberal Media

L. Brent Bozell III

CROWN
FORUM
NEW YORK

Copyright © 2004 by L. Brent Bozell III

All rights reserved. No part of this book may be reproduced or transmitted in any form or by any means, electronic or mechanical, including photocopying, recording, or by any information storage and retrieval system, without permission in writing from the publisher.

Published by Crown Forum, New York, New York.
Member of the Crown Publishing Group, a division of Random House, Inc.
www.crownpublishing.com

CROWN FORUM and the Crown Forum colophon are trademarks of Random House, Inc.

Printed in the United States of America.

Design by Lauren Dong

Library of Congress Cataloging-in-Publication Data

Bozell, L. Brent.
Weapons of mass distortion : the coming meltdown of the liberal media
1. Journalism—Objectivity—United States. 2. Mass media—Objectivity—United States. 3. Journalism—Political aspects—United States. 4. United States—Politics and government—1993–2001. I. Title.
PN4888.O25B69 2004
302.23'0973—dc22
2003024679

ISBN 1-4000-5378-1

10 9 8 7 6 5 4 3 2 1

First Edition

For Norma

Contents

PART THREE

ACTORS, NOT OBSERVERS
How the Media Try to Influence Events

WEAPONS OF
MASS
DISTORTION

Introduction

Weapons of Mass Distortion

I n an April 10, 2002, appearance on CNN's *Larry King Live,* ABC News anchor Peter Jennings gave a remarkable answer when he was asked about media bias.

"Historically in the media, it has been more of a liberal persuasion for many years," Jennings said. "It has taken us a long time, too long in my view, to have vigorous conservative voices heard as widely in the media as they now are. And so I think, yes, on occasion there is a liberal instinct in the media which we need to keep our eye on, if you will."

It was an astonishing statement. For years, media analysts had been pointing out the pervasive liberal bias found in mainstream news coverage. In fact, in 1987 I founded an organization called the Media Research Center specifically to bring balance and responsibility to the news media, and for some fifteen years the center had been carefully and systematically documenting the extent of media bias. But despite all those efforts, news leaders had vigorously denied any charge of bias, no matter how thoroughly documented. Actually, for the most part the Jenningses, Brokaws, and Rathers refused even to acknowledge the charges, which they could get away with at a time when the American public was less attuned to the leftward slant in the press.

But that time had passed. Now, here was Peter Jennings, one of the

1

most important journalists in the country, acknowledging on national television that, yes, the charge of liberal bias was true.

Then again, was the statement really all that astonishing? Well, yes, simply because no one of his stature had ever come close to admitting that liberal bias existed. (Though Walter Cronkite had acknowledged the leftist bias permeating the airwaves, he did so long after he had retired from CBS News.) But if one looks closely at Jennings's answer, it becomes clear that, to the distinguished anchor of ABC News, media bias really isn't much of a problem at all. It's just an "instinct" that is evidenced only "on occasion." Like a slow leak in a tire, it's not something that demands an immediate repair. It's just something "we need to keep our eye on."

Jennings also betrayed a fundamental misunderstanding of *why* media bias is a problem. For "too long," he said, "conservative voices" were not "heard as widely in the media as they now are." Quite true, but that statement is slippery on two counts. First, who does Jennings mean by "conservative voices"—journalists or their guests? There is no empirical evidence I've seen that there has been any marked increase of conservatives in the newsrooms—note that we're talking about *newsrooms*, not the pundits' roundtables—of ABC, CBS, NBC, CNN, MSNBC, CNBC, and PBS. Second, if by "conservative voices" Jennings is referencing the opinions of conservatives within news stories, even if journalists are giving more airtime to conservatives, it doesn't follow that the *coverage* of those "conservative voices" is any more positive. The implication of his statement is that conservatives now are getting a fair shot in the media, which, as we'll see in this book, is patently untrue. Even more important, having more conservative voices heard in the mainstream media is just one small step toward balanced news coverage. Liberal bias affects much more than simply how certain political figures are covered and how certain news stories are reported. The media's pervasive bias determines precisely which stories are (and are not) covered, and in how much detail. Indeed, the media elite deliberately attempt to set the national agenda through their coverage of the news.

I have learned this firsthand in a career spent closely analyzing the news media, but the point was driven home to me several years ago at a meeting with a Los Angeles newspaper. The Media Research Center had just released an exhaustive study regarding liberal bias in the news media, and I was scheduled to meet with the editorial board of the (now-defunct) *Los Angeles Herald-Examiner* to discuss the report's findings. When I arrived, however, I was ushered into the conference room and met by a solitary figure, a member of the editorial board obviously pegged with the unsavory assignment of listening to this pesky conservative. The ponytailed hair and the cold body language—he silently pointed me to a chair—hinted that this would be anything but a productive meeting. I made an opening statement, then passed him the voluminous report we were to discuss. Without bothering to open it, the editor shoved it back at me and unleashed a vitriolic harangue against conservatives. Niceties flew out the window as he snarled, "All you conservatives care about is making money!" Clearly we weren't going to discuss the report, so I asked him what liberals like him cared about. Without bothering to deny my description of his ideological persuasion, he quickly shot back, "You just don't get it: We are the social conscience of this country and we have an obligation to use the media."

At least this editor had the decency to admit what so many others steadfastly deny. Yes, the mainstream news media's view of conservatives is less than flattering—the liberal media see conservatives as "the great unwashed," as Republican congressman Henry Hyde aptly put it—and that is a big problem. But just as important, and too often overlooked, is the problem of how the media view themselves. The media elites feel they must be the "social conscience of this country"; they seem to have a higher calling beyond objectively reporting what happens on a day-to-day basis. Reporters, editors, and producers routinely display an arrogance driven by an inflated sense of self-worth. They are the enlightened, the elite. This attitude cannot help but distort the way the news is covered.

Media bias is more than just something "we need to keep our eye on." It is an endemic problem, and even now, when the media have actually come under some scrutiny, the problem is not being seriously addressed. Although media bias has become the subject of debate in this country, the terms of that debate are far too narrow. Usually it is focused on a small subtopic, like the number of conservative commentators on television, when news *commentary* isn't even the issue—it is in news *reporting* that the journalist must strive for objectivity. Or it is focused on a particular statement that galls—say, CNN boss Ted Turner's insulting Christians—but examining such a statement, while instructive, doesn't begin to plumb the depths of the problem of liberal media bias.

Peter Jennings might think that the problem of media bias is pretty much solved, but as this book will show, liberal media bias is alive and well. The evidence of such bias is simply staggering.

The Liberal Counterattack

Although overwhelming evidence indicates that liberal bias in the mainstream news media continues unchecked, something important *has* changed in recent years. It is not just that news leaders like Peter Jennings have been forced for the first time to answer questions about media bias. No, the Left has come to believe that a battle is on and has begun to attack those dreaded conservatives who dare to challenge the authority and legitimacy of the "mainstream" news media. But the liberal counterattack has been bizarre. Some on the Left, refusing to admit to the longtime liberal dominance over the mainstream news media, go so far as to claim that there is actually a *conservative* media bias. According to a series of books released in 2002 and 2003, the vast right-wing conspiracy has somehow managed to conquer the news media as well. It is important, and won't take long, to demolish this mythology.

First out of the gate was *The Nation*'s Eric Alterman with the book *What Liberal Media?: The Truth About* Bias *and the News,* a response to the number one bestseller from former CBS newsman Bernard Goldberg, *Bias: A CBS Insider Exposes How the Media Distort the News.* (In his book Alterman condemns me for praising the media's powerful, if short-lived, patriotism in the days following the September 11 horror.) The *New York Observer's* Joe Conason followed with *Big Lies: The Right-Wing Propaganda Machine and How It Distorts the Truth,* in which he tries to "debunk conservative mythology," devoting a whole chapter to the "palpably ridiculous argument" that "liberals control the media." (It's instructive that Conason says of this writer that the "belligerent, red-bearded Bozell, a nephew of William F. Buckley Jr., scarcely pretends to be anything more than an instrument of the Republican Party's conservative leadership," an extraordinary accomplishment given that I'm not even a Republican.) Finally we got comedian Al Franken's *Lies and the Lying Liars Who Tell Them: A Fair and Balanced Look at the Right.* A quick review of Franken's book begs the question: Is this man serious? And a related question: Just how serious is a movement that relies on this man as its spokesman? We will spend more time with Mr. Franken later in the book.

The Conason/Alterman/Franken argument that the media are conservative revolves around four major points, all of them fallacious:

1. *Liberal bias? Just look at all those conservatives in the media!* By far the most common trick of the Left is to focus on the "media," not the "news media." How many times do we hear liberals cite Rush Limbaugh, William F. Buckley, Robert Novak, Cal Thomas, Sean Hannity, and so on, as evidence of the conservative "dominance" of the media? What these liberals know full well is that all of these conservatives are commentators, not reporters; their work appears in opinion columns and on TV or radio talk shows—not in news stories in our newspapers or on radio or television news programs. None reports news, but rather they all react to it analytically and, by necessity, with prejudice. More: No conservative on talk radio denies his conservative stance, which puts every one of them in almost perfect juxtaposition with the liberals in the news media, almost all of whom deny their own bias. It is impossible to contend that conservatives dominate the news media—which is why liberals play with the terminology.

2. *Who cares about liberal reporters? It's all about those dastardly conservative media owners.* Alterman has a chapter titled "You're Only As Liberal As the Man Who Owns You." This is the stuff of Berkeley

coffee klatches. Contrary to the Marxist stick-figure caricature, corporate CEOs cannot be automatically stereotyped as supply-side right-wingers dressed in three-piece Armani suits smoking oversized stogies and swigging martinis at the Knickerbocker Club. And if you don't believe me, ask Michael Eisner or Ted Turner.

Even if we suspend our disbelief for a moment and go along with Alterman that the owners of media corporations are all right-wingers, what does that really tell us? Nothing, as CNN's Tucker Carlson rightly pointed out when Alterman tried to claim that right-wing media owners control "what gets on the news." On the February 5, 2003, edition of *Crossfire,* Carlson swiftly rebutted Alterman's argument: "Actually, having worked in media corporations . . . all my adult life, I can tell you, as I think you already know, most reporters don't take orders from the owners of their companies. Most reporters don't know who the owners of their companies are and have zero contact with them. So that's not a plausible claim."

The corporate ownership argument is closely linked to point #1. Liberals like to point out that a majority of newspaper editorial pages normally endorse Republicans in presidential campaigns, as if somehow this validates their theory that the owners are calling the shots. But these are editorial writers—not owners, and not reporters—making this call. Moreover, theirs is a one-day story in the editorial page; this tells us nothing about a paper's slant 365 days per year in the news section, which is all that matters.

3. *Don't believe us liberals; just listen to what some conservatives say about this silly "liberal media" accusation.* Conason quotes former Christian Coalition head Ralph Reed mouthing this analysis of the press: "My sense is that it's probably never as good as you think and it's never as bad as you think." But what does that *mean*? It is not content analysis; it's conjecture. And yet Conason believes that in saying this, Reed "acknowledged" that "the media have turned to the right."

Alterman misuses *Weekly Standard* editor Bill Kristol in the same way. Kristol once told *The New Yorker* that "the liberal media were never that powerful, and the whole thing was often used as an excuse by conservatives for conservative failures," a point with which most conservatives would disagree, but also a point focusing on the *impact* of liberal media bias, not its *existence*, which Alterman seems not to realize is a given for Kristol. Alterman also quotes Pat Buchanan suggesting that the media had been fair to him on the presidential campaign trail, but in no way was Buchanan denying the existence of a liberal media bias. In fact, over the years Buchanan has denounced the liberal media probably hundreds of times, but Alterman has somehow missed all of these quotes. I wonder if he also missed Buchanan's dismissal of *What Liberal Media?* In a column in June 2003, Buchanan called Alterman a poor judge of bias and averred that there is indeed a "liberal press," which includes "all three major networks, PBS, NPR and virtually all major U.S. papers—*Boston Globe, New York Times, Philadelphia Inquirer, Baltimore Sun, Washington Post, Atlanta Constitution, Miami Herald, Chicago Tribune, Denver Post, Los Angeles Times*. . . . Not only are the editorial pages of most major papers liberal, the news staffs are overwhelmingly so." Buchanan concluded that "Big Media remains a fortress of liberalism," which is not exactly a ringing endorsement of Alterman's thesis.

Franken, meanwhile, relies on an ex-conservative to guide him through the world of conspiratorial conservative media politics. But the ex-conservative in question, David Brock, is a highly suspect source, to say the least, for he is an accomplished liar. (Incidentally, Franken, he who condemns "liars" in his book, was forced to confess that he lied in writing the book. In July 2003 he wrote a letter of apology to Attorney General John Ashcroft, admitting that he had not been truthful when he had earlier asked for Ashcroft's views on abstinence for what he had claimed, falsely, was a book on the subject.)

4. *Gore had the election stolen from him and this proves the media's conservative bias.* Conason finds a conspiracy here: "For eight years, the nation's largest mainstream news organizations devoted substantial resources to bringing down a Democratic administration. Investigative units at ABC News and NBC News chased scandal stories so zealously that they became virtual adjuncts of the prosecutors and conservative groups attacking the White House. . . . That same enmity infected the coverage of Democratic nominee Al Gore during the 2000 presiden-

tial election. False stories designed to ruin Gore's reputation, including phony and distorted quotes, found their way from the Republican National Committee to the conservative media and seeped into the mainstream press."

That accusation packs quite a wallop—except Conason doesn't offer a single example to support his case.

Franken devotes an entire chapter to the 2000 presidential election, claiming that it "disproved" the argument that the media display a liberal bias. This thirteen-page study in incoherent ramblings offers no serious content analysis and beats to death one or two utterly irrelevant anecdotes (the media's handling of Al Gore and the Love Canal issue—stop the presses!).

Alterman devotes a chapter to the 2000 election and another entire chapter to the postelection standoff in Florida. Most of it is a rather hysterical tirade against George W. Bush's camp for being evil and Al Gore's camp for not being as clever as the evil Bush camp. Here and there, however, he slips in a quote or factoid as "evidence" of this conservative, anti-Gore bias. For example, he cites *The Press Effect*, a study by Kathleen Hall Jamieson and Paul Waldman which found that "in the five Sunday shows aired by the three networks [on December 3], the word 'concede' appeared in twenty-three questions." In twenty of them, Alterman points out, "the hypothetical conceder was Al Gore." Somehow he finds this to be rather damning evidence, but he does not consider that perhaps this was so because recount after recount continued to validate Bush's victory while Gore's attempts to overturn the election results were rebuffed time and again.

Since all three of these authors seize on the 2000 presidential election as "evidence" of their wacky claims, this book will address the topic in depth, in Chapter 11.

Strangely, even when denying a liberal bias in the media, these writers don't deny that most reporters are liberal. Alterman admits, "I concur that the overall flavor of the elite media reporting favors gun control, campaign finance reform, gay rights, and the environmental movement"—and he could have easily added abortion, tax hikes, big government, and a host of other liberal policies—though he does feebly submit, "I do not find this bias as overwhelming as some conservatives do." Franken spends a chapter ridiculing Bernard Goldberg and *Bias* but also writes, "I think Goldberg's most valid point is that reporters tend to have more liberal views than the public on social issues." His argument is reduced to this: *Okay, so the media* are *liberal on social issues, but they're conservative on economic issues, which are what really matter.* But even that is not true. To prove his point that "journalists are economically conservative," Franken cites a 1998 survey of Washington-area reporters by Virginia Commonwealth University professor David Croteau, who often performs studies for the Far Left (and misnamed) group Fairness and Accuracy in Reporting (FAIR). Yet Franken omits the most important numbers from Croteau's survey—because these numbers contradict his conclusion: When asked to characterize their political orientation on social issues, only 9 percent of the journalists said "right" while 87 percent said "left" or "center"; on economic issues, only 19 percent said "right" while 75 percent said "left" or "center." Despite what Al Franken would have us believe, few reporters are conservative on either social *or* economic issues. Interestingly, Joe Conason cites the same Croteau survey, but even he does not try to make the bogus Franken claim that it reveals journalists to be economically conservative.

The Coming Meltdown

The liberal argument about a conservative media bias is so flimsy as to be amusing. But the Left's counterattack is serious, and calculated.

Several times during the Clinton years, when some in the media threatened to depart from liberal orthodoxy by focusing on Clinton scandals—Gennifer Flowers, Troopergate, and Monica Lewinsky come to mind—Team Clinton lashed out at the media for being mouthpieces of the vast right-wing conspiracy. The charge was always preposterous, and deliberately so: It was a preemptive strike designed to intimidate the press into compliance. And it worked every time, as the mainstream media responded by either turning their guns on

Republicans (the Lewinsky scandal) or dropping the story altogether (Flowers, Troopergate) to prove their liberal bona fides.

No serious liberal believes that a conservative bias dominates the news media. Liberals know what this book will prove: Like the old *Outer Limits* television series, the Left still controls the transmission, still controls "all that you see and hear." Television is not the only domain of the liberal news media: The Left still dominates with the printing presses, and yes, still dominates the "news" programming on radio.

So why the hysterical claims of conservative domination of the media? Because liberals fear that their monopoly on news coverage is in jeopardy. For decades, the liberal hegemony over the news media has provided the political Left with the ability not only to slant news coverage portside but actually to *control the public conversation, both political and cultural, in America.* Being the "social conscience" of the nation—having the ability to direct the national agenda—is quite a power. Liberals don't want to lose that.

In fact, they are right to be scared. As this book will demonstrate, the liberal news media are headed for a meltdown. To be sure, even today the vast power of the liberal media cannot be underestimated. But the days of liberal spin always prevailing are coming to an end. This has nothing to do with some sinister right-wing conspiracy. Rather, the problem lies with those in the liberal news media themselves. So dismissive are they of any claim of liberal bias, no matter how well documented, that they regularly allow this bias to seep into news stories. Even when poll after poll reveals that Americans have lost confidence in the news media, the liberal media elites do not deign to cleanse their industry of the bias that plagues it.

Something else is changing that will speed the collapse of the liberal media's monopoly on news coverage in this country. Conservatives have traditionally accepted liberal bias in the mainstream news media as a fact of life; it has been a given that the Left controls the news industry just as it holds sway over academia and the arts. But this has bred a certain complacency toward the press that has spelled disaster for one conservative initiative after another. Remember the Contract with America?

Even though I firmly believe that liberal bias does not have to be a fact of life, and indeed have devoted my professional life to bringing balance to news coverage, I have at times had to throw up my hands and simply accept the liberal agenda of the news media.

One day in 1986 I received a call from public relations guru Craig Shirley, who told me that the *Wall Street Journal*'s Ellen Hume wanted to interview me about John T. ("Terry") Dolan, a friend of mine who had passed away a few days before. Dolan had founded the National Conservative Political Action Committee (NCPAC), where I went to work in 1980, the year NCPAC scored some of the most amazing political feats in recent history, credited with defeating four of the most powerful liberal Democratic senators in America, George McGovern, Frank Church, Birch Bayh, and John Culver. Dolan was just twenty-seven at the time, a relative unknown, but that success had made him one of the most sought-after politicos in the country. Now, less than six years later, Dolan was dead, one of the first public casualties of the AIDS epidemic. The media fascination was feverish and understandable, even if in some quarters the sense of triumph could barely be disguised. So when Shirley called me about the interview, I immediately declined. Hume persisted, insisting that she did *not* want to talk about the AIDS issue but rather wanted to explore what she thought was a fascinating contradiction: the media perception of Dolan as the fierce, angry, mean-spirited political genius versus the reality of Dolan, the fun-loving, gentle jokester. Stressing her pledge not to explore the AIDS issue, she asked Shirley if I would reconsider. Again I declined, but again she wouldn't accept my decision, this time asking Shirley to approach me with another suggestion: Could she meet me privately for breakfast, off the record, to give her an opportunity to convince me of her honest intentions? That seemed fair to both Shirley and me, and the following Saturday morning Hume and I met at the Jefferson Hotel. We were off the record, but I was guarded nonetheless. What, exactly, did Hume want?

The stories, she answered. Was it true what she'd heard about Dolan's sense of humor? (Well, depends.) About the water gun battles in the office hallways? (Well, yeah.) And the NCPAC staff squirt gun attacks against other organizations? (Uh-huh.) And the hamster colonies at the office? (Yup.) And the solemn funerals for deceased hamsters outside the NCPAC offices, complete with twenty-one-bottle-rocket salutes? (Yes indeed.) Soon our conversation was loose; ultimately we were both dissolving in laughter as I recounted story after hilarious story about this lovable prankster, the protocols of an off-the-record conversation long forgotten and replaced by permission to record. When it was over, Hume had her piece, and I had the satisfaction of knowing that my friend Terry's heart and soul would be the subject of this story.

Or so I thought. Several weeks later Hume's story came out, not in the *Wall Street Journal* but as the cover story for *Regardie's*, Washington, D.C.'s would-be upscale, glossy gossip magazine. It had nothing to do with Dolan's engaging sense of humor; it dealt with the alleged gay conservative conspiracy (the "Lavender Bund," as Hume called it) that had hijacked the conservative movement. The headline told the story: "Fear and Self-Loathing on the Far Right." I read, horrified— quote after quote had been twisted out of context to support her hit piece. I'd been had. From start to finish, Shirley and I had been set up. I called Hume and furiously demanded an explanation. Her answer was cold, short, almost uninterested. "I changed my mind," was all she would say before hanging up. So Shirley and I jointly wrote her boss, the *Wall Street Journal*'s proud liberal Al Hunt, explaining how Hume had openly deceived us, even hiding from us the publication behind the hit piece. Hunt's response was as dismissive as Hume's, a one-sentence back-of-the-hand answer making a simple point: We conservatives should have known better.

Well, conservatives now do know better. No longer do we merely have to accept the liberal agenda of the so-called objective news media. Nothing made this point more clearly than a startling statement by President George W. Bush in October 2003. Fed up with the way the national media were covering the rebuilding efforts in Iraq, Bush stated in a Hearst-Argyle interview that he was going to bypass them. "I'm mindful of the filter through which some news travels," the president said, "and sometimes you just have to go over the heads of the filter and speak directly to the people and that's what we will continue to do." The liberal press, predictably, fainted in disbelief. As John Roberts of CBS News put it, "It was the public relations equivalent of a declaration of war aimed at the national media." Many who read this book will have an altogether different perspective. They'll wonder why it took the Bush administration so long.

PART ONE

The
REAL SOURCE
of BIAS

How the Media View Conservatives and Liberals—
and Their Own Role in Society

1

"Always Professional, Never Personal"

"**T**HEY HATE YOU!"

A cheerful Robert Novak was shouting at me across the room, shaking up an otherwise dull Washington, D.C., cocktail reception. The CNN commentator and syndicated columnist had just entered the crowded party, and as soon as he saw me he broke into a broad smile and boomed those words to me. As I made my way over to Bob, he again shouted, "They hate you! They really hate you!"

It wasn't hard to guess who "they" were. But I was surprised that this was coming from the Prince of Darkness himself, a man who was confronting the leftist press long before I ever came into the picture, and I told him so. "That's what I mean!" he said, laughing heartily. "They're calling *me* to say how much they hate you!"

As much as we laughed about it, Novak was making an important point. Sure, it was an exaggeration: One would be hard-pressed to find members of the media who, simply because of politics, truly *hate* me— or Novak, or any other conservative, for that matter. But the mainstream media went unchallenged for so long that they were thoroughly unaccustomed to criticism from anyone, and many media figures are less than pleased with the mounting assaults on their credibility and trustworthiness. As head of the largest organization in America confronting and exposing the liberal proclivities of the press, I could understandably be their Enemy Number One.

My critiques of the media are not part of some personal vendetta, however. Indeed, I have great admiration for many members of the media whose political philosophies are diametrically opposed to mine. Take Sam Donaldson of ABC News, a journalist whom many conservatives love to hate. He is not just liberal in his thinking; on the air he is often bombastic and infuriatingly obnoxious. One shudders to think how many books, shoes, and baseball bats have been hurled at television sets over the years because of his pontificating.

But that is the public persona; the real Sam Donaldson is nothing like that. He is affable and courteous—and mischievous as well, as I learned years ago when we were pitted against each other on CNN's *Crossfire*. Just as the program's announcer was introducing me and the camera's red light clicked on to indicate I was on-screen, I felt Donaldson's knee slam into my own under the table, conveniently out of the camera shot. The jolt had its desired effect: CNN viewers' first glimpse of me was of a man with a contorted, perplexed, thoroughly goofy expression on his face. And when his camera turned on, there was Sam, calm and demure, with a polite, utterly professional—and extremely satisfied—smile on his face.

That was only one of many skirmishes Donaldson and I have had on television. Often the topic of our debate is liberal media bias. Where most liberals in the press refuse even to acknowledge this subject as suitable for discussion, Donaldson, to his credit, is willing to discuss media bias openly and candidly. For many years, in fact, he has come to the annual Conservative Political Action Conference (CPAC) to debate Bob Novak on the issue of media bias, and I have had the pleasure of moderating those debates. It's a testament to Donaldson that even if his comments are met with hisses and howls of derision from a thousand conservative activists, his performance—perhaps just the mere fact that he has the guts to enter the lion's den and defend his industry—inevitably triggers a standing ovation from the audience, and rightfully so. Liberals could learn a lesson from this man.

I certainly learned an important lesson from him. Back in 1996, as we were chatting in the CNN greenroom after another *Crossfire* debate, I asked why he had skipped that year's GOP national convention, which had been held just a few weeks earlier. He had been conspicuous in his absence; after all, this was the man who had been the scourge of Republicans because of his coverage of their conventions, and he obviously relished that role. His answer surprised me. Perhaps if we'd been in a public setting the response would have been different; certainly it would have been less impassioned. But we were alone, the setting was relaxed, and he let his guard down, recounting sorrowfully how, while he was in Sarajevo working on a story shortly before the convention, his producer had been shot and killed, a sniper's bullet penetrating the window of their vehicle. It would be impossible ever to know the truth, he said, but it stood to reason that the assassin had hit the wrong target. He acknowledged that his journalistic duty called for him to carry out his next assignment, especially one as important as a national convention, but he felt it was inappropriate, and he wanted to mourn the loss of his friend. It was a powerful story, to be sure, but I was mostly impressed by Donaldson's humility. In a note I wrote him afterward I told him of my heightened personal regard for him. His simple answer came back a few days later, direct and blazingly accurate: "Remember: Always professional, never personal."

"Always professional, never personal": It's a creed I've tried to follow ever since. For someone in Sam Donaldson's profession, it's particularly important. After all, journalists are charged with the responsibility of reporting the news objectively, of keeping their personal prejudices from influencing how they chronicle events and profile individuals and groups. The problem, of course, is that so much of what we see coming from the mainstream media *is* personal.

Nowhere has this been more of a problem than in the media's coverage of conservatives. Many attacks on conservatives, intentional or not, are personal because the animus against conservatives from many in the news media is all too real. Even today, at a time when the mainstream media have (finally) come under intense scrutiny for the way their liberalism affects their news reporting, attacks on conservatives are all too common.

Conservatives: "Poor, Uneducated and Easy to Command"

I've often been asked what it's like to deal personally with the institution we castigate professionally, and I can answer emphatically that
most members of the media are courteous, respectful, and professional.
Many are downright pleasant. But some are not. Walk into the studios
of National Public Radio for an interview and the looks you receive
from the aged hippies betray their desire to fumigate their offices the
moment you leave. And sometimes you don't even have to analyze
body language and facial expressions to gauge how the liberal media
really feel about conservatives.

I got a rare glimpse behind the curtain during an appearance on
CNN. I had been invited on the program *Reliable Sources* to discuss a
brand-new Media Research Center study of the networks' coverage
(both quantitative and qualitative) of religion. The study showed how,
year after year, the news media devote paltry attention to stories dealing with religion. Somewhat to my surprise, and certainly to my
delight, the media covered the report fairly, even positively. My fellow
panelists at CNN that day also agreed that the media were not giving
the issue of faith nearly the respect it deserved; it was the rare cable
television appearance where the discussion did not devolve into a fight.

But those in the CNN control room were not so respectful. I know,
because when we went on the air, in my earpiece I could still hear
everything being said in the control room. *CNN had forgotten to shut off
the transmission. Oops.* So while my fellow panelists and I had a serious
discussion about the media, I listened to the producers and other
staffers in the control room offer their commentary. Actually, they
screamed their commentary. Every time I made a statement it was met
with derisive insults—*"Goddamn Nazi!" "Fucking fascist!" "What an ass-
hole you are!"*—and hysterical laughter. Each CNN staffer tried to one-
up the last in the "Let's Abuse That Conservative Jerk Bozell"
sweepstakes.

When the program ended, I unhooked my microphone but held on to the earpiece. As I walked down the hallway toward the exit, I encountered one of the producers standing outside the control room. "Great show!" the producer oh-so-sweetly commented. I couldn't resist. I reached past him and swung open the control room door. There, crunched in the tight quarters, were a good half-dozen CNN employees chattering away. One look at me and they froze. Smiling, I tossed them the earpiece. "Next time, don't forget to turn it off during the show" was all I needed to say: The picture of this motley crew, bug-eyed, their mouths hanging open, will be with me forever.

Sure, the incident might have been an aberration. But a career spent studying the news business has shown me that members of the media do have, if not pure hatred, a real distaste for conservatives—not just the political positions they hold, but the people themselves. Most reporters, editors, and producers would never admit this, of course. But at the networks, the major newspapers, and the national magazines, journalists too often look across the country and instead of seeing hardworking, taxpaying conservatives from all walks of life—polls have told us for years that a strong plurality of Americans call themselves conservatives—they see the unsophisticated, the provincial, people whose dark passions can be easily stirred. They are the "poor, unedu-cated and easy to command," as former *Washington Post* reporter Michael Weisskopf, now a senior correspondent at *Time* magazine, famously called them in a 1993 article.

But a special vitriol is reserved for Republican or conservative leaders.

The liberal media often couch their disdain for conservative leaders in their slanted reporting on their policies, as we'll see in Part II of this book. But sometimes journalists just can't bottle up their hatred any longer. In September 2003, Jonathan Chait of the *New Republic* let loose on the Republican president, opening his column with this frank statement: "I hate President George W. Bush." Immediately he added, "There, I said it," clearly relieved to have rid himself of any pretense of objectivity and clearly speaking for legions of disgruntled liberal jour-nalists who hadn't "said it" so explicitly, at least in print or on the air. Chait went on: "I think his policies rank him among the worst presidents in U.S. history. And, while I'm tempted to leave it at that, the truth is that I hate him for less substantive reasons, too. I hate the inequitable way he has come to his economic and political achievements and his utter lack of humility (disguised behind transparently false modesty) at having done so. . . . I hate the way he walks—shoulders flexed, elbows splayed out from his sides like a teenage boy feigning machismo. I hate the way he talks—blustery self-assurance masked by a pseudo-populist twang. I even hate the things that everybody seems to like about him. I hate his lame nickname-bestowing—a way to establish one's social superiority beneath a veneer of chumminess (does anybody give their boss a nickname without his consent?). And, while most people who meet Bush claim to like him, I suspect that, if I got to know him personally, I would hate him even more."

Liberal journalists spewing such venom was a sure sign that they were revving up for another presidential election.

In fact, many liberals in the media had been revving up ever since the Democrats lost the 2002 midterm elections. Just after those elections, Bill Moyers used his taxpayer-funded platform on PBS's *NOW* to launch this diatribe: "The entire federal government—the Congress, the executive, the courts—is united behind a right-wing agenda for which George W. Bush believes he now has a mandate. That agenda includes the power of the state to force pregnant women to surrender control over their own lives. It includes using the taxing power to transfer wealth from working people to the rich. It includes giving corporations a free hand to eviscerate the environment and control the regulatory agencies meant to hold them accountable. And it includes secrecy on a scale you cannot imagine. Above all, it means judges with a political agenda appointed for life. If you liked the Supreme Court that put George W. Bush in the White House, you will swoon over what's coming. And if you like God in government, get ready for the Rapture. . . . Republicans outraised Democrats by $184 million [in the 2002 elections] and they came up with the big prize: monopoly control of the American government and the power of the state to turn their radical ideology into the law of the land."

The Republican administration isn't always the target. In a *New*

York Times opinion column in November 2002, Bill Keller called Senator James Inhofe, Republican of Oklahoma, "a dimmer version of Jesse Helms—an intolerant, xenophobic, might-makes-right ultra-patriot, but not as quick on his feet as Mr. Helms was in his prime." Keller thereby managed to slam *two* Republican leaders at once. Just eight months later, this same Keller was named as the paper's executive editor—as if we needed any further evidence of the liberal worldview that dominates the *New York Times* newsroom.

Helms was a familiar target for the media when he was in office. But in August 2001, David Broder of the *Washington Post* was aghast at the media's coverage of Helms's announcement that he would not run for another Senate term. Wrote Broder, "The squeamishness of much of the press in characterizing Helms for what he is suggests an unwillingness to confront the reality of race in our national life. . . . What is unique about Helms—and from my viewpoint, unforgivable—is his willingness to pick at the scab of the great wound of American history, the legacy of slavery and segregation, and to inflame racial resentment against African Americans." Broder is considered the dean of the Washington political press corps, so his words carry weight.

Sometimes the "objective" news media let slip their true feelings in their descriptions of conservatives. In September 2001, *Newsweek* used its website to promote a new book by the magazine's David Kaplan, *The Accidental President* (that "accidental president" being George W. Bush, of course). Next to an excerpt from Kaplan's book, a "Newsweek Interactive" feature offered capsule summaries of the nine Supreme Court justices. Perhaps not surprisingly, the liberal members of the court came off much better than did the conservative justices. Ruth Bader Ginsburg, for example, was correctly described as "one of the Court's most consistent liberals" but was lauded for having "established herself as a champion of women's rights and minority rights." Meanwhile, Justice Clarence Thomas was described as being "at the Rehnquist Court's conservative extreme, consistently taking a page from the far right's playbook on abortion, school prayer, gay rights and other issues." So a liberal is a "champion" of people's rights while a conservative is on the "extreme" and takes his marching orders from the "Far Right"? Sure, that seems like balanced reporting.

The aftermath of the 1995 Oklahoma City bombing illustrated the spiteful anticonservative strain that lies just beneath the surface for liberal journalists. In reporting the event, some networks and other major media—and, to be sure, President Bill Clinton—placed the guilt squarely on the shoulders of conservatives who, if not murderers themselves, had inspired terrorism with their hate-filled messages.

Up until the World Trade Center and Pentagon attacks in 2001, the Oklahoma bombing ranked as the greatest act of domestic terrorism in American history, and liberals used the horrific event to chain all of American conservatism to the ankle of Timothy McVeigh. While crews were still clearing rubble from the Alfred P. Murrah Federal Building, the Left was blaming every Republican politician who had ever cast doubt on the omnicompetence of Washington, every talk radio host who protested the punishment of tax increases, every speechwriter who suggested that government was the problem, not the solution. All would be implicated in the killing of those men, women, and children in Oklahoma City.

On April 23, 1995, a sad Sunday morning just four days after the disaster, Sam Donaldson proposed that conservative rhetoric had contributed to a climate that encouraged violence. Bob Schieffer seconded that on CBS. By that evening, President Bill Clinton had made the political calculations and was blaming the "purveyors of hate and division" for the massacre. Bryant Gumbel, then of NBC, named names two days later on national television: Rush Limbaugh, G. Gordon Liddy, Michael Reagan, Bob Grant, and Oliver North—those talk radio hosts "who cater to angry white men," Gumbel said. The *Los Angeles Times* endorsed these claims in a front-page news analysis: "The Oklahoma City attack on federal workers and their children also alters the once-easy dynamic between charismatic talk show host and adoring audience. Hosts who routinely espouse the same anti-government themes as the militia movement must now walk a fine line between inspiring their audience—and inciting the most radical among them."

Apparently the Republican Party leadership was to blame as well. *Time* magazine's Michael Kramer moved quickly to connect the dots between Oklahoma City and the GOP: "The burden of fostering [the bombers'] delusion is borne out not just by the nut cases that preach conspiracy but also to some extent by those who erode faith in our governance in the pursuit of their own ambitions." Columnist Carl Rowan stated, "Unless [Speaker of the House Newt] Gingrich and [Senate Majority Leader Bob] Dole and the Republicans say, 'Am I inflaming a bunch of nuts?,' you know we're going to have some more events [like the Oklahoma City bombing]. I am absolutely certain the harsher rhetoric of the Gingriches and the Doles . . . creates a climate of violence in America."

Then there was the Matthew Shepard story, one of the biggest news stories of 1998. Shepard, a gay student at the University of Wyoming in Laramie, was attacked and brutally beaten by two men on October 7 outside a bar. Tied to a fence, he was discovered and rescued by two passing cyclists, but he would die from his injuries in a hospital five days later. The crime unleashed a media firestorm.

Shepard's murder met all the liberal standards for a Big Story. As a gay man, he was a member of a self-identified minority, and therefore his murder qualified as a "hate" crime. That, in turn, gave the press the opportunity to raise the banner for one of its favorite causes while simultaneously tying opponents of gay rights to the murderers themselves.

Had Shepard been heterosexual, the murder would never have risen to the level of national news. It might have run in a few Rocky Mountain newspapers, only to fade quickly from sight. But this was the murder of a gay man in the wide-open spaces of the conservative American West, thus reinforcing the national media's prejudices about the Great Unwashed, as Congressman Henry Hyde once so deliciously described grassroots conservatives. Moreover, it provided the media with enough material for weeks of lecturing about the murdering bigots of the high plains.

A strong argument can be made that location was the driving angle of the story. Numerous "hate" crimes had been committed in large cities prior to Shepard's death. In New York City, for instance, there were nine "anti-gay" murders in 1994 and twelve more in 1995, according to the *New York Times*. Yet not one of those murders became a network story, never mind a cause. But Shepard's murder took place out *there*, far from the Manhattan skyline and the Washington Beltway, and illustrated the murderous, hateful tendencies of *those* people. Combine the elite media's contempt for "fly-over country" with a heavily publicized, conservative Christian effort then under way to help homosexuals break the gay lifestyle, and all the pieces were in place to accuse conservatives—personally—of creating a "climate of hate."

NBC's *Today* show set a new low for itself on October 13, 1998. NBC's David Gregory openly promoted the vicious argument of gay-left extremists blaming Christian conservative commercial campaigns and Republican leaders like Trent Lott for Shepard's heinous beating: "Even as friends of Matthew Shepard held a candlelight vigil in his honor, gay rights groups rushed to condemn the killing, portraying Shepard as a casualty of a new cultural war against gays and lesbians, a war declared this summer, declared by a coalition of religious-right groups, including the Christian Coalition, which funded advertisements in major newspapers and commercials on TV promoting a campaign to convert homosexuals to heterosexuality.

"The ads were controversial for portraying gays and lesbians as sinners who had made poor choices, despite the growing belief that homosexuality may be genetic," Gregory continued. "And the campaign followed the divisive comments of Senate Majority Leader Trent Lott, who said in an interview that homosexuals should be helped like alcoholics, sex addicts, and kleptomaniacs. Have the ads fostered a climate of anti-gay hate that leads to incidents like the killing of Matthew Shepard? Gay rights activists say the ads convey a message that gay people are defective."

Gregory's supposed reporting might as well have been a paid advertisement for the mudslinging extremists on the Left.

Today coanchor Katie Couric did her part when she interviewed wild-eyed Elizabeth Birch of the Human Rights Campaign Fund and Janet Folger, an architect of the gays-can-change ad campaign. Couric fed the perfect softball to Birch: "Do you believe this ad campaign launched by some conservative groups really contributed somehow to Matthew Shepard's death?" Birch quickly replied, "I do, Katie. These kinds of violent acts . . . happen because people's minds have been twisted with cruel stereotypes about gay and lesbian people. And this ad campaign has been pumped out all summer presenting gay and lesbian people as defective, as less than, as not fully human."

But isn't it a cruel, twisted stereotype to suggest that conservatives condone hatred and violence? Not according to Gannett's Deborah Mathis, apparently. Commenting on the case on the television talk show *Inside Washington*, Mathis said, "The Christian Right per se and some particular members on Capitol Hill have helped inflame the air so that the air that [the murderers] breathed that night was filled, filled with the idea that somehow gays are different, and not only are they different in that difference, they're bad, and not only are they bad, they are evil and therefore evil can be destroyed. . . . I mentioned Trent Lott, Jesse Helms, and Dick Armey particularly. The Christian Coalition, the Family Research Council, and the Concerned Women for America."

Too often, the media do nothing to challenge such extreme statements, and liberals are allowed to proceed making outrageous claims without admonition, even without comment. As a result, Democrats have picked up on this strategy, using the same level of poison rhetoric against their Republican counterparts. They do it simply because they have no fear of exposure from the Fourth Estate. On the contrary, they can expect the media to support their attacks.

Double Standards

It is a fact of life for Republicans that the slightest show of allegiance to the conservative philosophy will trigger outrage from the supposedly impartial press corps. The 1998 congressional elections illustrate just how little they need to do to upset the media.

In mid-October, in the last weeks of that campaign, the Republicans launched an advertising campaign urging voters not to "reward" Bill Clinton's behavior by voting for Democrats. The media were quick to denounce this Republican effort as negative "attack advertising." Peter Jennings used his lofty perch at ABC to warn viewers that it was "a $10 million advertising attack," and Keith Olbermann of MSNBC wondered why Republicans wanted to "coarsen" political discourse. CNN followed Speaker Gingrich with its cameras, demanding to know his role in this nefarious plot.

Of course, the networks hadn't fluttered an eyelash three years earlier when a vicious advertising campaign was launched against the GOP. Personally directing that campaign—which was waged before the 1996 presidential election was even under way—was President Bill Clinton himself, and it included an ad suggesting that Bob Dole and Newt Gingrich would allow Medicare recipients to die.

So why the outrage in 1998? If these oh-so-objective journalists found it wrong for the GOP to run negative ads, and scandalous for Speaker Gingrich to have participated in them, where were they when the president of the United States was personally directing an advertising broadside far greater in size, and far nastier in tone, against Bob Dole? (And for good measure: At least the Republicans raised their funds [1] in the United States and [2] legally—but the Clinton-Gore campaign finance scandals were another issue that the mainstream media refused to investigate in appropriate depth.)

Moreover, the Republicans' "advertising attack" was by no means the nastiest of the 1998 campaign. In late October the Democratic Party of Missouri launched an attack on the GOP that was truly dishonest and scandalous: "When you don't vote, you let another church explode. When you don't vote, you allow another cross to burn. When you don't vote, you let another assault wound a brother or a sister. . . . Vote smart. Vote Democratic."

There is nothing in the GOP video archives that comes close to this wretched attack. And yet when the Missouri Democratic Party aired this ad throughout the state, not a word was mentioned about it on ABC. Or on CBS. Or on NBC. Or on CNN. Only the Fox News Channel found this ad newsworthy and aired stories about it on

November 1 and 2, just before the November 3 election. Fox News political commentator Juan Williams—whose experience at the *Washington Post* hardly qualified him as a fire-breathing conservative—rightly said, "When you talk about things like church burnings, when you talk about attacking, lynch mob activity, that strikes deep and I think the fact that Democrats feel that that's what they have to do with the black community, it's a little bit insulting; it's patronizing to black people."

Indeed, the ad was hateful and divisive, but the major networks didn't see it as a story worth covering. In contrast, when a conservative says something that the media perceive to be hateful, they will stop at nothing in their quest to expose this evil, including attacking conservative organizations that don't join them in the condemnation.

Consider, for example, the reaction of Jonathan Alter, *Newsweek*'s media critic, to the Reverend Jerry Falwell's remarks that the September 11 terrorist attacks were God's punishment for America's sinful ways. In a *Newsweek* "Web Exclusive" on MSNBC.com on December 14, 2001, Alter attacked conservatives for not condemning Falwell. "The larger conservative movement has done little or nothing to repudiate the founder of the Moral Majority, and he's still in business," Alter said. "Talk about double standards."

Conservatives are hypocrites, and Alter was determined to prove it. "Imagine if the shoe were on the other ideological foot," he huffed, presenting a hypothetical scenario in which the Reverend Jesse Jackson on a liberal television program blamed conservatives for September 11, and Bill Moyers agreed (as Pat Robertson had agreed with Falwell when Falwell made his comments on *The 700 Club*). Were this the case, Alter suggested, Rush Limbaugh and others would demand that liberals denounce Jackson and Moyers, and liberals would.

But had Alter been paying attention he would have heard and read countless conservatives state their disapproval of Falwell's comment. He must have missed William F. Buckley's denunciation in *National Review* ("ignorant misapplication of Christian thought"), and missed John Podhoretz bristle in the editorial pages of the *New York Post* ("I'd like to express my revulsion at remarks . . . shameful . . . ignorant"), and missed the *Weekly Standard's* take ("contemptible"). I assume he never heard Limbaugh and the hundreds of other conservative talk-show hosts nationwide who took Reverend Falwell to task. He didn't hear a single conservative interviewed on television who decried the comments.

Falwell did apologize for his remarks, something Alter himself has never bothered to do for intemperate remarks he made in October 1998, after the Shepard murder. In a *Newsweek* essay entitled "Trickle-Down Hate," Alter wrote, "At first, it seems unfair to link the anti-gay remarks of political leaders to a heinous crime they don't condone. . . . But just as white racists created a climate for lynching blacks, just as hate radio created a climate for militias, so the constant degrading of homosexuals is exacting a toll in blood." (Note that Alter was resuscitating the ugly argument from 1995 that conservative talk radio somehow fostered a culture of violence and hatred.)

But, left unchallenged by their colleagues, liberals don't have to apologize, it seems.

The Real Purveyors of Hate

In closely monitoring the media all these years, the Media Research Center has noted some truly shocking statements coming from members of the liberal media. But what is even more shocking is that these statements prompt no outcry, no demand for apologies. If President Clinton could label conservative voices "purveyors of hate and division," one is left to wonder what he would make of the following statements from respected members of the mainstream media establishment:

> *"I think [Senator Jesse Helms] ought to be worried about what's going on in the Good Lord's mind, because if there is retributive justice, he'll get AIDS from a transfusion, or one of his grandchildren will get it."*
>
> —*NPR's Nina Totenberg,* INSIDE WASHINGTON, *July 8, 1995*

"I hope his wife feeds him lots of eggs and butter and he dies early like many black men do, of heart disease. . . . He is an absolutely reprehensible person."

> —USA TODAY *columnist Julianne Malveaux on Justice Clarence Thomas, PBS's* TO THE CONTRARY, *November 4, 1994*

"We have an attorney general [John Ashcroft] that is, I don't know, how would you describe him, demented? We have an attorney general who doesn't seem to understand the law."

> —THE NEW YORKER'S *Seymour Hersh to the Chicago Headliner Club, as quoted by Steve Rhodes in* CHICAGO, *May 2, 2002*

"The term wacko right-winger is redundant. For example, they're the only people who don't like being called compassionate. Someone remarked that many now defend the tobacco industry because its products kill people early, saving us dollars in having to care for aged people."

> —*Larry King,* USA TODAY, *March 8, 1999*

"There is a scene [in Roots*] where kidnapped African Kunta Kinte won't settle down in his chains. 'Want me to give him a stripe or two, boss?' the old slave, Fiddler, asks his Master Reynolds. 'Do as I say, Fiddler,' Reynolds answers. 'That's all I expect from any of my niggers.' 'Oh, I love you, Massa Reynolds,' Fiddler tells him. And instantly, my mind draws political parallels. Ward Connerly, I think to myself. Armstrong Williams. Shelby Steele. Hyperbole, some might say. I say dead-on. 'Clarence Thomas,' I say to my Cousin Kim. And she just stares at me. She may be a little tender yet for racial metaphors. I see them everywhere."*

> —WASHINGTON POST *reporter Lonnae O'Neal Parker on watching* ROOTS *with her twenty-year-old cousin, August 8, 1999*

"I've got to know, Pat, why is this John Edwards/Lauch Faircloth race so important to the Republicans, other than the obvious that Senator

Faircloth is considered to be one of the junior Grand Wizards of the vast right-wing conspiracy?"

—MSNBC's *Keith Olbermann to former Democratic pollster Pat Caddell, October 26, 1998*

"The right wing has lied repeatedly in an effort to move public opinion on this issue [of partial-birth abortion]. . . . Lie No. 1: Conservatives care about life. The renowned quipmeister, Rep. Barney Frank, Massachusetts Democrat, once said, 'Conservatives' interest in life begins at conception and ends at birth.' Truer words were never spoken."

—*Syndicated columnist and PBS* To the Contrary *host Bonnie Erbe, March 29, 1997*

Why does the political Left feel so bold in expressing its viciousness against the Right? Because there is no fear of a media backlash. It's just not that objectionable, in the media's eyes, to attach blame to Republicans for church arsons, cross burnings, murders, and terrorist strikes; after all, those acts are natural consequences of the GOP's conservative agenda, aren't they?

2

Two Standards for Two Sides

I T IS A quantifiable fact that the news media routinely find fault
with the actions and personal behavior of conservatives even when
the accusations are mere allegations. George W. Bush and his
alleged drug use; Vice President Dick Cheney corrupted by Big Oil;
Richard Scaife godfathering the vast right-wing conspiracy; Ronald
Reagan and the October Surprise of 1980—these are but a handful of
the countless examples of how the media take liberal myths aimed at
tarnishing the reputations of conservative leaders and report them as
credible charges. It is also quantifiably true that these same reporters
generally overlook charges of inappropriate behavior by liberals even
when hard evidence is provided. This can be explained in only
two ways: (1) There's an Orwellian impulse at play with the press—
speculation is truth, and truth is speculation; or (2) the media have a
natural antipathy toward those on the Right but empathy for those on
the Left.

Whichever it is, the result is clear: The media have different standards for the two sides. Again and again the news industry has revealed
its bias.

Throughout the Clinton years we heard the nonstop mantra about
the "politics of personal destruction" being waged by conservatives—the
"Clinton haters," as you'll recall. But when liberal activists—including,
oftentimes, journalists—rain personal hellfire on conservatives, those

same reporters so shocked—shocked!—by conservatives' misbehavior during the Clinton years fall silent.

When left-wing activist Janeane Garofalo was asked to guest-host CNN's *Crossfire* on August 20, 2003, she used her platform to say this: "The lie that brought us into war was that Iraq was a threat to us. . . . It was an attempt at a corporate takeover. This was about oil. It wasn't about human rights. It's not about human rights. . . . Team Bush is more radically corrupt than Richard Nixon ever tried to be. . . . It is, in fact, a conspiracy of the Forty-third Reich."

Quick: Find me evidence anywhere of the media denouncing Garofalo for that little piece of hatred.

Okay, but Janeane Garofalo is a vocal liberal activist. What about journalists at major newspapers? About a month earlier, on July 22, *Boston Globe* columnist James Carroll wrote, "More than 50 air raids, each with more than 30 Iraqi civilian fatalities, each expressly approved by [Secretary of Defense Donald] Rumsfeld. Absolutely terrible tragedies, every one. And also—more evident by the day—every one a war crime." No one in the media found that untoward either.

Filmmaker Michael Moore has fashioned an entire career out of making hateful statements about conservatives. Just three days after the September 11, 2001, terrorist attacks, Moore posted this vicious screed against the president on his website: "Am I angry? You bet I am. I am an American citizen, and my leaders have taken my money to fund mass murder. . . . Keep crying, Mr. Bush. Keep running to Omaha or wherever it is you go while others die, just as you ran during Vietnam. . . . And now you are asking for 'unity' so you can start another [Vietnam]? Do not insult me or my country like this!" The news media reported this tirade but did not condemn Moore for it.

The news media similarly found nothing wrong when two of their own, reporters Karen Tumulty and Viveca Novak of *Time* magazine, managed to tie President Bush to the deadly sniper attacks that paralyzed the Washington, D.C., area in the fall of 2002: "Gun-rights advocates have been emboldened by an administration that is sympathetic to their cause. The closeness was underscored by the fact that the military-style gun used in the sniper attacks—named, unfortunately for the White House, Bushmaster XM15—was manufactured by a company owned by Richard Dyke, a Bush fund-raiser."

Politics of personal destruction, anyone?

When in the spring of 2002 the Energy Department released records demanded by Democrats showing that its officials met with energy industry leaders but not energy-loathing environmental extremists, you could almost hear the "Aha!" from major newspapers and networks. If it wasn't illegal, it was certainly unethical and confirmed every suspicion about the Bush administration's unholy alliance with Big Oil.

"Energy Contacts Disclosed: Consumer Groups Left Out, Data Show," warned the front page of the *Washington Post* on March 26, 2002.

That morning CBS's *The Early Show* covered the story as well. When cohost Jane Clayson said, "Apparently there's not much in [the records]," Bryant Gumbel protested, "Yeah, except they do show that the administration consulted business leaders and not consumer groups." CBS White House reporter Bill Plante underlined the point: "There were almost no consumer or conservation groups but there were a lot of energy industry people who were big campaign contributors."

That night, *CBS Evening News* substitute anchor Ed Bradley ominously found "a new chapter in the long-running controversy over President Bush's energy policy and who was consulted about it in secret." Reporter Wyatt Andrews announced that "one statistic stood out like a lopsided sports score. At least thirty-six times, Energy Secretary Spencer Abraham met representatives of the energy industry to discuss the policy, compared to zero meetings with environmental groups." Andrews also repeated complaints from the environmental group Natural Resources Defense Council (NRDC) that the documents were "heavily censored," reporting that "environmentalists call this a cover-up." Interviewing an NRDC activist, Andrews tossed this soft pitch: "Do you think the amount of blackout breaks the law?"

A few hours later on CNN's *NewsNight*, Connie Chung chirped like a Henry Waxman pom-pom girl about how "thousands of documents released last evening are only making a hot issue hotter." Chung asked *Washington Post* reporter Dana Milbank, "Tell me, do these documents confirm the worst suspicions of influence peddling?" When Milbank said twenty-nine of the thirty-six companies consulted were donors, Chung excitedly repeated, "Once again, twenty-nine out of thirty-six!"

The evidence against the Bush administration was damning—or so the mainstream media would have had you believe. Leave it to the *Washington Times* to expose this left-wing witch hunt. On March 26, the *Times* ran a front-page story that focused on a critical fact available to all those other reporters had they been interested in the truth more than in political gamesmanship: "The Bush administration sought the advice of environmental groups in drafting its energy plan, but several declined to participate . . . just-released documents show. . . . The Energy Department contacted Greenpeace, the Sierra Club, Environmental Defense, the World Resources Institute, Resources for the Future and four other groups to discuss conservation and energy efficiency."

In other words, there was no story there. Despite what the *Washington Post*, CBS News, and other major news outlets reported, the Bush administration did *not* actively exclude environmental groups; rather, the only reason that environmental groups did not meet with the Energy Department was that those groups *turned down the invitations to the meetings!* As the *Washington Times* reported, environmental groups "rebuffed administration overtures."

Of course, the liberal media couldn't be bothered to report the truth because the facts got in the way of their agenda, which was to reveal the Republican administration as one that practices the worst forms of influence peddling and has no concern whatsoever for the environment. But Republicans are held to a different standard.

Demolishing the Clinton Myths

The media's double standard is so pervasive that it's impossible to deny. In the eyes of the political Left, any sin committed by, or scandal involving, the liberal can be excused in the name of the higher calling of his principled policy prescriptions. The Kennedy family has benefited from this standard for generations; in recent times no politician has capitalized on it more than President Bill Clinton.

For the conservative, however, the reverse is the rule. Any personal peccadillo—no matter how small, no matter how long ago, no matter how unproven—is to be raised as a matter of journalistic imperative. Moreover, the merits of any public policy prescription are immediately suspect out of the belief that the conservative at his core is not driven, cannot be driven, by the desire for the public well-being. See: Reagan, Ronald.

Already one hears the howls of protest from the Left. How, they ask incessantly, can anyone suggest such bias after the way the media filleted Bill Clinton? After all, the earth stopped its rotation for almost fourteen months while the media handled the Monica Lewinsky scandal. Liberals emphasize this point in order to conclude the following: (1) The media were never "pro-Clinton," as conservatives charge; (2) the conservative accusation that the media covered—and covered up— for Clinton is preposterous; and (3) the coverage Clinton received from the press was far more negative than that afforded to either Reagan or Bush, thereby showing that the media are conservative.

Let us demolish these myths.

First, despite the fact that Clinton officiated over the single most corrupt administration in American history, the supposedly hard-charging media gave us eight years of calming Muzak. We've just seen how news media pilloried the Bush administration because it was supposedly in cahoots with Big Oil; now compare that to the handling the Clinton administration received on matters that should have been real controversies.

The Clintons had their picture taken with a cocaine smuggler, Jorge Cabrera. Was it a scandal? Far from it. A Nexis search reveals that over the course of a full year ABC did only one story on the Clintons and Cabrera and made only one other mention; NBC had one *mention;* CBS did *nothing;* and twenty-four-hour CNN had three stories and six other mentions. The print media, with hundreds of thousands of pages to fill over a year's time, were no different: six mentions in *USA Today;* one story and five mentions in the *Washington Post;* two stories and four mentions in the *New York Times;* and seven stories and four mentions in the *Los Angeles Times.*

Major Clinton donors like Loral Space and Communications handed missile secrets to the Chinese, and the Chinese handed their soft money to Hillary's aides; when questioned, the Clintons sent "heavily censored" documents to investigators, reducing the evidence to pulp. But the mainstream media didn't cry "cover-up" or even think the story was worth attention.

In 1993, as the Clintons prepared a massive scheme for socialized medicine in this country, they refused to meet with the Heritage Foundation, the Cato Institute, and Citizens for a Sound Economy—or just about anyone else objecting to their efforts to nationalize one-seventh of the U.S. economy. But the *Washington Post* did not feature a front-page headline blaring that these groups were "left out" by the Clinton administration. (Isn't it just a bit odd that liberals expect to be coddled and consulted when they've lost the White House, but think of Democrats meeting with conservative groups as less than politically necessary?)

Then, of course, there was the Monica Lewinsky scandal, which many liberals consider to be irrefutable evidence that the media's treatment of President Clinton was far from favorable. Actually, the Lewinsky scandal was two scandals: (1) Clinton's adulterous behavior and (2) Clinton's dishonesty—both lying to the American people and lying *under oath.* He was formally impeached on charges relating to these two scandals, and ultimately he confessed his guilt as an adulterer *and* a liar.

In Chapter 10, we'll explore in depth the media's handling of the Lewinsky case, showing how it is a myth that the press was unduly harsh on Clinton during that scandal. But for the time being, let's focus on some other cases that provide—or should provide—context for understanding the Lewinsky case. Bill Clinton was philandering long before he unpacked his bags at 1600 Pennsylvania Avenue. How did the news media see all this? Liberal journalists point to the media's supposedly comprehensive coverage of Clinton's extramarital relationships as evidence of the media's responsible and objective reporting. Is this true? Actually, the evidence demonstrates that the news media were uninterested in or dismissive of serious charges that Clinton was a philanderer, or something much worse than a philanderer. The most credible charges came from four women aside from Monica Lewinsky: Gennifer Flowers, Paula Jones, Kathleen Willey, and Juanita Broaddrick.

Flowers appeared on the national scene in January 1992, when the tabloid newspaper the *Star* ran an article about her alleged long-running affair with Bill Clinton. The media have claimed repeatedly that they reported the story at length during that year's primary campaign, but that's just not true. A Media Research Center study of the coverage in the week after the *Star* story hit the stands (January 24–30) found that the four broadcast networks (ABC, NBC, CBS, and PBS) ran a *total* of fourteen stories on the scandal on their evening news shows—a pittance. (As a means of comparison, in just four days, August 18–21, 1999, CBS News *by itself* ran at least fourteen stories on Republican candidate George W. Bush's rumored and unsubstantiated cocaine use, according to a Nexis search.) Worse, eight of the fourteen stories about the Flowers allegations were brief, anchor-read reports, not full news stories. These reports often highlighted the money Flowers received from the *Star*, thus calling into doubt her credibility.

During this period the weekly newsmagazines (in their February 3 issues) were openly dismissive of Flowers's allegations against the Democratic contender. *U.S. News & World Report*'s article was entitled "Money for Mischief." "We're Voting for President, Not Pope," was the headline judgment of *Newsweek*'s editors. And a *Time* article was even more direct: "Who Cares, Anyway?"

The media sent a clear signal: Gennifer Flowers wasn't to be trusted or even accorded serious consideration. That helped Clinton when he went on CBS's *60 Minutes* to deny her allegation of an affair. The only trouble was that, apparently, Flowers was making a legitimate claim. Six years later, when testifying under oath in the Paula Jones sexual harassment case, President Clinton reportedly acknowledged having had a sexual relationship with Flowers. Oh well. If Bill Clinton lied on *60 Minutes* that night in January 1992, it certainly wasn't the last time he took to national television to lie to the American people.

While the media dismissed Gennifer Flowers, they were downright hostile to Paula Jones. The former Arkansas state employee charged that Clinton, as Arkansas governor in 1991, had lured her to a hotel room and made crude sexual advances. Initial press descriptions revealed the same elitist prejudice that we would later see in coverage of Matthew Shepard's death. The words of James Carville—"Drag hundred-dollar bills through trailer parks, there's no telling what you'll find"—were repackaged and repeated by the media themselves.

To the media elites, Jones was another of the Great Unwashed, an Arkansas hillbilly, plain old white trash bent on money and fame. Evan Thomas of *Newsweek* was one of the ringleaders. On a 1994 episode of *Inside Washington,* the Harvard-educated Thomas called Jones "some sleazy woman with big hair coming out of the trailer parks" and claimed she was "not a very credible witness." But Thomas wasn't alone in looking down his East Coast nose. *Time* columnist Margaret Carlson made the same point on CNN's *Capital Gang*: "I think at least the American people are more likely to believe the President than they are to believe, you know, someone without a job, from Arkansas, whose lawyer says she's not in it for money, but clearly she's in it for something—fame, celebrity, money, something."

The fact that Jones would eventually pose nude in *Penthouse* and appear on Fox's embarrassing celebrity boxing spectacle would make many of these critics feel vindicated. But while Jones may not be a particularly pleasant person to defend, the point is that the media vilified her because of her appearance and background, who she was and where she was from. Imagine if members of the media said these sorts of things about a person from a minority background; you can bet the bank the commentators would immediately—and rightfully—be branded racists.

The networks really didn't want to cover the Jones case, and in fact, even after Jones accused Clinton of sexual harassment, they sat on the story for three months. (The only exception was ABC, which devoted all of sixteen *seconds* to the story prior to May 1994.) In an interview with Tim Russert on CNBC, NBC's Tom Brokaw explained why. "Why didn't we put it on earlier? It didn't seem, I think to most people, entirely relevant to what was going on at the time," Brokaw said. Who were "most people"—the public? If so, why, during the Clinton impeachment trial a few years later, were "most people" suddenly interested in what Congressman Henry Hyde was doing in his private life decades earlier? Or in Congressman Dan Burton's private life? Or Congressman Bob Barr's? Do "most people" care only about *Republican* scandals?

It becomes clear that when Tom Brokaw talks about "most people," he's not referring to the American public; he is referring to his colleagues in the press.

Another credible Clinton accuser was Kathleen Willey, a campaign volunteer who also worked at the White House early in the Clinton administration. Willey burst onto the national scene after a rare two-segment interview on the March 15, 1998, edition of *60 Minutes,* in which she told her interviewer that President Clinton fondled her breasts and put her hand on his genitals in a study next to the Oval Office.

"Wow! That was something!" exclaimed NBC's *Today* show cohost Matt Lauer the next day. But if that really was "something," why wasn't the Willey story taken seriously when it first broke *more than seven months earlier?*

On July 30, 1997, the *CBS Evening News* reported in a brief story (without naming Willey) that Paula Jones's lawyers had subpoenaed Willey to testify. Of course, reporter Bill Plante issued the requisite disclaimer: "But unless and until this case is settled, this is only the beginning of attempts by attorneys on both sides to damage the reputations and credibility of everyone involved." That same day, CNN's *Inside Politics* put a Willey brief at the end of the show and gave it twenty-six seconds on the evening newscast of *The World Today.* The next day, CBS and NBC aired brief updates underlining Willey's angry reaction to the Jones subpoena. Again, CBS couldn't be bothered even to give Willey's name. That was still better than ABC, which aired nothing whatsoever.

In its August 11 issue, *Newsweek* detailed Willey's story, which led to some more news coverage but not to any substantial investigation. Only when *60 Minutes* decided to run its interview, seven months later, did the Willey story get serious attention.

Juanita Broaddrick's story went far beyond the harassment charges of Willey and Jones: the Arkansas nursing home operator claimed that in 1978 she had been raped by Bill Clinton, then the attorney general of Arkansas. Broaddrick's tale was a credible one; she had told a small number of friends shortly after the alleged attack took place, which had led to a deposition before the Paula Jones legal team. When Jones's lawyers cited a "Jane Doe #5" whom Clinton had supposedly assaulted, NBC's Lisa Myers ran a story on Saturday, March 28, 1998, revealing Broaddrick as Jane Doe #5 and detailing the assault charge and how it had become public. Myers also interviewed Phillip Yoakum, an acquaintance whom Broaddrick had told of the alleged attack in 1981.

ABC ran a story on the charges on both March 28 and March 29, and CBS ran a story on the 29th. Yet both networks framed their stories not around Broaddrick's explosive charge but around White House outrage.

And what happened next? Nothing. For several months, utter silence. Behind the scenes, however, Myers was working diligently on the story, pursuing Broaddrick and finally arranging an interview with her set to air on January 20, 1999.

But it didn't air then. NBC was suddenly overcome by hand-wringing, self-doubt, and, one can imagine, more than a little pressure from the Clinton White House. Matt Drudge exposed NBC's stalling tactics on his website in late January, and it suddenly became the hot topic on talk radio and Internet sites. Radio talkmeister Don Imus knew about the story—he'd read it on the Drudge Report like everyone else—and asked *Meet the Press* host Tim Russert about it in a February 2 interview. "If and when we lock up a story, we'll go with it," Russert said. "If we don't, we won't."

While NBC dawdled, Fox News picked up the story. On the night of February 2, Fox reporter Rita Cosby ran a Broaddrick story on *Special Report with Brit Hume*. Although Cosby did nothing more than recite the basic facts that Myers had laid out nearly a full year earlier, the Fox News story soon became the center of more Internet buzz and rumors, since everyone knew that NBC had the interview with Broaddrick in the can but was not airing it. Drudge posted a story on his site shortly after the Fox report aired, claiming that the White House, in the person of Press Secretary Joe Lockhart, had threatened the cable network in an attempt to keep it from running the story.

Despite the buzz and rumors, the story—a credible rape charge against the president of the United States—remained dormant for a couple of weeks. Then on Friday, February 19, Dorothy Rabinowitz ran a story on the *Wall Street Journal* editorial page that detailed her interview with Broaddrick, who, feeling betrayed by NBC, had decided to talk to other outlets.

The very next day, the *Washington Post* ran a front-page story based on interviews it had conducted with Broaddrick the previous spring. The *Post* included a story by media critic Howard Kurtz citing NBC insiders who claimed that Myers and Russert were both frustrated by their inability to get the Broaddrick piece aired. According to the insiders, every time Myers had the story completed, the NBC bigwigs raised the evidentiary bar higher.

Surely a front-page *Washington Post* story on such an incendiary subject would lead to a media frenzy, right? Wrong. The rules were different for the Clinton White House. NBC's *Today* gave the story eighteen seconds that morning. Its own *Nightly News* ignored it, as did ABC's *World News Tonight*. That night only the *CBS Evening News* and CNN's *World News Today* put together segments based on the *Post* story.

And over the next ten days, the major networks basically ignored the story, refusing to investigate it or expand on it. Although a Nexis search revealed that NBC News featured seventeen mentions of Broaddrick between February 19 and February 28, that figure taken alone is highly misleading. In fact, eight of the Nexis hits were from the February 28 *Meet the Press*, on which a gaggle of politicians, journalists, and political activists discussed the rape charge. Four more were from *Today*, including three from its February 25 show. There was only one *story* on NBC's *Nightly News*; this came on February 24, the night

Myers's interview finally ran on *Dateline NBC,* when Tom Brokaw dedicated a whopping *twenty-seven words* to the story.

Meanwhile, according to Nexis, ABC mentioned Broaddrick four times from February 19 through February 28, while CBS managed only one mention. That's right. A credible charge of sexual violence leveled against a sitting president drew only one story from CBS, and that was on the night of the front-page *Post* story.

So much for the negative media coverage of Bill Clinton.

The Pariah Becomes a Media Darling

While Clinton as president probably enjoyed the most sympathetic press since the days of John F. Kennedy, he certainly isn't the only liberal to benefit from a double standard. The mainstream media reviled David Brock when he worked as a conservative reporter investigating Clinton. But when Brock changed his political philosophy and became a Clinton apologist, the author was suddenly showered with attention and affection from the media.

Brock first burst on the scene when he wrote *The Real Anita Hill,* a 1993 exposé of the woman who nearly wrecked the confirmation of Supreme Court Justice Clarence Thomas. Brock's book on Hill was all but ignored by the mainstream media, especially the television networks. His appearances were sparse and almost always in conjunction with a liberal critic of the book, such as Hill lawyer Charles Ogletree, who repeatedly called Brock a liar during a *Today* show interview in May 1993. Talk show heavyweights Larry King (CNN) and Charlie Rose (PBS) flatly refused to book Brock unless he appeared with liberal critics.

In contrast, pro-Hill authors Jane Mayer and Jill Abramson of the *Wall Street Journal* were given the red carpet treatment, invited to appear on almost every available media forum in late October and early November of 1994 to discuss their book, *Strange Justice: The Selling of Clarence Thomas.* Mayer and Abramson appeared on Larry King, Charlie Rose, and *Nightline,* as well as ABC's *Good Morning America* and CBS's *This Morning.*

At about the time Mayer and Abramson's book was published, Brock became a hero in conservative journalism. He proceeded to complete an investigative report for the *American Spectator* magazine that exposed the ongoing lies about Bill Clinton's serial adultery. For the story, Brock interviewed Arkansas state troopers who had been part of Governor Clinton's security detail and who claimed they had set up extramarital trysts for the governor. "Troopergate" became yet another Clinton scandal, but the liberal media continued virtually to ignore both Brock and the evidence he compiled. While talk radio was on fire with the story, the mainstream press was practically silent. If any coverage was given, as it was on CNN, the story was—again—the Clinton White House's "outrage," not the scandal itself.

But after years on the Clinton-scandal beat, Brock's investigative ambitions took a sharp turn—left. His 1996 book, *The Seduction of Hillary Rodham*, began with the author praising Mrs. Clinton as a "high-achieving, straight-A student, world-class organizer, determined operator, and gifted proselytizer" who was guilty only by association with her much guiltier husband. The book marked Brock's bizarre ideological transformation, and it wasn't long before he learned to love Bill, too. In June 1997, he turned on his friends personally and viciously, penning "Confessions of a Right-Wing Hit Man" for *Esquire* magazine, followed in March 1998 by a public letter of apology to President Clinton for bringing up his dangerous liaisons. "I do know that I didn't learn a damn thing worth knowing about your character" was one of Brock's more famous lines.

With these articles, Brock torched all his bridges to conservatives, but he began a new love affair with the very networks that had once reviled and ignored him. By turning on the Right, he had become a welcome guest on television. There he was, this time alone, on all three network morning shows; and on *Meet the Press* and *Face the Nation;* and on cable, telling his rapt new audience that he regretted all those awful things he reported about Arkansas's finest. No conservative was allowed on the set to rebut the nonsense.

When he published his next book, *Blinded by the Right: Confessions of an Ex-Conservative,* in the spring of 2002, he received similar fawning treatment. Brock appeared on the *Today* show and CNN *News-*

Night on back-to-back days. He was on CNN's *Crossfire* and *Reliable Sources* and on Tim Russert's CNBC show. The *New York Times* ran a special feature on him, as did *USA Today*. The *Los Angeles Times* ran a massive book review. On and on it went, with hundreds upon hundreds of mentions given to the man who wrote a book in which he proclaimed himself a liar.

How very odd. The press coverage of the strange saga of David Brock only underscores the point that the liberal media just don't care about the truth. What mattered in this case was that a former Clinton detractor changed his mind, and in doing so he suddenly became worthy of the airtime he had been denied previously. It didn't matter, for example, that revelations in the years since publication of the Troopergate story had only borne out Brock's case in that *American Spectator* piece. (Who could deny, by 2002, that Bill Clinton was reckless, that he used his position of power for personal, sexual gain?) Nor did it matter that *Blinded by the Right* was full of merciless—and often unfounded—personal attacks on his former comrades, including close friends. There were no media outbursts over such insults, of course, because they were now being directed at conservatives.

What a Difference a Lawsuit Makes

As the Brock case shows, the mainstream media will embrace certain undesirables as long as doing so will further their liberal agenda. During the Clinton years, the media treated Larry Klayman and his Judicial Watch litigation machine as Exhibit A of the vast right-wing conspiracy, as obsessive haters who were trying to frustrate Bill Clinton as he brilliantly went about "doing the work of the American people." The validity of Klayman's lawsuits and discovery processes by and large was irrelevant. He was to be ignored, period. But he would not be ignored and brazenly continued agitating. This made him a menace. *Time* magazine began one profile by saying, "Even in the fang-baring world of Bill Clinton's most dedicated pursuers, Larry Klayman is in a class by himself." And that was one of the nicer things said in the press about this man.

But in July 2002, Klayman filed suit against Vice President Dick Cheney, charging him with misleading investors in his previous role as CEO of the Halliburton energy concern, and—*blam!* How quickly he moved from *bête noire* to *cause célèbre*. As with Brock before him, Klayman was now credible. Conservatives, according to this judgment, are useful sources—but only when they attack fellow conservatives.

Shortly after the Cheney suit was filed, NPR newscasts were leading with Klayman on the hour. On July 10, Dan Rather placed him at the top of the CBS newscast, while ABC and NBC included their Klayman stories before the first commercial break. The fact that the network news programs were mentioning Judicial Watch was significant in itself, but even more interesting was how the networks chose to describe Klayman's organization.

On the rare occasion that Judicial Watch had been mentioned on the networks during the Clinton years, the telling label of "conservative" had almost always been attached. There was nothing inaccurate about that—Klayman actively solicited support from conservatives and served conservative goals—but the term served as a warning label to viewers ("Caution: Partisanship ahead—be skeptical").

But when Klayman sued Cheney, the ideological tag mysteriously vanished. Suddenly, there was no need for the warning label. Judicial Watch was now described as simply a "watchdog group," or a "Washington watchdog group," or a "legal group."

And every network, with the exception of Fox, was guilty of the switch. (The italic phrases here and on the next two pages have been added for emphasis.) On CNN, Judy Woodruff on March 3, 1998, had spoken of "lawyers for *the conservative group Judicial Watch*" who had questions about President Clinton and some FBI files. On July 10, 2002, however, Woodruff introduced a story about the suit against Cheney by stating, "The reviews of President Bush's speech on that subject [corporate responsibility] were still coming in today as *a watchdog group* said that it was suing Vice President Dick Cheney."

ABC had been particularly vigilant about applying the "conservative" label when talking about Judicial Watch suits against Democrats. In an October 24, 1996, story, reporter Brian Ross had referred to "Larry Klayman, *a conservative lawyer* who filed the lawsuit." In an

August 27, 2001, story on Anne Marie Smith, the flight attendant who claimed she had had a relationship with Congressman Gary Condit, reporter Pierre Thomas had described Judicial Watch's role in that episode in this manner: "Smith . . . appears to be fighting back, with support from *the conservative legal foundation Judicial Watch.*" Just a day later, while interviewing Smith's attorney on *Good Morning America,* Diane Sawyer had not only labeled Judicial Watch but also intimated that the organization's participation in the case could be a sign that something sinister was afoot: "The fact that you are joined in this request for a grand jury by Judicial Watch, according to the *New York Times* . . . 'adds a decidedly political edge to the case.' Is this a *Republican vendetta* of some kind? *A right-wing vendetta?*"

What a difference a lawsuit makes. Peter Jennings, on July 10, 2002, swallowed the supposedly necessary conservative label in his lead-in: "Now to this issue of Vice President Cheney. *A legal activist group called Judicial Watch* filed a lawsuit today against the Vice President and Halliburton, the energy company he used to run." The next day, newsreader Robin Roberts dropped labels, too. "*The watchdog group Judicial Watch* is suing Cheney and the energy company he once headed," Roberts said.

Over at the *CBS Evening News* it was more of the same. Phil Jones, in a December 6, 1996, story about Judicial Watch's suit against Clinton, had told viewers that "Judge Royce Lamberth issued an order to the Department of Commerce to produce documents being sought by *Judicial Watch; it's a conservative group* investigating foreign contributions to Democrats and the Clinton presidential campaign." Bob Schieffer also used the term on March 23, 1998, calling Judicial Watch a "*conservative watchdog group.*" But on July 10, 2002, CBS correspondent Wyatt Andrews expressed the media's changed attitude toward Klayman's now-nonideological group when he reported, "Vice President Cheney, already facing a six-week-old SEC investigation, was sued by *a watchdog group* alleging investor fraud."

Tom Brokaw and NBC hadn't even bothered to describe Judicial Watch as a "watchdog group" during the Florida election fiasco in December 2000. "Back in Florida, the news media and at least one *conservative advocacy group* have restarted the recount," Brokaw said. In the subsequent *Nightly News* story, Kerry Sanders noted that "a *conservative legal group, Judicial Watch,* is counting here as well, trying to figure out, it says, what standard Broward officials used when they counted the ballots and found Al Gore the winner." On that famous July 10, though, anchor Brian Williams, sitting in for Brokaw, told his viewers, "*A watchdog group* that tormented the Clinton administration filed suit against Vice President Cheney over alleged accounting irregularities at Halliburton." Campbell Brown followed Williams's lead: "*The legal group Judicial Watch* that made headlines helping Paula Jones with her lawsuit against President Clinton today sued Vice President Cheney. . . ."

In the eyes of the liberal media, Judicial Watch was suddenly big—and believable—news because it had attacked a conservative Republican vice president. By ushering the group to the top of the newscasts and dropping the ideological warning, the networks were saying to the news consumer: *Stop, listen. This is important and authoritative, all seriousness and no gamesmanship.*

Some might think Klayman, always a fax-melting attention-seeker, was guilty of entering undergraduate studies in the David Brock School of Betrayal in return for Media Accolades. But Klayman had not totally changed teams, for his website still touted his work against the Clintons. Far more noteworthy than Klayman's seeming turn against the Bush administration was the media's flip-flop; their worst-to-first treatment of Judicial Watch was truly jaw-dropping. A man whom they once considered unsavory as the legal counsel to the vast right-wing conspiracy earned the top news slot during July of 2002 simply because he filed a suit against a conservative instead of a liberal.

Law-breaking or Youthful Hijinks? Depends on Who's Doing It

The dismissive and uninterested media coverage of Clinton's scandals when he was a candidate has never been extended to conservatives. At the earliest stages of a campaign, conservatives are supposed to answer questions about unsubstantiated rumors and confess to every youthful mistake so the media can sit in judgment. And once conservatives are in their sights, there is absolutely no statute of limitations, nor is there any forgiveness for questionable personal behavior because of principled policy stands.

Those who say that all political candidates, regardless of party affiliation, must now endure intense questioning about their backgrounds should look more carefully at the media's role in the 2000 presidential campaign. The mainstream media investigated and developed in detail unfounded rumors of cocaine use by a young George W. Bush, while admissions of Al Gore's long-term marijuana use were all but ignored.

In August 1999, the national media pounced on Bush over swirling rumors that he had used cocaine in his youth. Reporters echoed the *Washington Post* reporters who urgently suggested to Bush that "we need to ask the cocaine question." Even though the *Post* and others had searched far and wide for any hint of evidence, no witness, no accuser, had stepped forward.

Candidate Bush refused to participate in what he called the "game" of fighting off one vile rumor after another. Instead, Bush stated simply, "When I was young and irresponsible, I was young and irresponsible." Many in the media skewered Bush for this statement. For example, on a *Nightline* episode devoted to the Bush rumors, Ted Koppel lectured, "Why not accept his one-size-fits-all declaration that when I was young and irresponsible, I was young and irresponsible? Perhaps, we might say, because he has never accepted youth and irresponsibility as legitimate excuses for illegal behavior."

But curiously, while Bush endured intense questioning about these unsubstantiated rumors and his seemingly unacceptable explanation, the media did not challenge Gore when he responded to the pot-smoking allegations with a very similar-sounding dodge: "When I was young, I did things young people do; when I grew up I put away childish things." Ted Koppel did not devote a whole edition of *Nightline* to parsing that "one-size-fits-all declaration."

Imagine what would have happened had an accuser come forward and said not only that he had indulged in drugs with George W. Bush but also that the Bush family had pressured him to lie about it. The media reaction, correctly, would have been merciless. In a matter of days—hours, maybe—Bush would have been forced to quit the race, thoroughly disgraced.

Yet this is precisely what happened with Gore. When *Newsweek* magazine (the *Washington Post*'s corporate cousin) spiked an excerpt from its own reporter Bill Turque's biography of Al Gore dealing with Gore's use of marijuana, a witness named John Warnecke, a Gore friend for many years, spoke out. More damning still, Warnecke alleged that he and Gore had regularly smoked marijuana together right up to Gore's initial run for Congress in 1976 (and once even during that campaign). Warnecke also maintained that he had been called in rapid succession by Al Gore, one of his campaign aides, and his wife, Tipper, all urging him not to talk to the press. But now the story was out . . . and the networks were silent. Even most of the print publications that noted the accusations chose not to include Warnecke's claim that he had been pressured to keep the truth from reporters.

Unfortunately, the media's double standard on personal lives extends to political offspring as well. To be sure, how to cover scandals involving children of public figures is a difficult question. What is not in dispute is that there cannot be one set of rules for one camp and another for the opposition.

When George W. Bush's daughter Jenna was cited for underage drinking in an Austin, Texas, bar on May 30, 2001, the media rushed to cover the story. This was a newsworthy event, journalists and pundits proclaimed, and they were probably right, distasteful as the story was. Jonathan Alter, *Newsweek*'s poster child for liberal media bias, declared on MSNBC that any improperly obtained margaritas by Chelsea Clinton would have been a big story, as well. "Any time somebody in the public spotlight, even if they don't intend to be there, has some connection with law enforcement, you can bet that it will be a news story."

Well, that's not really true—not if your father is a liberal Democrat. In October 1995, Maryland police caught Sarah Gore, the sixteen-year-old daughter of the vice president, with an open can of beer. "She broke our rules and she broke the law. She's extremely miserable and unhappy," Tipper Gore told the local Fox affiliate. The *Washington Post* covered the story but focused on Sarah, the star athlete and great student. The networks, broadcast and cable, said absolutely nothing. Neither did Alter.

In 1996, only the vaguest whispers surfaced that Al Gore III, then just thirteen, was suspended from school for possession of marijuana. British newspapers suggested that the vice president had effectively asked editors for restraint. Fast-forward four years to August of 2000, when Al III had a far more serious brush with the law, driving ninety-seven miles per hour in a fifty-five-mile-per-hour zone in North Carolina. Who was a greater danger to the public? Jenna Bush snatching margaritas with her fake ID, or a seventeen-year-old kid playing Mario Andretti on the highway? And yet, in the middle of an election year, newspapers didn't do much more than run a perfunctory AP wire story about young Gore's reckless driving, while the major networks didn't breathe a word of the story. So much for the Alter rule.

You could even make a retroactive argument for Karenna Gore, since an August 2000 *Time* magazine profile noted, "By the time she hit the teen years, her spirited nature veered into open rebellion. Karenna lectured her parents on how their rules infringed on her First Amendment rights. She was big on 'adventuring,' climbing out of her window to shimmy down a manhole into the D.C. subway system for after-hours partying." I suspect these were not Kool-Aid parties, and we'll probably never know because no one bothered to look into the matter.

How then do the media justify the avalanche of stories on Jenna? ABC's Elizabeth Vargas felt the need to point out that "it has become an issue because President Bush himself has admitted that he had a drinking problem as a man, quit drinking when he was forty, was in fact arrested for driving under the influence." If that's so, why did no one hit the soapbox to ask if Al Gore III's alleged marijuana handling was learned from Dear Old Dad? No one asked what kind of "adventuring" influences the Gores instilled in their daughter, either.

Was the Jenna Bush arrest a credible story? Yes. But no one should pretend that the media have applied a consistent standard based on the involvement of law enforcement. Bush's daughters will continue having to live up to a higher standard. Republicans always do.

When Ethics Matter

Not only do conservatives have to meet higher standards of personal conduct, they also have to meet higher ethical standards. Just ask Newt Gingrich, who as House Speaker found himself at the center of a feeding frenzy because of an allegation that he had violated tax laws with a televised history course he offered, "Renewing American Civilization." The network news departments made sure everyone in the civilized world knew the Speaker was a possible, if not probable, lawbreaker. Indeed, in just six weeks between mid-December 1996 and late January 1997, Gingrich's ethical problems inspired no less than 234 separate news reports on the networks' morning and evening news shows, a veritable avalanche of reporting. Ultimately, Gingrich would agree to pay the House of Representatives a $300,000 fine.

Then the IRS jumped in with its own investigation. But after three and a half years of investigation, the IRS cleared Gingrich and his allied nonprofit groups of any violation of the tax laws in the controversy over his television history course. In other words, Gingrich was *innocent.*

So, after having run 234 news reports highlighting the accusations during a six-week period, a fair and balanced media would surely make a major effort to correct the record, to report the resolution. How many stories did fair and balanced ABC, CBS, and NBC devote to Newt Gingrich's vindication? Zero. Only CNN's Brooks Jackson filed a decent TV report on the early evening show *Inside Politics*. "It was legal after all," Jackson began. "Newt Gingrich's oh-so-controversial college course that he started back in 1993, before he was Speaker. Remember how Democrats denounced it?" Jackson then highlighted old footage of Democrats David Bonior ("Mr. Gingrich engaged in a pattern of tax fraud") and John Lewis ("We now have a Speaker under investigation for lying to the outside counsel, investigating his involvement in a massive tax-fraud scheme"). But with so few reporters focusing on Gingrich's exoneration, Democrats—and the media—didn't have to worry too much about issuing apologies.

An in-depth examination of the Gingrich story provides even more evidence of the media's inherent and unethical double standard. When Gingrich's troubles first arose and the House fined him $300,000, Bob Dole, the former senator and Republican presidential candidate, offered to loan Gingrich the money; at the time, Dole was lobbying for a tobacco company on Capitol Hill. The media outcry over this proposed loan, with all of the conflict-of-interest overtones, was immediate and intense.

On CNN's *Late Edition,* for example, Steve Roberts, then with *U.S. News & World Report,* noted Dole's job with a law firm lobbying on the tobacco settlement and asked, "Do we really want a Speaker of the House who owes $300,000 to a guy who's a principal in a major lobbying firm?" On *Inside Washington, Newsweek's* Evan Thomas bemoaned the fact that Dole had retired from public service to "become an influence peddler so he can post bail for Newt Gingrich."

But just two years later, in 1999, onetime lobbyist Terry McAuliffe—the Clintons' fund-raiser extraordinaire, who would later be rewarded for his abilities as a rainmaker by being named chairman of the Democratic National Committee—did something that raised important ethical questions: He pledged *$1.35 million* of his own money to secure a mortgage on the Clintons' New York home.

Media outrage? Media anger? Hardly.

Typical of the mainstream media's response was the *Washington Post's* September 3 account of the deal. While noting that the Clintons would finance the purchase "with major assistance from the Democratic Party's top fund-raiser," the *Post* saw nothing controversial in the deal. The only potential problem for the Clintons, according to the story, was whether "all the attention to the house hunt might be contributing to a lame-duck image for a president in his seventh year." Yes, that *would* be a problem for the *Washington Post* and its Democratic president, wouldn't it? But how about the other questions that McAuliffe's financial assistance raised?

First of all, the arrangement made some curious about why a sitting president would make himself so financially dependent on one individual. But more troubling was the fact that at the time the Department of Labor was investigating a McAuliffe business venture that had allegedly fleeced a union's pension fund. Was it appropriate for the president of the United States to accept more than a million dollars from someone connected to a government investigation? But the mainstream media did not address any potential conflict of interest in their reports on the Clintons' house purchase. (Ultimately the two union officials with whom McAuliffe had his business arrangement would agree "to pay hundreds of thousands of dollars in penalties for their actions" and the union would "reimburse its pension fund by nearly $5 million," as *National Review*'s Byron York later reported.) What Bob Novak called "McAuliffe's mixing of government, politics, union affairs and personal business" also could have prompted the news media to ask questions about the Clintons' benefactor, but those questions were not immediately forthcoming. Nor did the media make much of the fact that McAuliffe's financial assistance could represent the ultimate in-kind contribution to the future Hillary-for-Senate campaign.

The pundits actually labored *not* to raise the controversy. A notable exception was Jack Germond, the gruff liberal columnist who on the September 11, 1999, episode of *Inside Washington* predicted that Mrs. Clinton was "going to start to get a little static from the Republicans on Terry McAuliffe putting up the $1.3 million for their house. No other Senate candidate could do that and get away with it. If that were a Republican we'd all be screaming at the press." He added that if a conservative "were getting that kind of money we'd all be saying that's illegal." In response, the pride of National Public Radio, Nina Totenberg, corrected Germond on just how the hypocrisy would work: "Well, that's not illegal. We'd all be saying it smells."

But the Clintons' deal apparently didn't "smell" to most of the commentators. In *Newsweek*, Newt-basher Evan Thomas gave McAuliffe's role the kind of glib once-over that would make Democratic spinmeister Paul Begala proud: "An amiable Clinton golfing buddy who, perhaps as much as any friend, stood by the President during the

Lewinsky scandal, McAuliffe is also raising money for Hillary's Senate campaign. While unorthodox, McAuliffe's sugar-daddy role on the Clinton house appears to be perfectly legal."

Meanwhile, ABC called on its "objective" political analyst, former Clinton aide George Stephanopoulos, to offer his "hard-hitting" analysis of the house purchase. Stephanopoulos sounded like the Clintons' real-estate agent: "It's a nice traditional house, it's private, near a lot of golf courses for the president, and finally they've got a swimming pool. . . . Hillary has wanted a swimming pool for a long time."

Clearly, on this deal as on so many other matters, the Clintons were not under intense media scrutiny. In this case, however, other groups stepped in to fill the watchdog role that the news media had abdicated. Some conservative groups questioned the ethics of the Clintons' financial arrangement with Terry McAuliffe, with the nonprofit group Democracy 21 filing a complaint with the Federal Election Commission. At last the questions that the mainstream media had refused to raise were being asked publicly. The next month the Clintons announced that they had sought new financing on the New York house; McAuliffe's money was no longer part of the deal.

It was a small victory for ethics—but not one for which we can thank the liberal media.

3

A Case Study in Liberal Bias

W HEN THE SUBJECT of media bias comes up, liberals often turn the discussion to the rise of conservative talk radio and the Fox News Channel. Essentially their argument is that even if the mainstream news media do betray a liberal bias (something most liberals still aren't willing to concede, despite the overwhelming evidence of such bias), it doesn't matter because conservative voices are somehow balancing the dialogue.

That is ridiculous. Remember, we're talking only about *news* media. Conservative talk-radio hosts, along with conservatives on television like Bob Novak and Sean Hannity, are *commentators*, not "reporters" in the "news" media. Moreover, these conservatives openly, cheerfully acknowledge their biases, something that liberals in the mainstream media refuse to do.

Okay, but what about the news programs on the Fox News Channel? Well, even if we assume that Fox News is as conservative as liberals charge—and this is an assumption I am not willing to make—it is just one network standing athwart the liberal spin provided by ABC, CBS, NBC, CNN, CNN Headline News, CNBC, MSNBC, and PBS. Yes, Fox News *is* having an effect, and its influence will only grow in the coming years. But right now it is a bit player compared with the Big Three networks.

Interestingly, one who has made this very argument about the relative insignificance of Fox News is the ultraliberal Eric Alterman. In the introduction to his book *What Liberal Media?* Alterman writes, "The combined audience of the three network [evening] news programs is well over thirty million Americans. . . . It is also more than ten times the combined total prime-time audience for Fox News Channel, CNN, and MSNBC."

Exactly. Mr. Alterman gets something right for a change.

The statistics that Alterman cites illustrate an important point: Despite the rise of alternative news outlets, most Americans today still get their news from the liberal mainstream media, especially the network news programs. And here the liberal bias is pronounced, which is why any study of media bias must pay close attention to how the news is covered on ABC's *World News Tonight*, NBC's *Nightly News*, and the *CBS Evening News.*

Of the Big Three news anchors, the longest-serving is Dan Rather of CBS. Rather's *CBS Evening News* drew headlines in July 2003 when it posted its lowest numbers in at least a decade (and maybe ever), averaging 6.5 million viewers. But think about those "low" ratings: Even during a time that the Associated Press called "generally the least-watched TV weeks of the year," well over *six million people* each night were tuning in to hear Dan Rather dispense his peculiar brand of liberal spin.

Indeed, liberal spin is exactly what viewers often get from Rather. For that reason, he makes for an instructive case study in liberal bias. Looking closely at how the anchor of a venerable network news operation betrays his liberal bias reveals a lot about how the mainstream media work.

But there is another reason to focus on Rather. Conservatives often make the mistake of assuming that if a journalist is as passionately liberal on some fronts as Rather is, it follows that he must be uniformly liberal on all issues. To study Rather's record is to understand that this is just not so.

Skewed Reporting and Twisted Logic

Dan Rather is an intelligent, experienced journalist who got to the top of his profession through hard work, determination, and perseverance. Born in the small town of Wharton, Texas, in 1931, he worked as a reporter for the Associated Press, United Press International, the *Houston Chronicle,* and a Houston television station before going to work for CBS in 1962. Nineteen years later, in March 1981, he became the anchor of the *CBS Evening News.* In the years since then he has also anchored *48 Hours,* been a correspondent for *60 Minutes II,* and filed countless radio news and analysis pieces for the CBS Radio Network.

Aside from being known as one of America's leading newsmen, Rather is known for his colorful, often perplexing phrases—"Ratherisms." A particularly close Senate race, the CBS anchor observed, was as "hot and tight as a too small bathing suit on a too long car ride back from the beach." A Republican primary in Michigan was "tighter than Willie Nelson's headband." George W. Bush's lead on Election Night 2000 was "shakier than cafeteria Jell-O." Then there are Rather's animal lines, which often leave viewers scratching their heads. In a 1998 appearance with David Letterman, Rather declared that Independent Counsel Kenneth Starr could have found Monica Lewinsky without the Paula Jones case, but "that's like if a frog had side pockets he'd probably wear a handgun. It didn't happen that way." In 2000, describing the vice presidential debate between Democrat Joe Lieberman and Republican Dick Cheney, he noted, "Senator Lieberman used the phrase 'big time.' Cheney shot him back a look as if to say—looked at him like he was a hitchhiker with pets." And sometimes Rather has abandoned the animal theme to offer the truly bizarre, as when, characterizing the likelihood of his remaining as CBS anchor too much longer, he told the *Los Angeles Times,* "You can sooner expect a tall talking broccoli stick to offer to mow your lawn for free."

Rather's down-home language (no matter how inscrutable) may make him seem benign, but the fact that the CBS anchor has consistently used his position as news leader to flack for Democrats and liberal causes is a serious problem. Even more troubling is that all the while he has stubbornly denied that liberal media bias—his own liberal bias—exists. In 1995, for example, he told Denver radio host Mike Rosen, "When you start talking about a liberal agenda, and all the, quote, 'liberal bias' in the media, I quite frankly . . . I don't know what you're talking about." The next year, after former CBS correspondent Bernard Goldberg wrote a *Wall Street Journal* editorial about liberal bias at CBS News, Rather told CNN's Larry King that he had a simple response to Goldberg's charges: "Bullfeathers." Goldberg's 2001 book, *Bias: A CBS Insider Exposes How the Media Distort the News*, revealed how much the *Journal* editorial had upset the CBS anchor: "Dan Rather, the man who assured me 'we were friends yesterday, we're friends today, and we'll be friends tomorrow,' hasn't spoken a word to me. I could have taken out a full-page ad in the *New York Times* saying Dan Rather wears black stiletto, do-me heels and red miniskirts behind the anchor desk, and he wouldn't have gotten as mad as when I said we have a bias problem in the media."

Rather's temper surely must have flared in the summer of 2002 when an old CBS hand, *60 Minutes* commentator Andy Rooney, pointed out the obvious. "I thought he [Goldberg] made some very good points," Rooney said on the June 5 *Larry King Live.* "There is just no question that I, among others, have a liberal bias. I mean, I'm consistently liberal in my opinions. And . . . I think Dan [Rather] is transparently liberal. Now, he may not like to hear me say that. I always agree with him, too, but I think he should be more careful."

What could have prompted Rooney to call Rather "transparently liberal"? How about the way Rather supported the Democrats? Compare these descriptions of the Republican and Democratic tickets in the 2000 election.

"The official announcement and photo-op today [was] of Republican George Bush and his running mate Richard Cheney," Rather told viewers on the July 25 *CBS Evening News.* "Democrats were quick to portray the ticket as quote 'two Texas oilmen' because Cheney was chief of a big Dallas-based oil supply conglomerate. They also blast Cheney's voting record in Congress as again, quote, 'outside the American mainstream' because of Cheney's votes against the Equal Rights for Women Amendment, against a woman's right to choose abortion—'against abortion,' as Cheney prefers to put it—and Cheney's votes against gun control." Almost as an afterthought, he added, "Republicans see it all differently, most of them hailing Bush's choice and Cheney's experience."

Just two weeks later Rather gushed about the Democratic ticket. "Democratic presidential candidate Al Gore officially introduced his history-making running mate today, Senator Joseph Lieberman of Connecticut," Rather said on August 8. "History-making because Lieberman is of Jewish heritage and faith. The two started running right away. In their first joint appearance they gave a preview of the Gore-Lieberman fight-back, comeback strategy. Their message: They represent the future, not the past, and they are the ticket of high moral standards most in tune with real mainstream America."

Rather's liberal perspective has been equally apparent in his coverage of issues. When President Bush issued his policy on clean air in 2001, Rather slammed it: "President Bush insisted today that he was not caving in to big-money contributors, big-time lobbyists, and overall industry pressure when he broke a campaign promise to regulate carbon dioxide emissions from power plants. But the air was thick today with accusations from people"—like Rather?—"who believe that's exactly what happened." When the House passed Bush's budget in 2001, the CBS anchor made sure to tell his viewers that the federal budget blueprint "includes his big tax-cut plan, partly bankrolled, critics say"—again, those critics!—"through cuts in many federal aid programs for children and education." This was the same budget that Rather had described, when Bush first presented it, as "his cut-federal-programs-to-get-a-tax-cut plan."

Abortion is another case in point. In the past Rather has flatly assumed the abortion lobby's position, equating abortion rights with women's rights. For example, in 1990 Rather asked Democrat Paul Simon, then a senator from Illinois, whether he felt Supreme Court nominee David Souter's abortion views paralleled those of President George H. W. Bush's chief of staff, John Sununu, "which means he's anti-abortion or anti–women's rights, whichever way you want to put it."

When George W. Bush took office eleven years later, Rather was still concerned about abortion. On January 22, 2001, he told CBS viewers, "This was President Bush's first day at the office and he did something to quickly please the right flank in his party: He reinstituted an anti-abortion policy that had been in place during his father's term and the Reagan presidency but was lifted during the Clinton years."

Bush's move was a political move, according to Rather, made to placate the right wing of his party. But eight years earlier Rather had described Bill Clinton's move to make abortions more readily available not as a political maneuver to mollify the left wing of his party but simply as a campaign promise kept. "On the anniversary of *Roe v. Wade,* President Clinton fulfills a promise, supporting abortion rights," Rather had said on the January 22, 1993, *Evening News.* "It was twenty years ago today, the United States Supreme Court handed down its landmark abortion rights ruling, and the controversy hasn't stopped since. Today, with the stroke of a pen, President Clinton delivered on his campaign promise to cancel several anti-abortion regulations of the Reagan-Bush years."

Yet nowhere has Rather's liberal bias been more evident than in his support of Bill and Hillary Clinton. On May 27, 1993, just a few short months into the Clinton administration, Rather publicly demonstrated how much he adored the First Couple. *Washington Post* reporter John Carmody revealed how during a CBS affiliates' meeting to announce that Connie Chung would coanchor the evening newscast with Rather (which would prove to be a disaster for the network), President Clinton said to Rather, via satellite, "I think you two will be great together. I'm excited about it." Rather positively glowed. "Thank you, Mr. President. Thank you! Thank you!" he exclaimed. "Mr. President, if we could be one one-hundredth as great as you and Hillary Rodham Clinton have been together in the White House, we'd take it right now and walk away winners." And that embarrassing display of obsequiousness wasn't enough for Rather, as he later said to the president, "Tell Mrs. Clinton we respect her and we're pulling for her."

Five years later, Rather proved that he hadn't lost that squishy feeling. On December 8, 1998, he took to CNN's *Larry King Live* to lavish praise on Hillary Clinton. When King asked him who he thought should be *Time* magazine's "Person of the Year," Rather gave a somewhat rambling response that nevertheless revealed how smitten he was with Mrs. Clinton. "I would not be astonished to see Hillary Clinton be the Democratic nominee in 2000," he told King. "Listen, I agree that Al Gore is the odds-on favorite. He's probably going to be the nominee. But . . . here we are talking about a race almost two years away. Hillary Clinton, as far as I'm concerned, she's the Person of the Year. . . . You talk about a comeback kid—she makes her husband look like Ned in kneepants in terms of comeback from where she was early in the Clinton administration. You know, you add it all up, and you can make a case that Hillary Clinton might, *might*—mark the word—be the strongest candidate for the Democrats."

But Rather knew Mrs. Clinton would never be the Democratic Party's presidential nominee in 2000—she would wait a few years before going after the Oval Office—so he had an alternative idea. Perhaps she could be appointed to the Supreme Court. Referring to the Democrats' presumptive nominee, Rather asked King, "If you were Al Gore, what would you do [for Mrs. Clinton]?"

"Make her, ask her to be vice president. Is that what you think? Is that where you're leading me?" King replied.

"No," Rather said. "I think maybe I would say, 'You know, we want the goals of the Clinton administration to be achieved and to go forward. I need your help, first lady, friend of mine, Hillary Clinton, and if I'm elected president, I will make you the next chief justice of the United States Supreme Court.' That's what I'd do, but Al Gore is a better man than I am and I doubt that he'd do it."

Dan Rather's regard for the Clintons remained undiminished after they left the White House. On May 15, 2001, the CBS anchor went on Fox News Channel's *The O'Reilly Factor* to make this astonishing statement about Bill Clinton, the president who had admitted to lying to his family and to the American people (not to mention lying under oath): "I think he's an honest man." When host Bill O'Reilly demanded to know the logic behind this bizarre contention, Rather said, "I think at core he's an honest person. . . . I think you can be an honest person and lie about any number of things."

Twisted logic, to be sure. Most Clintonites by that point had given up on the argument that their fearless leader was an honest man, but not America's longest-serving news anchor.

The Anchor as Democratic Fund-raiser

There is an ongoing debate within journalistic circles as to how much members of the press should involve themselves in the world of politics or public policy. The purists maintain that journalists should distance themselves entirely, should avoid any "semblance of impropriety," because reporters must at all times be seen as objective, as having no personal interest in subjects they might have to cover. Others, however, believe that certain rules—such as the one that prohibits reporters from accepting speaking fees—are silly and unfair. After all, as long as reporters can demonstrate an ability to remain detached from the organization providing the honorarium, or as long as they recuse themselves from covering the organization altogether, is accepting a small speaking fee really harmful?

But on other matters of journalistic ethics there is no debate. One firm rule is that journalists can never publicly use their celebrity or their clout to advance a political cause.

That, however, is precisely what Dan Rather did on March 21, 2001. That night he appeared as the main speaker at a $20,000 fund-raiser for the Travis County Democratic Party in Austin, Texas. Even the *Washington Post* saw this breach as front-page material, but when he was confronted with the story, Democrat Dan had some curious things to say. Sounding an awful lot like Al Gore after the infamous Democratic fund-raiser at a Buddhist temple in California, Rather claimed he hadn't realized beforehand that the event was a fund-raiser. But, according to the *Post,* he "stopped short of calling his appearance a mistake or saying he would not have attended had he known in advance that he was being used to raise money." Why stop short of making such an easy, perfunctory statement? Probably because one of the event's hosts was Robin Rather, the anchor's daughter and a "Texas environmentalist and marketing executive" who reportedly was eyeing a run for mayor of Austin.

Rather also tried to get out from under the story by emphasizing how he had had his picture taken the night before with Texas's Republican governor, Rick Perry. Yet the newsman didn't help raise $20,000 for Perry, so there wasn't even a hint of balance. Then Rather claimed, "Over a long period of time, I've met with political groups large and small, Democratic and Republican, Green Party, mugwumps, you name it, because that's what reporters do." But there's an enormous difference between *meeting with* a political group and using your position to *raise money* for that group. Reporters shouldn't headline fund-raisers for political parties, period.

In truth, plenty of other prominent journalists have flouted journalistic ethics and attended fund-raisers for liberal interest groups. Before Rather showed up at the Texas Democrats' fund-raiser, the leftist group TransAfrica had drawn Bernard Shaw, Bryant Gumbel, and Ted Koppel; the Children's Defense Fund had featured Roger Rosenblatt and Jane Pauley; and the NAACP Legal Defense Fund had held a fund-raiser with ABC's Carole Simpson as the headliner. But Rather's transgression was in another league altogether, because he was raising money for a political party. The invitation to the event had said, "Please join us for an evening with DAN RATHER," while the accompanying RSVP envelope had asked for donations of up to $1,000 for the county's Democratic Party.

Nor was this the first time Rather's sympathy for Democrats of the Texas variety had led him to a fund-raiser. In November 1988, gossip columnist Liz Smith reported that a "gang" which included Dan Rather and his wife got together in New York City and "gathered up money in buckets" for Ann Richards's (ultimately successful) 1990 run for governor.

Perhaps the most annoying thing about Rather's appearance at the Texas fund-raiser was the arrogant double standard it revealed. One day before appearing at that Texas fund-raiser, Rather had issued this news report: "On Capitol Hill, it took seven years, but the shame of Enron finally got Congress to pass a campaign finance reform bill today. The legislation bans soft money, the unregulated, special-interest donations to national political parties." Yet less than twenty-four hours later, there he was, helping to raise this "soft money" that he had denounced. And how many times had Rather and his colleagues throughout the establishment media railed against "partisan politics"? Ultimately, Rather conceded his mistake. "I made an embarrassing and regrettable error in judgment by going to this event," the CBS anchor said in a statement published in the April 5, 2001, *Washington Post.* "It was a serious mistake, which I acknowledge. No one believes more strongly in CBS News standards than I do, and I have let those standards down." But he never said so on the air, to the viewers to whom the apology was owed.

"A Patriotic American Without Apology"

As Andy Rooney said, Dan Rather "is transparently liberal," having raised money for the Democratic Party and fawned over Democratic politicians like the Clintons. Rather's liberalism, much as he might deny it, has most certainly affected how he has covered the news over the years. But as passionate as he might be about liberal causes and Democratic politicians, the CBS newsman has not provided liberal spin 100 percent of the time he has been anchoring the *Evening News.*

This is an important point, for many conservatives who are rightly concerned about media bias believe that liberals in the media can *never* offer reliable news coverage. This is simply untrue. Liberal bias is undoubtedly an enormous problem in the mainstream media, but media bias is also a complex issue. Looking carefully at Dan Rather's record reveals this complexity.

No discussion of Rather would be complete without a review of his exemplary performance in the aftermath of the September 11, 2001, terrorist attacks on the United States. In truth, the CBS newsman was a source of inspiration in the weeks after September 11. He twice broke into tears on David Letterman's *Late Show* on September 17, once while reciting "America the Beautiful." Several days later he told a panel of journalists on CNN's *Reliable Sources* exactly how he felt about the war on terrorism on which the United States had embarked. "I am willing to give the government, the president, and the military the benefit of any doubt here in the beginning," Rather said, quite appropriately. "I'm going to fulfill my role as a journalist, and that is ask the questions, when necessary ask the tough questions. I'm going to do my job as a journalist, but at the same time I will give them the benefit of the doubt, whenever possible in this kind of crisis, emergency situation. Not because I am concerned about any backlash—I'm not—but because I want to be a patriotic American without apology." For Rather, there would no round-table discussions with experts offering equivocations about the causes of terrorism.

As the U.S. military went into Afghanistan, Rather remained true to his word. Whereas some of his media colleagues seemed distant in their coverage, the CBS anchor spoke for the vast majority of Americans when he expressed unabashed concern, support, and respect for our troops. In closing the October 8, 2001, *Evening News,* for example, he eloquently saluted our fighting men and women, and reminded viewers what those young Americans were fighting for: "After a second wave of U.S. aerial bombardment in the Afghan night, the American mind runs on two tracks: First, our thoughts and our love are with our warrior men and women, our sons and our daughters, brothers and sisters, husbands and wives, fathers and mothers over there. We see them at work and we are reassured by their professionalism and skill. We know some may come back in flag-draped caskets, but we reluctantly and sadly accept that as a reality of a war forced upon us. Less familiar to Americans are concerns of protecting home and hearth here. Our worst fears tell us that the enemy within could strike again. On a day when President Bush swore in the first director of Homeland Security in our history, thoughts turn to the words of the late newsman Elmer Davis: 'This will remain the land of the free only so long as it is the home of the brave.' "

Two nights later, Rather again focused on the war on terrorism: "Normal now includes terrorist threats, bombing runs, and rumors, and a slow-running river of sadness for those lost. And for the lives we knew so recently, though it seems now long, long ago. It has been only a month since so much has changed, but it has been the longest month. And with America's fighting men and women in peril far from home tonight, we know we must steel ourselves for many more long months."

On March 5, 2002, over photos of servicemen killed in battle in Afghanistan, an emotional Rather delivered one of the most moving narratives in recent network news history: "The U.S. death toll in the war against terrorists stands now at thirty, including seven who died in Operation Anaconda and joined the ranks of America's fallen heroes. Sergeant Bradley Crose, an avid reader, loved motorcycles, always wanted to be an Army Ranger. His father says Crose was 'the most precious thing I could give my country.' Army Specialist Marc Anderson, it was his dream too to be an Army Ranger as his father was. Before that, Anderson was a teacher. He wanted to help kids. Army Sergeant Philip Svitak told his mother, 'The terrorists have to be stopped. If anything happens to me, I'm proud to die for my country.' Svitak leaves a wife and two young sons. Senior Airman Jason Cunningham, his mother says he loved his job, loved his country. 'He was a good kid,' she said. Cunningham leaves a wife and two daughters. Navy Petty Officer First Class Neil Roberts went into the service right after high school. He is survived by a wife and an eighteen-month-old son. Air Force Technical Sergeant John Chapman received two commendation medals. His sister says the family knew he was risking his life. Chapman had a wife and two daughters. A former teacher said Army Private First Class Matthew Commons was a solid kid who loved his country. 'Matt,' she said, 'is a good example of what's right about America.'

"They were some of America's best. They gave this country everything. We close our broadcast tonight thinking of them and of their valor. Dan Rather reporting for the *CBS Evening News*. Good night."

Without a doubt, as we became further removed from the horrific events of September 11, 2001, and the emotions became less raw,

Rather occasionally let his liberal bias slip back into his coverage of the war on terrorism. (Most troubling was the interview he conducted with Iraqi dictator Saddam Hussein in February 2003, just before the war; Hussein did not have much of a problem with the American newsman's softball questions.) But by and large he provided fair and respectable news coverage. It is no coincidence that when in late April 2003 the Media Research Center graded the television networks' coverage of the war in Iraq, Rather earned the honorable mark of B-plus.

In their report on the Iraq war coverage, Brent Baker and Rich Noyes of the Media Research Center provided a striking example of how Rather's coverage was much less gloomy and far less speculative than that of at least one of his fellow anchors. On March 24, 2003, the fourth day of the war in Iraq, Rather opened his newscast with this upbeat description of the American-led military campaign: "Barreling toward Baghdad. Fast-moving U.S. ground forces fight their way to within miles of the capital. Up above, air raids try to cut up and cut off Iraqi divisions. Iraq insists Saddam is alive, well, and in control." But over at ABC, Peter Jennings seemed to be reporting on an entirely different war: "On *World News Tonight,* the U.S. attacks all over Iraq, the drive on Baghdad is cautious. There is opposition and there is weather. The Iraqi leader is alive and on television. Who knows how well he is. The U.S. believes he is still in control. Two more Americans are captured, their helicopter shot down. So many others are coming back full of bullet holes. And the pictures of the POWs. So public now, such pain for the families."

As it turned out, of course, Rather's reporting was not simply more optimistic than Jennings's; it was far more accurate. The drive to Baghdad was indeed swift, as the U.S.-led coalition liberated the Iraqi capital just two and a half weeks later. Whatever problems the United States ultimately encountered in trying to establish a democratic system in Iraq, the main military campaign in March and April of 2003 was anything but "cautious." Rather got it right, and he should be commended for that.

After the major combat operations ended and the long postwar reconstruction began, Rather continued to offer welcome relief from the relentless negativity of the liberal media. For example, on September 19, 2003, Kimberly Dozier of the *CBS Evening News* reported on crime in Baghdad, speaking from what she called "some of the most dangerous streets on earth." "Iraqis have traded fear of the despot for fear of their fellow man," Dozier said, "and U.S. troops seem powerless to protect them. Thieves grab up to seventy cars every twenty-four hours, usually when someone's in them. . . . Since the war, Baghdad's hospitals have been flooded with shooting victims, more than eight hundred a month end up dead, as many as the entire previous year. Also on the rise, kidnapping." After interviewing the father of a kidnapped Iraqi child, Dozier concluded her piece with this dramatic denunciation of the American troops in Iraq: "His liberators, the Americans, have failed to protect what he values most. He sees no reason for them to stay."

Dozier's story offered an extremely gloomy picture of the situation in Iraq. But Rather followed up the report with a much needed caveat to American viewers: "A reminder that television sometimes has trouble with perspective, so you may want to note that in some areas of Iraq, things are peaceful." It was a simple, eloquent statement that gave viewers a framework for looking at such a negative news report. If only other journalists besides Dan Rather had been able to consistently offer balanced reporting instead of portraying every situation in the most dire terms possible.

"Play No Favorites and Pull No Punches"

After Dan Rather was discovered to have headlined the Democratic Party fund-raiser in Texas, *National Review* editor Rich Lowry told the *Washington Post* that Rather "is perceived as the most buffoonishly biased of any of the anchors, as far as conservatives are concerned. He's the favorite media piñata for people on the right. He arouses their ire."

Lowry was right: To many conservatives, Dan Rather is the avatar of liberal media bias. Yet it is important to remember that Rather is an intelligent, talented journalist who does get the story right in many cases. Liberal media bias, as Rather's case reveals, is not a black-and-white issue; not *every* news story advances the liberal position, and not *every* journalist in the mainstream media abandons good reporting to flack for liberal causes.

But Rather's case also makes clear why liberal media bias is so troubling. Precisely because he is an intelligent, talented journalist, Rather should know better than to make his liberalism so "transparent" (to use Andy Rooney's term) to the millions of *CBS Evening News* viewers. He also should know better than to abandon his journalistic instincts when looking at his own industry. Instead of examining the clear documentation of liberal media bias, he simply offers stubborn denials that any bias could possibly exist. Rather once said, in one of his denials, "I'm all news, all the time." If so, then why doesn't he study the evidence to see what the "news" really is about media bias? The Media Research Center alone has produced dozens of scientific studies, often examining tens of thousands of stories at a time, proving the liberal bias dominating the mainstream news media. Not once has a study—or any of the hundreds of thousands of data therein—been disputed.

While Dan Rather might bluster that "I do subscribe to the idea of 'Play no favorites and pull no punches' " (which he did on the June 24, 1999, edition of CNN's *Crossfire*), the sad fact is that he has too often favored liberals and liberal causes. As the Media Research Center said in its detailed report on his two-decade tenure at the CBS anchor's desk, Rather has on the whole been a "liberal advocate masquerading as a journalist." (The report offers far too many incidences of Rather's liberal bias to list here, but readers who wish to see more outrageous examples of the CBS newsman's bias can find the report on the Media Research Center website, www.mediaresearch.org.)

For a man who is charged with delivering the news objectively to millions of Americans each night, such partisan advocacy is a major problem. Sadly, Dan Rather is not the exception but the rule in the mainstream media. And as we'll see in the next section of the book, the widespread liberal bias among journalists greatly skews how they portray politics and policy in this country.

PART TWO

BIAS in
ACTION

How the Media Promote Liberal Issues

4

Abortion: Extremists Become the Mainstream

"Since September 11 the word terrorist has come to mean someone who is radical, Islamic, and foreign, but many believe we have as much to fear from a homegrown group of anti-abortion crusaders."

    —*Jami Floyd, 20/20, ABC, November 28, 2001*

"Abortion rights activists now believe some leaders of the mainstream anti-abortion movement are inciting supporters on the fringe to violence."

    —*Richard Schlesinger,* CBS EVENING NEWS, *October 26, 1998*

"Bob Casey has died tonight. . . . The former two-term governor of Pennsylvania [was] a Democrat but a devout Catholic and thus was ultraconservative on the topic of abortion."

    —*Brian Williams,* THE NEWS WITH BRIAN WILLIAMS, *MSNBC, May 30, 2000*

"The anti-abortion movement has been creeping to the edge of bloody fanaticism for a decade."

    —*Jane Pauley,* DATELINE NBC, *January 3, 1995*

"The city editor stepped in. Minus a few descriptive words, here's the essence of what he said: Look, the pro-choice people are pro-choice. The people who say they're pro-life aren't really pro-life. They're nothing but a bunch of hypocritical right-wing religious fanatics, and we'll call them whatever we want to call them."

—Scripps-Howard religion columnist Terry Mattingly, on a ROCKY MOUNTAIN NEWS *editor answering Mattingly's questions about labeling of the abortion battle,* QUILL, *July/August 1993*

ON MAY 22, 2003, the editor and executive vice president of the *Los Angeles Times,* John Carroll, was so appalled by his newspaper's front-page story on an abortion bill in Texas that he sent a memo to his staff with the subject line "Credibility/abortion." The abortion piece, Carroll wrote, had demonstrated the "occasional reality" that the *Times* is a "liberal, 'politically correct' newspaper." The editor chastised his staff: "The apparent bias of the writer and/or the desk reveals itself in the third paragraph, which characterizes such bills in Texas and elsewhere as requiring 'so-called counseling of patients.' I don't think people on the anti-abortion side would consider it 'so-called,' a phrase that is loaded with derision." Addressing a larger issue, Carroll insisted that "we are not going to push a liberal agenda in the news pages of the *Times.*"

Carroll is to be commended for taking a stand against bias in his newspaper. The trouble is, too few media leaders take such a firm position. As a result, reporters and editors are free to let their bias influence their coverage of a whole host of important issues, as we'll see here in Part Two of the book.

It is no accident that a story on abortion prompted Carroll's outrage. Abortion receives more slanted coverage from the mainstream media than perhaps any other issue. Why does this happen? Carroll was right when he said to his staff that they "live in a political atmosphere that is suffused with liberal values (and is unreflective of the nation as a whole)." For decades, the mainstream media have been far removed from the nation as a whole, and this disconnect becomes clear in their coverage of abortion.

A groundbreaking 1981 study by Robert Lichter and Stanley Rothman—the study became the basis for their landmark book *The Media Elite*—found that 90 percent of the journalists surveyed at the network news divisions, the major newspapers, and the newsmagazines favored abortion. And subsequent studies over the years have only confirmed that members of the mainstream media are overwhelmingly pro-abortion. In 1985, the *Los Angeles Times* conducted the most extensive poll of journalists in history, surveying 2,700 journalists at 621 newspapers across the country, and found that 82 percent of the reporters and editors favored abortion. A 1992 study by David H. Weaver and G. Cleveland Wilhoit of Indiana University, published in *Media Studies Journal*, found that 91 percent of journalists favored abortion. And in 2001, Stanley Rothman, working with fellow researcher Amy E. Black, published another study, this one revealing that 97 percent of the reporters and editors at major national newspapers, newsmagazines, and wire services were pro-abortion.

A careful review of the media's coverage of the abortion issue reveals that this overwhelming personal bias cannot be kept out of news stories. (Indeed, a mere perusal of the quotations at the beginning of this chapter confirms the point.) So ingrained is the support for abortion that some journalists don't even bother to hide it. *New York Times* health reporter Gina Kolata conceded the obvious in a 1998 interview with *National Journal.* "If you read their pieces, you can usually figure out what they [reporters] think," she said. "Anybody who reads the *New York Times* who doesn't think the *New York Times* is pro-choice, they are out of their minds. . . . We send messages all the time about what we think."

To be sure, the abortion debate in this country is heated, with passionate advocates on both sides. Abortion "presents a profound philosophical, religous and scientific question," as John Carroll wrote in his memo to the *L.A. Times* staff. And Carroll was right on another point: Any news organ that is "intelligent and fair-minded" will "respect people on both sides of the debate."

For most journalists and editors, however, abortion is an accepted medical practice that only religious lunatics and Neanderthal conservatives oppose. So entrenched is this view that news stories are often little more than recitals of talking points from NARAL Pro-Choice America (formerly the National Abortion and Reproductive Rights Action League). This is particularly disturbing because, as much as it might reflect the opinions of most journalists, it is actually the perspective of the hard Left in this country. In other words, what the press sees and reports as "mainstream" on the topic of abortion is *extremist.*

The polls reveal how the news media do not speak for an overwhelming majority of Americans when they push for "abortion rights." For example, a July 2003 Fox News/Opinion Dynamics poll showed that 44 percent of Americans identify themselves as "pro-life"—which is exactly the same percentage that identify themselves as "pro-choice." But Americans are not simply divided on the subject of abortion; in fact, the country is nudging ever closer toward the pro-life view, as a *New York Times* poll indicated. This *Times* poll, which ran on the front page on January 16, 1998, showed a notable shift from general "acceptance" of abortion. While 61 percent favored the choice of abortion in the first trimester (28 percent were opposed), that support collapsed to only 15 percent for the second trimester (with 66 percent opposed). And for the third trimester, support evaporated: only 7 percent were in favor, with 79 percent against it. Those numbers do not tell the whole story, however. The survey showed that fully 50 percent of the public labeled abortion as "murder," something that goes completely against media-think. And more people believed that abortion concerned the "life of a fetus" (the pollster's term) than "a woman's ability to control her body." So the politically inspired "pro-choice" moniker doesn't work too well either.

Even some longtime abortion advocates have had to acknowledge that more and more Americans are moving toward the pro-life position. In July 2003, the president of the Center for the Advancement of Women, Faye Wattleton—who for many years was the head of Planned Parenthood—released a national survey that found that 51 percent of women do not support abortion at all or support it only in cases of rape or incest or when the life of the mother is at stake.

This was a stunning study—but the liberal media did not deem it newsworthy that a majority of American women were now pro-life. Faye Wattleton had never had difficulty getting media attention for her pro-abortion positions, but reporters had no interest in talking to her about this report. When the study was released, ABC, CBS, and NBC didn't cover the story at all, and CNN conducted only one interview with Wattleton.

We simply don't get the truth on the abortion issue from the liberal media.

Ideological Labels: The Media's Warning Signs

One problem with the way the media cover the abortion issue comes with those descriptive labels they choose to apply. Pro-life groups and spokesmen are regularly given the political warning label "conservative" and hardly ever enjoy the "pro-life" language they prefer. And if a member of the media does use the term "pro-life," it will almost assuredly spark indignation. Witness, for example, the reaction of *Washington Post* television critic Tom Shales to PBS anchor Jim Lehrer's use of the term during a 2000 presidential debate. Shales accused Lehrer of committing a "blunder" for saying to George W. Bush, "You're pro-life." "Generally," Shales wrote, "reputable journalistic organizations do not use this term to refer to those opposed to abortion. Would Lehrer have turned to Gore and said, 'You're anti-life?' He should know better."

Conversely, abortion advocates are almost never labeled "liberal" and are routinely described as advocating "abortion rights," which is the language they prefer. The Media Research Center conducted a comprehensive survey on this topic, looking at 1,050 news stories in the *New York Times*, the *Washington Post*, and *USA Today* between 1995 and 1996. Each of those 1,050 stories mentioned at least one of eight organizations—four pro-life groups and four abortion-advocacy groups. The survey found that the pro-life groups were labeled "conservative" in 47 percent of the stories, while abortion advocates were labeled "liberal" less than 3 percent of the time. Moreover, if one takes out of the equation the National Right to Life Committee—which is rarely labeled, mainly because of its self-explanatory name—the percentage of stories labeling pro-life groups "conservative" climbs to 66 percent.

Another problem is how selective the media are in portraying abortion as a divisive issue. The mainstream media regularly present the abortion issue as dividing only one political party—the Republican Party, of course. In the 1996 elections, for example, network reporters gave saturation coverage to the struggle within the Republican Party over platform language on abortion, but not on disagreement among Democrats, even though the Democratic Party was far from unanimous on the issue of abortion. The Media Research Center's *Media Watch* newsletter examined network news coverage in the three months leading up to the 1996 conventions and found that the debate within the GOP drew sixty stories while the Democrats' debate attracted only one. In prime-time convention coverage, the networks brought up the Republican abortion platform fight on fifty-five occasions in San Diego, but not once did they raise the subject of discord within the Democratic Party ranks in Chicago, even though fully one-third of the federally elected Democratic delegation was pro-life. And while the Democrats' platform calls for taxpayer funding of abortion—a position opposed by 75 percent of all Americans, according to a 1998 poll by Wirthlin Worldwide—never will the Democratic Party's platform be labeled as extremist. That label is reserved for the GOP.

The case of the late Bob Casey, the former governor of Pennsylvania and perhaps the last pro-life lion in the Democratic Party, illustrates the media's pro-abortion agenda better than anything else. In 1992, the party's powers-that-be refused to allow Casey to speak at the Democratic convention in New York. The decision drew minuscule press coverage, garnering only one interview on NBC and an interview and four mentions on CNN. By contrast, a Media Research Center study found that abortion was a major focus of coverage during the

1992 Republican convention in Houston, when on more than twenty occasions network analysts charged the Republicans with trying to "exclude" people (read: pro-choice people) from their party.

Casey was again shut out of his party's convention in 1996, despite having written a *Wall Street Journal* op-ed attacking the Democrats' gag rule on abortion just before the convention opened. (Which party is "intolerant" on abortion?) Once again, the networks ignored the story. It would have interfered with the bigger picture the national media were trying to give to the American people—whether that bigger picture was accurate or not.

Free Advertising for the Left

So intertwined are abortion forces and the media that the pro-abortion message and the media message are interchangeable. In March 1999, NARAL bought ad time to attack the abortion positions of Republican presidential candidates Elizabeth Dole and George W. Bush. Most political consultants would warn that running commercials so far in advance of the election wasn't an effective use of funds. But it paid off tremendously this time. NARAL spent a minuscule amount of money, but the attendant media coverage—nineteen months before the election—was worth millions in free advertising.

CNN's Judy Woodruff, for example, was practically in lockstep with the NARAL message. On the March 22 *Inside Politics,* Woodruff never called NARAL "liberal" but faithfully attached the "conservative" label to Pat Robertson and the National Right to Life Committee. After she played portions of two of the NARAL ads, she suggested that the GOP was treading a fine line. "The abortion issue presents a troubling complication for a Republican Party anxious to win back the White House," Woodruff said. "While anti-abortion activists make up a large part of the GOP base, other more moderate voters, especially women, have drifted away from the party, in part because of its hardline image on issues like abortion." That's precisely what NARAL was saying.

NARAL's key theme—one that networks like CNN and NBC presented exactly—was that old quadrennial chestnut: The Republicans are "too extreme" on abortion. But given NARAL's tried and true tactic of calling anyone to its right "extreme," the networks should have asked the obvious question: Where do NARAL's opinions fit on the political spectrum? NARAL is so radical it cheers the idea of taxpayer-funded security equipment for multimillionaire abortionists, something I suspect garners zero support with the public. But you'll *never* see the media describe NARAL as "extreme." Reporters won't even call the group "liberal."

Role reversals make excellent illustrations of the point. Imagine that in 2003 the Christian Coalition or Gary Bauer's Campaign for Working Families announced an ad campaign making the point that John Kerry and Howard Dean were "too extreme" on abortion. What kind of *positive* network airtime do you suppose the campaign would get? What kind of free publicity could these pro-life groups expect selling their point of view? To answer those questions, consider that on occasions in the past the networks have refused even to *sell* pro-lifers advertising time.

And this does not even take into account the aspects of the abortion debate on which the American public is squarely on the side of pro-lifers. Most notably, on the issue of partial-birth abortion—that gruesome procedure wherein delivery is induced, the baby's skull is punctured and his brains are sucked out—polls reveal that a vast majority of Americans support the pro-life position. For instance, an October 2003 Gallup/CNN/*USA Today* poll showed that a full 68 percent of the public wanted to outlaw partial-birth abortion while only 25 percent were in favor of keeping it legal. Given that Americans opposed the procedure by a ratio of almost 3 to 1, it stands to reason that the media would portray partial-birth abortion as "controversial" and a ban on the procedure as being representative of the public mood. Right?

Wrong. The major media have reversed the picture: The *ban* on partial-birth abortion, not partial-birth abortion itself, has become controversial.

Thus, in the fall of 2003, when Congress passed and President Bush signed into law a ban on partial-birth abortion, the mainstream media's one-sided coverage favored the pro-abortion minority. After the Senate passed the ban, on October 21, *Newsweek* ran a story headlined "A Firefight Over Abortion." The story quoted four abortion advocates but only one representative of the pro-life position, even though a bipartisan majority had voted for the ban (the Senate vote was a decisive 64–34). *Newsweek* also defined the Senate's ban from the perspective of the pro-abortion minority, calling it "a major public-relations setback for abortion rights." The media were even more aggressive after President Bush signed the bill into law on November 5. Most newsreaders insisted on speaking of "the procedure opponents call 'partial-birth abortion,'" but NBC anchor Tom Brokaw refused even to utter the phrase "partial-birth abortion," referring instead to "the controversial procedure, late-term abortion" and to "that kind of abortion." Over on CNBC, anchor Campbell Brown offered this "teaser" going into a commercial break: "The emotional fight over abortion: The president signs a controversial ban into law, but will it stand, and what does it mean for a woman's right to choose?" In a second teaser Brown said, "And still ahead, President Bush gives abortion opponents the law they've wanted for years, but will it stand? We'll find out where a controversial ban goes from here." After reporter David Gregory's story, which focused on the lack of female officeholders on the stage during the bill signing, Brown was back to discuss the legalities of it all. She said to a guest, "Let me begin by asking what I think is the bottom-line question here: Are we heading now down the slippery slope where abortion may at some point be outlawed?"

With the media faithfully repeating the pro-abortion message of radical groups, perhaps it is no surprise that the Democratic Party has been hijacked by radicals on this issue. For all the media attention devoted to the "extremists" who supposedly drive the Republican Party's pro-life platform, little is said about how the Democratic Party has become the abortion-on-demand party, kowtowing to every item on the pro-abortion agenda. The abortion lobby is so powerful, so entrenched, that it has virtual veto authority when it comes to Democratic candidates for national office. To be a viable candidate, a Democrat must cooperate, partial-birth abortions and all—or else. As Bob Casey explained in his 1998 book, *Fighting for Life*, despite the presence of pro-life Democrats, "Often it seemed like the Democratic National Committee had become little more than an auxiliary of NARAL."

Witness the case of Senator Evan Bayh of Indiana, whose name was floated as a possible Democratic vice presidential candidate in the summer of 2000. Bayh was young, attractive, and energetic, a politician whose prime-time appearance at the podium during the 1996 Democratic convention signaled that he was a rising star . . . and he didn't have a chance of becoming Al Gore's running mate in 2000. Bayh's problem? In 1999 he had made the strategic mistake of voting for a ban on partial-birth abortions. Even though he had sided with the pro-abortion position on all four of the other abortion-related votes in 1999, the abortion lobby immediately vetoed Bayh. NARAL's Alice Germond met with the Gore campaign to express "our feelings that Evan's record is problematic for us," she told the *Baltimore Sun*, surely understating NARAL's objections. Patricia Ireland of the National Organization for Women offered a thinly veiled threat that stressed the feminist hard Left's position of influence within the Democratic Party: "Among our activists, there would be a decided lack of interest in campaigning for him and getting out the vote."

Because of the inordinate influence of these radicals, nationally ambitious Democrats like Jesse Jackson, Dick Gephardt, Bill Clinton, and Al "I Was Always Pro-Choice" Gore have abandoned whatever pro-life "imperfections" they had to become rubber stamps for the abortion-on-demand lobby. Up until now the liberal media have enabled pro-abortion extremists to exert such extraordinary influence. But with the country turning against abortion, the radical abortion lobby and its ardent defenders in the liberal media could have more difficulty dictating the nation's agenda in the future.

5

Taxes: Ignore the Evidence

"If the president [Bush] is looking for another salesman to help him with his tax package, I've got a candidate—that old Iraqi information minister. He knows how to sell a fraud. . . . This is a giveaway to wealthy investors and contributors."

> —*Al Hunt of the* WALL STREET JOURNAL *on CNN's* Capital Gang, *April 19, 2003*

"It is scandalous to think we are indulging ourselves at the expense of the elderly. . . . How can we look at ourselves in the mirror if we keep shoving tax cuts into our pockets while letting poor, elderly people go without doctors and medicine?"

> —*David Gergen,* U.S. NEWS & WORLD REPORT, *April 1, 2002*

"Adios, surplus. When retired boomers dine on dog food, will they say thanks for that $600?"

> —NEWSWEEK'S *"Conventional Wisdom," September 3, 2001, assigning President Bush a "down" arrow for his tax cut*

"That's what's pernicious here, is seizing on this [economic downturn] as a way to get a tax cut. . . . [Bush] could create something self-

85

fulfilling, talk down the economy because he wants to use that as a tool to get a tax cut that we don't really need and is a bad idea."

—*Evan Thomas of* Newsweek *on* INSIDE WASHINGTON, *December 23, 2000*

I WENT TO THE CNN studios on Capitol Hill as arranged, to tape an interview in which I was to discuss a breaking Hollywood scandal. After I went through makeup, an intern led me to the studio, where I immediately sensed a problem. I was in one of the larger studios, which are normally reserved for the live shots, not for the simple "setup" interviews of the sort I was scheduled to give. But before I could react, the producer had me seated and had the IFB piece (that's shorthand for "interrupted fold back") in my ear, allowing me to hear three other voices—the other guests.

That's when I knew I was in real trouble.

I was in the wrong room doing the wrong interview. We were going live in a matter of moments, and I had no earthly clue what I was there to do. All I knew was that there were three other guests coming in from three other cities around the country.

Soon I heard the tinny soundtrack blasting in my ear, and we were on the air. The anchor cheerfully welcomed viewers to CNN's *Showbiz Today*, where today she would be asking four film critics to evaluate— gulp!—the nominees for the upcoming Academy Awards. One small problem, though: "Film critic" Bozell had not viewed a single one of the Best Picture nominees and had no idea what was going on with the other categories! But I was stuck, and so for the next half hour, I bluffed. I didn't want to answer "I have no clue" to every question, so I winged it, proffering one uninformed opinion after another. I was especially proud of myself when I spoke of being impressed by the cinematography of one particular film and won enthusiastic agreement from my fellow critics, causing me to wonder if any of them had watched these movies either.

This story comes to mind whenever I ponder how some in the news media cover economics.

Tonight's News: Brought to You by the Democratic Party

The mainstream media's economic coverage is routinely muddied, ill-informed, and inaccurate. Too often, it seems, those in the news business who report on the economy don't have a solid grounding in economics. But more disturbing is that with taxes and the economy, as with so many other issues, the media care less about the truth than about the political agenda they are trying to further. Rather than offering Americans balanced, objective reporting, the news media serve as flacks for the Democratic Party.

The media certainly took the opportunity to lambaste President George W. Bush for offering the American people tax cuts. Nina Totenberg of National Public Radio (NPR) pretty neatly summed up the liberal media's reaction to the Bush tax cuts when she said, on the May 17, 2003, edition of the television program *Inside Washington,* "This is a really stupid way to run a budget."

And the news media made sure the American people knew just how "stupid" the tax cuts really were. The Media Research Center examined how the three major networks' evening newscasts covered President Bush's tax-cut proposal in January 2003 and determined that the liberal perspective (that is, the Totenberg perspective) was afforded far more time than were conservative counterarguments—and that journalists themselves often echoed the anti-tax-cut talking points. Between January 2 and January 15, the ABC, CBS, and NBC nightly news programs aired twenty-eight stories on the Bush tax cut, and in these stories a liberal mantra was repeated over and over: Bush's tax cut comforts only the rich. Viewers heard this point a whopping twenty-seven times from news sources and another ten times from reporters themselves. Meanwhile, viewers heard just seven sources (all Republicans, none in journalism) challenge this contention. That's a five-to-one liberal skew on this issue.

The media also repeated the Left's claim that the "costly" tax cuts would worsen the deficit. During the study period viewers heard this liberal point made a dozen times—nine times by liberal guests, another three times by reporters directly. For example, ABC reporter Terry Moran ominously warned, "White House officials [are] . . . confident that the president will get a lot of what he wants, but there's a cost to that kind of success—a ballooning deficit." Only four times did anyone challenge this myth, and all of these responses came from GOP sources. Again the tilt was in favor of the liberals, in this case by a factor of three to one.

Conservatives fared only slightly better when it came to the issue of a tax cut as economic stimulus. During the study period, the networks featured sixteen comments from news sources (mostly President Bush himself) to the effect that a tax cut would spur economic growth, and one reporter actually saw merit in this argument. But the liberal media could not let this argument go unchallenged: Viewers heard the tax-cut-as-stimulus idea denigrated twenty-five times—twenty-two times by news sources and three times by reporters.

It is always this way. Coverage of the proposed Bush tax cut in the spring of 2001 showed the media at their government-loving best, as they obscured the details of a ten-year program designed to reduce the average American's tax burden. Rich Noyes of the Media Research Center's Free Market Project looked at every ABC, CBS, and NBC evening news story from January 20 to March 31 on the tax-cut debate, and the picture was not pretty. In the ninety-three tax stories filed over those seventy days, network correspondents and anchors described the tax-cut package as "big" or "very big" on thirty different occasions. In contrast, not one broadcast reporter during that period labeled President Bush's cut as "modest" or "small"—even though the tax cut was *too* small, according to many conservatives.

Moreover, the networks quoted liberal critics who charged that the Bush tax cut was "massive" or "huge" *five times as often* (seventy-nine times) as they quoted tax-cut supporters making the opposite point (fifteen times): that the tax cut was tiny as a percentage of the trillions

Washington would spend in the next decade. And network audiences heard complaints from liberals such as Senator Tom Daschle that the tax cut favored the wealthy *twice as often* (thirty-one times) as they heard the contrary point of view (fifteen times)—this despite data showing that Bush's plan offered a greater percentage of tax reduction to lower- and middle-income families. (CBS got around that problem—by not once reporting the data!) The TV "experts" almost never told viewers that the $1.6 trillion tax cut would be spread out over ten years. Nor did the networks point out that the National Taxpayers Union had found the Bush tax-cut proposal to be much smaller than either the Reagan or the JFK tax cut.

In the eyes of the press, it seems, the wealthy and successful are never suitable recipients of a tax cut, even after Democrats have singled them out for hikes. None of the networks reported during the seventy-day period covered in the Media Research Center study that the last income tax increase in 1993 had targeted only higher-income families. Not one millionaire anchorman relayed that the top 5 percent of earners shouldered more than half of the tax burden or that the top 1 percent of earners paid almost 35 percent of all federal income taxes.

The most slanted network was CBS, led by Democratic fund-raiser Dan Rather. How's this for the network's commitment to objectivity?: Rather led off President Bush's economic address to Congress on February 27, 2001, by calling it "a TV pitch for a tax-cut gamble." The next day, CBS even censored its very own poll, which found strong support for the tax cut; the network did not mention the poll on the *Evening News* (though CBS did run it on *The Early Show*), relying instead on a woman-on-the-street interview concluding that the tax cut was—you guessed it—much too big.

Undermining the Conservatives

While the media champion taxation, they rarely bother to cover the continual expansion of government and the detrimental effect this growth has on the federal budget. During the last four years of the Clinton administration, money poured into Washington at an unparalleled rate because a powerful economy was generating massive wealth and therefore huge tax revenue. The good times resulted in a budget surplus that the media happily associated with Bill Clinton and the Democratic Party, as if either one had enacted policy initiatives responsible for the growth.

What the media didn't mention, however, was that government spending soared during that time, climbing 22 percent between 1995 and 2001, according to the National Taxpayers Union. In 2001 alone, nondefense discretionary federal spending increased by 6.6 percent—which, while less than the 8.7 percent increase in President Clinton's last budget, was a hefty jump, especially in a slowing economy.

Still, by late summer 2001, the media were claiming that the budget surplus had been squandered, which meant only one thing: The tax cuts must be halted. Indeed, with federal revenues no longer pouring into Washington to create unprecedented surpluses, the liberal elite were horrified that Congress had ever allowed a tax cut to pass in the first place.

NBC's Tim Russert reflected the media orthodoxy. Russert normally excels in his quest for balance, playing the role of devil's advocate with both sides, but this is the same man who has been known to fill restaurant napkins with charts to prove to dining companions just how damaging the Reagan tax cuts were. On the September 2, 2001, *Meet the Press,* Russert pummeled Bush budget director Mitch Daniels with the latest calculations from the leftists at the Center on Budget and Policy Priorities, and then he asked Senator John Kerry about the need for a "trigger," or a tax-cut repeal. Kerry, a Democrat, agreed that such a repeal was necessary, but then the senator blew it. He suggested the sluggish economy might benefit from a tax cut on capital gains. Russert was horrified. "Another tax cut?!" he cried. He did everything but throw a glass of water in Kerry's face to snap the man out of his delusion.

Such questions and reactions were not unusual from Russert. A Media Research Center study found that, from January 1 through July 28 of 2002, Russert asked thirty questions dealing with the tax cut. Every single one came from the Left, wondering if the cuts were too big and if they should be repealed.

NBC starlet Katie Couric was even more doctrinaire on the *Today* show. "The bitter reality is that there's now almost no money for either party's priorities," she insisted to journalist Howard Fineman. "And that complicates everything. So aren't all these [tax-cut] discussions almost moot points?" It was a dramatic statement, but it overlooked the almost $2 *trillion* squeezed out of our paychecks annually. Still, liberals somehow find that the feds have "almost no money."

And that, too often, is the problem with the media's coverage of taxes and the economy. While journalists parrot dire Far Left warnings about tax cuts, they usually ignore important economic data showing that tax cuts spur economic growth. More important, in narrowly focusing on tax cuts, the media completely overlook the critical issue of federal spending.

At the same time that Katie Couric and others in the media were complaining about the federal government's supposed lack of money, the National Taxpayers Union showed that the gluttonous federal government's total outlays were headed nowhere but up—from $1.5 trillion in 1995, to $1.8 trillion in 2001, to a projected $2.2 trillion in fiscal year 2006 (and this was before the additional spending undertaken in the wake of the September 11 terrorist attacks). In other words, the government's madcap spending, not relatively tiny tax cuts, threatened surpluses. This gem from the National Taxpayers Union report tells the story: Had all the bills introduced in both chambers during the 106th Congress been passed, Congress would have increased spending by $973 billion a year. Eric Schlecht of the National Taxpayers Union explained: "In other words, the Bush tax cut will save taxpayers $511 billion between 2002 and 2006, while the 106th Congress proposed to spend $4.9 trillion over the same period— thereby reducing the surplus by nearly ten times that amount."

The national media simply ignore such devastating economic data. Hell-bent on the proposition that tax cuts cause deficits, the media use their powerful platform to try to undermine any new initiatives to reduce taxes. Bush succeeded nonetheless—at least early in his presidency. But the biased and ill-informed economic coverage Americans receive from the news media only clouds our understanding of these vital issues.

6

The Environment: Don't Question
the Radicals

"*The Bush administration is carrying on what the* Los Angeles
Times *this week called 'the most concerted exploitation of the public's
land, air and water since fundamental protection laws went into
effect three decades ago.'*"

—*Bill Moyers, PBS's* NOW, *August 23, 2002*

"*We launder our views through, quote, 'objective critics.' And certainly
the press is pretty green, the press is pretty pro-environment and I
don't think there's any question that they, as a body, feel that Bush is
wrong on the environment, with varying degrees of willingness to
give him credit—and I'm excluding the conservative press, the*
Weekly Standard *and so forth. But generally the rank-and-file press
is pretty green and they're going to use the Europeans to take the
Bushies to task.*"

—*Evan Thomas of* NEWSWEEK *on CNN's* RELIABLE SOURCES,
June 16, 2001

"*Glaciers are receding. Oceans are rising. Alaska is thawing. As officials from nearly 180 nations start to gather Monday in Bonn, Ger-*

*many, to confront the vexing problem of global warming, the issue is
no longer whether it is real, but what should be done about it.*"

—Traci Watson and Jonathan Weisman, "Six Ways to Combat
Global Warming," USA TODAY, July 16, 2001

BRYANT GUMBEL: *"At the risk of starting an argument, are you a
believer in global warming?"*
MARK MCEWEN: *"Absolutely."*
JANE CLAYSON: *"Of course."*
JULIE CHEN: *"Yeah."*
GUMBEL: *"So am I. . . . And you wonder what it's gonna take. I mean,
is it gonna take some kind of a real catastrophe? I mean, does an ice-
berg have to come floating down the Hudson before somebody stands
up and goes, 'Oh yeah?'"*

—Exchange on CBS's EARLY SHOW, April 18, 2001

R ADICAL ENVIRONMENTALISM is practically a religion for the
national media. While the media adopt a cynical approach to
fanciful notions like, say, Christianity (as we'll see in the next
chapter), they brook no skepticism when it comes to the great green
church. Environmentalist extremists, grant-seeking climatologists, and
wild-eyed defenders of flora and fauna are treated as prophets of God,
even if, time and again, their predictions are proven flat-out wrong.

Many environmental issues are serious matters that deserve sober
discussion, but too often we get only drama and daydreams from the
media, as even the most hyperbolic claims from environmentalists are
credulously reported. In part this is because the media are always looking for a gripping story, and surely ecological disasters and dire predictions are more exciting than careful, balanced examinations of
empirical evidence. The worse a disaster sounds, the better it sells. But
floods and storms don't make the news just because the video footage
is dramatic. Rather, these natural disasters become news because they

provide the radical environmentalists' fellow travelers in the media yet another opportunity to criticize U.S. policies—to argue that the United States must ratify the Kyoto treaty on greenhouse gas emissions, ban sport utility vehicles, institute one-child limits on families, and pay homage to the kangaroo rat.

So doctrinaire are the media in their radical environmentalism that we see an almost total absence of balance in environmental reporting. The typical environmental piece includes video shots of sludge pouring into streams, a few oil-covered otters, a sick duck, and an unusually hot summer day. On most occasions, the video is accompanied by a voice-over from some environmentalist, whose agenda is never discussed, proclaiming that the end is near. Every so often, a spokesperson for a business group or government agency is allowed eight or ten words to refute a preposterous claim, but the claim has already been packaged as reasonable, so opposition to it becomes controversial. Although many regulations championed by environmentalists are radical and overwhelmingly antibusiness, the media present them unquestioningly. Meanwhile, news accounts increasingly present the modern world—the same world that has wiped out diseases and exponentially reduced human suffering—as the problem instead of the solution.

As a result of the media's radical agenda, environmental reporting has become tediously predictable. For example, whenever a heat wave hits some part of the world, a spate of stories about "global warming" surely follows. This was certainly the case in August of 2003, when Europe endured a period of unusually hot weather. In an NBC piece in which reporter Patricia Sabga warned that extreme temperatures in the summer "may become the norm," talking head Sean Seabrook, identified on-screen as a "meteorologist," asserted, "Scientists appreciate now that global warming is taking place, and I think these occurrences of heat waves will become more frequent, so this may be a sign of things to come." Meanwhile, on ABC's *Good Morning America,* reporter Hilary Brown declared, "Climatologists say that all this is the direct result of global warming."

Over and over again the media present a direct cause-and-effect argument: Modern civilization's dependence on fossil fuels is dramatically changing the world's climate, and with devastating consequences. Environmental news stories blithely cite the conclusions of "scientists" and "climatologists" to support this claim, as if the world's scientific community were unanimous in its analysis of global warming. But that is hardly the case. Indeed, plenty of renowned scientists question how much of global climate change is man-made, and many also challenge the notion that global warming poses a grave threat to the future of the planet. Still, since the media have no interest in the sort of balanced reporting that might call into question the radical environmentalists' orthodoxy, we almost never hear from these scientists. Instead we get simplistic statements like Hilary Brown's that Europe's heat wave was the "direct result" of global warming—something environmentalist ideologues would be hard-pressed to prove. (Interestingly, this last point was one NBC's Patricia Sabga was forced to concede in a follow-up story, when she stated that "scientists say there's no clear evidence to link these higher temperatures to man-made climate change." Of course, Sabga was quick to add, "They are warning, however, that these higher temperatures are likely to become the norm.")

As troubling as the media's biased environmental reporting is when prompted by a heat wave, it becomes particularly problematic when it relates to—and ultimately affects—our nation's environmental policy.

Doomsday Predictions

After taking office, President George W. Bush demonstrated that he would not acquiesce to environmental extremists on certain important issues. To be sure, the Bush administration was not always clear on how it was pursuing its environment policy, as it sent a confusing mix of signals. The media were quite right to report on the seeming inconsistencies. But they did not criticize Bush simply for inconsistencies; instead, they assumed their familiar role of advocates for liberal causes. Wherever Bush veered from liberal orthodoxy on the environment, he endured unfair and unbalanced news coverage.

It began early in Bush's term. In April 2001, just three months after

President Bush took office, *Newsweek* announced that Bush's approval rating on the environment was dropping and suggested that his administration's refusal to enact Clinton-era policies was causing the damage. But was the problem Bush's handling of the environment or the media's coverage of Bush's handling of the environment?

Consider the debate over arsenic levels in drinking water. Was it a dramatic "rollback" (as many charged) to refuse to institute a radical change in arsenic standards when no one else had bothered to change the standards in fifty years? If lower arsenic levels were so critical, why did Bill Clinton wait until his last week in office to implement them? And if there was such an urgent need for the new standards, why wouldn't they have been implemented until 2006?

NBC News, like the rest of the national media, ignored these questions. Instead NBC let an environmental extremist go unchallenged in making this statement: "The Bush administration is really risking millions of lives by not implementing the new standards." *Risking millions of lives?* It was a preposterous claim, for the Clinton administration itself had argued that the new standard would save twenty-eight lives per year. Moreover, as David Shuster of Fox News reported, many water experts were skeptical of even that relatively modest claim, questioning the science on which the Clinton administration based its call for a new arsenic standard. The Bush administration's experts questioned the science, too, which is why the administration decided to conduct a review to determine what the arsenic standard should be.

But the media weren't concerned with those finer points. They left the field to the environmental wackos and their doomsday predictions, giving the clear impression to the American people that "bought-by-business" Bush favored a looser, and therefore more dangerous, arsenic standard. If the media had been interested in the truth, they would have shown that the Bush administration had actually changed *nothing* about America's drinking water.

President Bush endured his harshest attacks—and some of the most biased media coverage ever—after refusing to approve the Kyoto Protocol on "global warming." Yet in the scathing news coverage that the Bush administration received, rarely was it mentioned that Bill Clinton had never even bothered to send the Kyoto treaty up to Capitol Hill for ratification—because the Clinton White House knew the Senate would refuse to approve it! In August 1997 the Senate passed a resolution, by a vote of 95–0, saying it would not ratify a treaty that excluded "developing" countries like China and India or that seriously harmed the U.S. economy—and the Kyoto treaty did both of those things.

Despite the Senate's overwhelming, bipartisan rejection of the Kyoto Protocol and the Clinton administration's realization that the treaty wasn't viable, the mainstream media reacted as if President Bush were leading an extremist crusade against the environment. For example, CBS's John Roberts opened his report on March 28, 2001, with this statement: "Global temperatures on the rise, glaciers retreating, storms more frequent and severe—a looming crisis, say many scientists, of the greenhouse effect. Yet claiming potential harm to the economy, the White House today confirmed it will abandon the global accord to curb emissions of carbon dioxide, the number one greenhouse gas." While the Bush administration did voice concern that the Kyoto treaty would harm the U.S. economy—just as the Senate had a few years before—the CBS report did not even allude to valid concerns about the supposed environmental benefits of the treaty. With huge polluters like China exempt from emissions limits, Kyoto seemed, to many critics, a severely flawed and inadequate treaty.

John Roberts's screed was just one of the many potshots the media took at Bush on this issue during the late winter and spring of 2001. The Media Research Center's Free Market Project looked at the networks' coverage from Inauguration Day (January 20) through Earth Day (April 22). It found that the global warming fearmongers drew six times as much attention as those who thought the nightmare scenarios were either exaggerated or wrong. In three months of evening news coverage, 86 percent of network reporters or sources expressed the view that global warming was a dire threat, while only 14 percent—just seven statements out of forty-nine—challenged that dominant story line, and weakly at that. And in the twenty sound bites awarded to liberal environmental activists, not once was such an activist labeled "liberal."

Perhaps the most interesting numbers in this study centered on the Fox News Channel, the focus of so much liberal ridicule for being "GOP-TV." On Fox's *Special Report with Brit Hume,* 63 percent of reporters and sources spoke of a dire global warming threat, while only 37 percent voiced any dissent. Presumably giving 37 percent of the time to conservative dissenters qualified Fox as having an ardently "conservative" bias. But then, to the liberal media, radical environmentalism is the truth, the whole truth, and nothing but the truth.

This remained evident long after the controversy over the Kyoto Protocol. In June 2003, global warming became a lead story once again when the Bush administration changed a sentence in an Environmental Protection Agency (EPA) report. The administration replaced "Climate change has global consequences for human health and the environment" with "The complexity of the Earth system and the interconnections among its components make it a scientific challenge to document change, diagnose its causes, and develop useful projections of how natural variability and human actions may affect the global environment in the future." Given the disagreements within the scientific community about the causes and consequences of global warming, the Bush administration's revised sentence was quite reasonable. But to the media, who do not acknowledge any departures from the radical environmentalists' position, the change was scandalous.

CNN's Aaron Brown offered perhaps the most ridiculous interpretation when he equated those skeptical of the liberal environmental orthodoxy with flat-earthers. On *NewsNight,* Brown haughtily intoned, "Once upon a time a scientist named Galileo said the earth was round and the political leaders of the time said, 'No, no, Galileo, it's flat.' And Galileo got life under house arrest for his little theory. Today, the vast majority of scientists will tell you the earth is getting warmer, and most would agree that industry is at least in part to blame. So far nobody's gone to jail for saying that, which doesn't mean the idea isn't squarely at the center of a political dustup—and not an insignificant one at that, because if the charges leveled against the White House are true, an important environmental question is being twisted or ignored for the sake of politics." Now, forget that Galileo said no such thing about the earth. (By Galileo's time, people accepted that the earth was round; the famed astronomer received his sentence for upholding the Copernican theory that the earth revolved around the sun.) It is more disturbing that "objective" news anchors like Brown can use their platform to promote radical environmentalists rather than to report the news without bias.

In addition to deriding the environmental policies of the Bush administration, the media were sure to explain the dark motives behind those policies. The story line was usually the same: Bush's moves to "repeal" environmental "protections" were inspired by those greedy, evil Big Oil polluters who funded his campaign. Once again we see how the media have different standards for different sides. Throughout the Clinton years, if a conservative attacked the president's integrity in this fashion, he or she was immediately labeled a "Clinton hater" and denounced as making reckless, insulting charges of unethical behavior without evidence. But when Bush came into office, the Left felt free to attack him on the environment or any other issue. No charge could be reckless if it involved Bush.

Actually, these rules of engagement were in effect long before George W. Bush came to Washington. When Newt Gingrich's Republican majority swept into Congress, the Sierra Club and its for-profit public relations agents at the networks reacted with shock, amazement, dismay, horror. Private lobbyists were advising the GOP on environmental policy? For shame! The press dutifully reported the "scandal." But when the Democrats ran the House and left-wing radicals at the Sierra Club and Greenpeace were setting legislative policy, not a peep came from the press about private lobbyists' involvement in writing laws. That is because, to the liberal mind-set, business represents the private interest, the profit motive: selfish, greedy, corrupt, and dangerous. The leave-no-tree-behind environmentalists, on the other hand, are automatically serving the "public interest," no matter how extreme their agenda.

That liberal mind-set certainly influenced how the media portrayed the EPA under George W. Bush compared with the EPA under Bill Clinton. On August 11, 2003, President Bush announced that Governor Mike Leavitt of Utah was his nominee to become the new head of the EPA, and the media immediately labeled Leavitt a "controversial" choice. Charles Gibson of ABC's *World News Tonight* put it this way: "President Bush has announced his new nominee to head the Environmental Protection Agency, and it may be controversial." Gibson went on to discuss the "controversial stewardship" of Leavitt's predecessor at the EPA, liberal Republican Christine Todd Whitman. Over at CBS, Dan Rather wasn't content just to call Leavitt and Whitman controversial; he went after the entire Bush EPA. "President Bush today nominated Utah governor Mike Leavitt to head his controversial Environmental Protection Agency," Rather reported. "Leavitt has already been criticized by environmentalists for his land-use policies."

Now compare that to the news coverage given to Carol Browner, Bill Clinton's EPA administrator throughout his two terms. When this former staffer for the ultragreen Al Gore was nominated as head of the EPA, the media did not refer to her as a "controversial" selection. Yet Browner was perhaps the most left-wing EPA head in that misbegotten agency's history. In the spring of 1997, she instituted new regulations on air pollution that were so heavy-handed and antibusiness that left-center Congressman John Dingle of Michigan and several Democratic governors joined the Republicans in opposition. The political battle raged for months. Amazingly, not once during this prolonged debate—not even when Browner's critics pointed out how she was exaggerating the strength of the supposed scientific evidence supporting her proposal— did the news media refer to Carol Browner as "controversial."

Who Needs Credibility?

Environmental reporting is most damaging when the media actively try to influence U.S. environmental policy, as they did throughout the first few years of the Bush administration. But less consequential environmental coverage can also reveal just how unconcerned the media are with credibility and objectivity.

One of the most embarrassing episodes came in the spring of 2000, when ABC News president David Westin hired actor Leonardo DiCaprio, famous for his role in the blockbuster movie *Titanic*, to interview President Bill Clinton for an Earth Day special. DiCaprio's grasp of the issues was, to say the least, lacking.

It seems that, in the eyes of Westin and ABC, DiCaprio was qualified to conduct the interview simply because the actor was remarkably popular with the all-important young adult demographic. It certainly had nothing to do with the actor's scientific or political expertise. In the March 1995 issue of *Details* magazine, this policy genius was asked about then–House Speaker Newt Gingrich and gave this insightful analysis: "Who's Newt Gingrich? Oh, wait a minute, I've seen Newt on TV. He's that funny-looking guy. I haven't really been following politics lately." At the kickoff press conference for Earth Day 2000, DiCaprio interviewed Earth Day organizers with multiple insertions of "wow," "cool," and "scary stuff."

DiCaprio's answers in an Internet chat on the official Earth Day website suggested he hadn't exactly hit the books to determine his position on the interaction of chlorofluorocarbons in the upper atmosphere. "I watched a lot of television programs, documentaries, and movies on wild life [*sic*] and the environment and was shocked to find out what we were doing to Earth," he explained. "Now I am in a position to make a difference, and I really want to." When asked what, besides global warming, was his major environmental concern, DiCaprio again underlined his video education: "Saving endangered species. I saw a program when I was very young about the wildlife that is now extinct."

And that qualified Mr. DiCaprio to serve as an expert on the environment for the venerable ABC News.

When word leaked that an actor was interviewing the president of the United States for one of the most respected news divisions in the country, however, it became a major controversy. Many in the media considered it an outrage, arguing that David Westin and ABC News had blurred the line between journalism and entertainment.

But when reporters blur the line between journalism and political advocacy, their outrageous actions prompt no response.

7

Religion: To Be Ridiculed, Not Respected

"In November, researchers announced that they had made the first human embryo clones, giving immediacy to warnings by religious conservatives and others that science is no longer serving the nation's moral will. At the same time, the United States was fighting a war to free a faraway nation from the grip of religious conservatives who were denounced for imposing their moral code on others."

—*Rick Weiss,* WASHINGTON POST, *January 17, 2002*

"What are you, a bunch of Jesus freaks? You ought to be working for Fox."

—*CNN founder Ted Turner on Ash Wednesday, 2001, to CNN employees with ash marks on their foreheads*

"Corporations pay public relations firms millions of dollars to contrive the kind of grass-roots response that [Jerry] Falwell or Pat Robertson can galvanize in a televised sermon. Their followers are largely poor, uneducated and easy to command."

—*Michael Weisskopf,* WASHINGTON POST, *February 1, 1993*

I N ALL OF American political and social life, there is nothing the elite media find more difficult to accept, or tolerate, than the Christianity practiced by most Americans. Nothing—not multinational corporations, not tax cuts, not talk radio—creates the instant skepticism and derision that Americans of faith do.

Popular culture, whether in television, film, or art, constantly derides and attacks faith. The art world is particularly relentless in its attack, especially in its attack on the Catholic Church. As *U.S. News & World Report* columnist John Leo wrote in 1999, "Today's art world orthodoxy increasingly seems to require a contempt for Christianity in general and Catholicism in particular." Examples of such contempt, according to Leo, are "so mainstream that it's barely noticed. Recent examples include the Virgin Mary coming out of a vagina, Mary encased in a condom, Mary in pink panties with breasts partially exposed, an Annunciation scene with the Archangel Gabriel giving Mary a coat hanger for an abortion. . . ."

While not as overt as artists, the news media exhibit similar disdain. They portray religious people, especially evangelical Christians and practicing Catholics, as dogmatic and therefore intolerant. Christianity has become an institution to be exposed, denounced, attacked, and ridiculed whenever possible.

The media found a new opportunity to attack Christian conservatives in August of 2003, when Chief Justice Roy Moore of Alabama fought to keep a Ten Commandments monument on display at the Alabama Supreme Court. Moore went so far as to defy a federal court order to remove the monument, earning himself a suspension—and a great deal of unfavorable media coverage. In an interview with Moore, ABC's Robin Roberts charged, "Some would also say that you're trying to restore morality and that you are forcing your agenda upon people." *Restore morality?* Horror of horrors!

Over at CNN, Aaron Brown drew a parallel that would become a familiar part of the attacks on Moore, saying that the judge's actions were "a replay" of those of Alabama governor George Wallace in 1963. Thus Moore's defense of the Judeo-Christian tradition had been equated with—lowered to—Wallace's defense of racial segregation.

This was the official line of the political Left. Morris Dees of the left-wing (but you'll never see it described this way) Southern Poverty Law Center repeated this mantra everywhere he could—and plenty of network news shows welcomed him on to blast Moore. On NBC's *Today* show, Dees charged, "George Wallace, like Judge Moore, was a demagogue and is a demagogue. He [Moore] uses religion; Wallace used race." Several days later Dees offered this rant on CNN's *Breaking News:* "It's more akin to George Wallace, who simply defied the federal court as a demagogue for the purpose of advancing his political career, and that's all Judge Moore is doing here." And Aaron Brown of CNN was not the only member of the news media to pick up this attack. On MSNBC, Keith Olbermann described the situation at the Alabama courthouse as "the scene that has evoked memories of George Wallace standing against integration and William Jennings Bryan prosecuting evolution in Tennessee." Even when the *New York Times* allowed Moore to dispute the comparison to Governor Wallace, the paper was quick to undercut that claim. The Alabama justice was quoted as saying, "Wallace stood for division. We stand for unity. This is more like what Martin Luther King did," but the *Times* reporter immediately stated, "Taylor Branch, a Pulitzer Prize–winning biographer of Dr. King, scoffed at that suggestion."

There was simply no way that the national news media were going to allow Judge Moore to have a fair say. Instead they seized the chance to portray Moore and his supporters as zealots. CNN's Brown dramatically asked the judge, "Don't we also, all of us, stand for the rule of law? And, in this case, the rule of law has come from every federal court that has looked at this, and they have ruled against you. How in good conscience can a judge defy the court?" So confident was Brown that Moore was an abomination that he felt secure in speaking for "all of us" and righteously invoking the "rule of law." But five years earlier, during President Clinton's impeachment, journalists like Aaron Brown were baying about how the scandal was "all about sex" and clearly had no interest in the rule of law that "all of us" supposedly stand for.

Brown and others were overlooking another, more immediate factor: According to a CNN/*USA Today*/Gallup poll, a staggering *77 per-*

cent of Americans *disapproved* of the federal court order to remove the Ten Commandments monument from public display. In other words, Judge Moore was not speaking for an extreme, Far Right minority; he had the support of more than three-quarters of the American people. Nevertheless, the media simplified the story of the Ten Commandments standoff so they could attack Christians who had the nerve to speak about morality and the importance of God.

The media's antireligious instincts were also on display in the coverage of the 2000 presidential race. When, in a December 1999 debate, George W. Bush named Jesus Christ as the philosopher who had most influenced his life, he gave the answer that is obvious to anyone of faith. But that response gave the media the willies.

NBC's Tim Russert is a Roman Catholic who has spoken publicly and profoundly about his faith. Yet when the Republican candidates debated again in January, even he felt it necessary to question repeatedly if Bush's faith in Jesus isolated him from voters of other faiths and religions. "Fifteen million atheists in this country, five million Jews, five million Muslims, millions more Buddhists and Hindus," Russert said to Bush. "Should they feel excluded from George W. Bush because of his allegiance to Jesus?" Russert went so far as to suggest that Republicans were overdoing this religion business, asking candidate Gary Bauer, "Are you concerned that many people in the country are watching that exchange and saying, 'You know, that's a little more about religion than it is about politics and that concerns me'?" Bauer's response was the right one: "Well, Tim, in all due fairness, you guys [the media] brought those issues up."

Russert's colleague Brian Williams, in his postdebate coverage, evinced the mainstream media's hostility toward traditional morality when he noted that the Republicans were "rather strident tonight: anti-gay, pro-Jesus, and anti-abortion and no gray matter in between." (Note that it was not enough for Williams to disdain the lack of a "gray area"; it was important to insert the subtle slam—"gray matter"—at the Republicans' intelligence. Perhaps Williams's dig at Republicans was unintended, but that would merely reflect how bias can easily slip into news reporting.)

What message was the public supposed to take away from this line of thought? It was the quadrennial media lesson: Republican primaries are polluted with the Christian Right, whose Bible-toting intolerance will cost the GOP in the fall. "Stridently pro-Jesus" Republicans frighten average Americans by dragging too much religion into the public square.

There's a real paradox here. Convinced that viewers will grab their remotes if the subject is the complexities of Medicare Plan B, the media devote an enormous amount of attention to the candidates' lifestyles, personalities, and private likes and dislikes. Yet probing in this direction isn't allowed to lead candidates to talk of personal faith, meaning that the reporters are missing—or dismissing—something important.

Some liberal journalists sneer when conservatives speak of their Christian faith because, to them, a *true* Christian is one who would implement liberal policies. Speaking about the "controversy" that George W. Bush created when he cited Christ's influence on his life, *Wall Street Journal* editor Al Hunt joked on CNN's *Capital Gang,* "Now if Jesus is a political thinker, I assume he's for the Comprehensive Test Ban Treaty—'blessed are the peacemakers.' I assume he's pro–earned income tax credit—'blessed are the poor.' " In *Time* magazine, columnist Jimmy Breslin pretended that Christ was on the campaign trail in Iowa and was angry at Republicans like Bush for invoking His name while also supporting the death penalty: " 'How can he say he carries me, Jesus Christ, in his heart,' candidate Christ asked, 'when at the same time he stands by while people are put to death?' "

Then there's National Public Radio (NPR). There's *always* NPR; these folks can't see the point of invoking Jesus unless someone is proposing a radical redistribution of wealth. During the 2000 campaign, reporter Lynn Neary acted as a press agent for the leftist Industrial Areas Foundation, which had assembled religious leaders to announce that faith without statism was "empty piety." Bishop David Benke of the Lutheran Church–Missouri Synod declared that if a candidate "is going to lead through a faith statement, then it'd better be a leading through action. That's authentic piety." Rabbi David Saperstein said of Bush, "How do you invoke that name [of Jesus] and still justify the inequities that plague this country? How do you invoke the real name of religion and the words of religion and the dreams of religion and . . . sit by in good conscience and allow such inequities to continue?"

Needless to say, these comments went unchallenged in the NPR piece.

"What a Fucking Idiot"

The anti-Christian bias in the media is so pervasive that a network host can insult Christians on national television in front of millions— with impunity.

On the June 29, 2000, edition of CBS's *Early Show,* host Bryant Gumbel was conducting his standard interview with a conservative guest, which is to say that he was on the attack. The subject was the Supreme Court's decision to uphold the Boy Scouts' ban on homosexual scoutmasters. The pro-family guest—that is, Gumbel's target—was the Family Research Council's Robert Knight, who had the audacity to defend the morality behind the decision. Throughout the interview Gumbel was openly hostile to Knight, which is not surprising given that he's openly hostile to anyone to the right of Kweisi Mfume.

At the end of the contentious segment, CBS cut away to Mark McEwen, who began his weather report. But then the camera unexpectedly cut back to Gumbel just as he was rising from his seat and unsnapping his microphone. And there was the unsuspecting Gumbel, live on national television, sneering and mouthing the words *"What a fucking idiot!"*

Imagine for a moment a network journalist making that same comment after interviewing an official from the Gay and Lesbian Alliance Against Defamation (GLAAD). Is there even a *scintilla* of doubt that the network would summarily fire the journalist? Or that it would immediately hand-deliver a half-dozen apologies to the homosexual movement? Or that it would require the entire news operation to attend a sensitivity course to prevent this kind of intolerance in the future?

So what did CBS do about Gumbel's insult? Nothing. The thing is, Robert Knight was a conservative and a devout Christian, and therefore unimportant. To the networks, making offensive comments about Christian conservatives is about as serious as insulting wallboard. Even in the face of the outrage voiced by pro-faith conservatives nationwide and the demands for a formal apology to Robert Knight and the Family Research Council, CBS and Gumbel uttered not a word of regret. Gumbel was allowed to leave for his vacation without saying anything, and CBS's official response—after much prodding from critics—was a truly stunning nonapology: "During a weather segment on Thursday morning's *Early Show*, a brief camera shot with no audio of Bryant getting up from his chair accidentally appeared on air. He was making a casual remark of some sort, but it is unclear what the comment was and, in any case, it bears no relevance to the content of *The Early Show*."

First of all, it doesn't matter that Gumbel didn't know he was live on camera when he made the statement after the Knight interview. Nor does it matter that the microphone was off; the video alone made it perfectly clear to the millions of viewers exactly what Gumbel was saying. So CBS's response was disingenuous. But even if one accepted the statement as sincere, it was completely illogical. After all, if Gumbel's remark was unclear, as CBS claimed, just how did the network know what relevance it bore to the content of the show? No matter. The Christian Bashing System had spoken.

CBS and Bryant Gumbel made no attempt—none—to apologize for, or even mask, a bias. It didn't matter that *The Early Show* was CBS's morning news program, which purported to give its viewers impartial coverage. Gumbel himself didn't feel the need to say a word on the topic, perhaps because he had been getting away with making nasty, biased comments about Christians for years. For example, back in February of 1993, when outgoing Republican National Committee chairman Rich Bond made some critical comments about conservatives, the ever-objective Gumbel characterized Bond's remarks this way: "As he stepped down as RNC chair, [Bond] had some parting

shots for the religious Right and fringe fanatics like Phyllis Schlafly."
A year later, discussing the political scene, he announced, "We're back
in just a moment to talk about the president's problems with the
extremists of the religious Right."

Smearing the Catholic Church

Conservative Christians aren't the only religious group hammered by
the media. The Roman Catholic Church is viewed as an unhip
anachronism—it has the poor taste to have rules and insist its members follow them—and has emerged as a major target for the media's
religious bigots.

Stories on Catholics usually focus on a sexual angle, with pedophilia
claims always sure to grab headlines. To be sure, documented cases of
sexual abuse within the Catholic Church are horrifying, and church
officials guilty of such crimes, or of helping cover them up, deserve
everyone's harshest rebukes. Still, the media's feeding frenzy on the
subject, which was most frenzied in 2002, obscured the obvious fact
that the overwhelming majority of Catholic priests—not to mention
Catholics in general—not only were innocent of abusive crimes but
actually continued to be good, faithful servants. Moreover, many in the
media used the revelations of sexual abuse to attack the Catholic
Church in general.

For example, on March 29, 2002, Eleanor Clift took to
Newsweek.com to slam the Catholic Church in America, saying that
Pope John Paul II had acted like "a U.S. president stacking the courts"
by appointing so many American bishops who were "ideologically conservative." Clift quoted an anonymous diocesan priest to express her
horror at these "ideologically conservative" bishops: "As a group, they're
like the Taliban," the priest said of his superiors. "If you want to succeed in this system, you never talk about the ordination of women—
and abortion and birth control are like the third rail." Those issues, of
course, were of paramount concern to Clift; she railed that because of
the pope's appointments, "social change will be wrenching, if not
impossible."

Around the same time, the *New York Times*'s Maureen Dowd accused Pope John Paul II of "institutional deceit" and called his American priests a "perp walk of sacramental perverts." She concluded, "The one place the church needs to go to save itself—shedding its dysfunctional all-male, all-celibate, all-closed culture—is the one place it's unwilling to go." As a columnist, Dowd was allowed to rev her rhetorical engine. That made her piece differ in tone from the news reports on the Catholic Church. But even while differing in tone from Dowd's piece, the news reports often reflected the same secular ideology.

On May 6, 2002, for instance, *Newsweek* featured a "news story" called "Sex and the Church: A Case for Change" by managing editor John Meacham. In it, Meacham wrote, "Some Catholic traditionalists are trying to manage the scandal's fallout by arguing that the sexual predation of children and teens by priests is largely a homosexual issue. Such a stance . . . forecloses talk about the future of celibacy, married priests or, at the farthest edge, ordaining openly gay clergy and blessing same-sex unions. By pointing their fingers mainly at homosexuality, these church leaders are avoiding discussion of the questions that should be front and center: the roots and costs of a culture of sexual repression and secrecy."

But it doesn't stop there. There is nothing, it seems, to which the media won't give credence where attacks on the Catholic Church are concerned. The most shocking example came when CBS's *60 Minutes*, supposedly a beacon of journalistic integrity, promoted the outlandish claim that the church had a role in the Holocaust—specifically, that Pope Pius XII didn't lift a finger to prevent the killing of Jews during World War II.

In March 2000, Ed Bradley of *60 Minutes* did a feature on the book *Hitler's Pope*, by British journalist John Cornwell. In his previous book, which explored whether Pope John Paul I was murdered, Cornwell had revealed himself as a professional Vatican hater; in a review of that book, *Time* magazine had noted that Cornwell portrayed the Vatican as "a palace of gossipy eunuchs" and "a sea of brilliant bitchery." But Ed Bradley made no mention of this on *60 Minutes*, preferring to call Cornwell a "practicing Catholic." Even that was a preposterous label, as the Catholic League for Religious and Civil Rights showed when it pointed out that in 1991 Cornwell had said he was "increasingly convinced that human beings were morally, psychologically, and materially better off without a belief in God. . . . As I entered middle age nothing short of a miracle could have shaken these firm convictions."

How CBS found this unshakeable atheism the thinking of a "practicing Catholic" is truly beyond logic. Cornwell's anti-Catholicism was blatant, but *60 Minutes* advanced his smear of the Catholic Church nonetheless. If at the same time an author of Cornwell's disposition had come to *60 Minutes* with a book about Bill Clinton, CBS would have had no trouble dismissing him as a "Clinton hater," as a vicious tool of a "vast right-wing conspiracy." The author wouldn't have been allowed within five hundred yards of any of the CBS sets.

But Cornwell got on the air; more troubling, the program so often praised for its investigative reporting did little to question his theories, even though there was plenty to question. Ed Bradley devoted most of his piece to advancing the claims made in *Hitler's Pope,* even giving Jewish activist Gerhard Riegner of the World Jewish Congress the opportunity to endorse Cornwell's contentions. Bradley dutifully interviewed Vatican expert Peter Gumpel, who said the book was "totally worthless"; that, *60 Minutes* would have us believe, constituted "balance." But in actuality, this merely followed the pattern found so often in biased news stories: give in-depth, respectful treatment to a position, then provide a spokesperson for the opposition a small window to rebut what has been presented as a thoroughly reasonable claim. Besides, Cornwell's charge—that Pius XII didn't prevent Hitler's killing of Jews because the pope was an anti-Semite who felt the Jews deserved everything they received—was false, and one cannot balance a lie with the truth.

The low point came when Bradley explained, "Cornwell says that the turning point in his research came when he found a letter written by the future pope when he was a papal representative in Germany after the First World War. In it, he poured scorn on the physical characteristics of a group of Jewish socialists, describing their leader as 'pale, dirty, with drugged eyes, vulgar, repulsive, with a face that is both intelligent and sly.' " Then Cornwell dragged out the smears: "It was the sort of expression that would—one would find in *Mein Kampf* during the same period." Bradley underlined the point: "So you're saying that what Hitler wrote would have been similar to what Pius XII—the man who would become Pius XII—wrote?" Cornwell: "Absolutely."

While Bradley and CBS were treating Cornwell as a serious historian, they should have paid more attention to the verdict of *Newsweek* religion specialist Kenneth Woodward, who had reviewed *Hitler's Pope* in late 1999. Woodward judged Cornwell's charge of Pope Pius's anti-Semitism "bizarre," and he also called the book "a classic example of what happens when an ill-equipped journalist assumes the airs of sober scholarship. . . . Errors of fact and ignorance of context appear on almost every page. Cornwell questions [Pope Pius's] every motive, but never doubts those who tell a different story. This is bogus scholarship, filled with nonexistent secrets, aimed to shock." Woodward further documented how "Cornwell makes nothing of the fact that Allied planes dropped 88,000 copies of the pope's first encyclical over Germany, in the hope that [Pope Pius's] guarded anti-Nazi message would get through to the people." He also pointed out that, as even Cornwell acknowledged, Pius XII put himself and the Catholic Church in danger by secretly aiding a 1940 plot to overthrow Hitler.

In other words, to call Pius XII "Hitler's pope" was absurd. As much as news outlets like *60 Minutes* proclaim devotion to solid, substantiated journalism no matter where it leads, too often reporters pursue only their own agendas, even if that means smearing institutions like the Catholic Church.

CBS challenged the integrity of Christ's vicar, but that pales in comparison to what ABC did in the fall of 2003. On November 3, 2003, ABC News devoted an hour-long special to the proposition that Jesus was married to Mary Magdalene—oh, and the Son of God and Mrs. Christ had a kid.

Not even Jerry Springer could top that one.

Where, oh where, did ABC "News" get its facts for this program? A novel. Yes, a novel. *The Da Vinci Code*, by Dan Brown, tells the story of a clandestine society formed after the Crucifixion that for centuries has protected this secret, which the oppressive, lying Catholic Church wouldn't want getting out. This society supposedly included Leonardo da Vinci, who, we are told, left clues to the secret in his paintings.

The Da Vinci Code is advertised as a mystery, but the real mystery in all this is how a respected news division could devote an hour to such a stupid and bizarre story.

The program's host, ABC reporter Elizabeth Vargas, claimed that she would reveal "surprising truths" about Jesus, Mary Magdalene, and Leonardo da Vinci, but over and over it was apparent that ABC had not uncovered a thing. Geraldo Rivera found more in Al Capone's vault than ABC dug up about the Catholic Church. There wasn't enough evidence in this special for a two-minute story on the E! channel, let alone a sixty-minute ABC News broadcast. Even the *New York Times* trashed the spectacle as "woolly and underthought," saying it "mixes fable with history in an absurdist way."

Without any real facts to work with, ABC resorted to shoddy methodology. For example, the network interviewed a pile of art historians to investigate Dan Brown's claim that the figure of the apostle John in da Vinci's *Last Supper* is really a woman, but Vargas admitted that "we could only find one art historian" who agreed with Brown. Nevertheless, that one expert with whom everyone else disagreed got five minutes to expound on this oddball theory.

The ABC program was a journalistic atrocity, a complete abandonment of professionalism—in short, an embarrassment. While promoting the special, Vargas gushed, "For me, it's made religion more real and, ironically, much more interesting—which is what we're hoping to do for our viewers." There you have it: ABC News isn't interested in truth; as long as something is "interesting," ABC News doesn't much care whether it is utter fiction.

Different Rules for Conservative Christians

Conservative politicians who are also religious receive a double whammy from the press. In addition to having their political views scrutinized, they are blasted for their personal religious beliefs, as if these are some sort of character defect. The media's treatment of President Bush's attorney general, John Ashcroft, has been a classic case in point. Reporters and journalists have revealed that in most cases they know next to nothing about Pentecostals—and what little they do know, they don't like.

Ashcroft's religion became an issue right after he was nominated as attorney general. Let's be clear. The problem with Ashcroft was not his faith. It was his *Christian* faith. And the controversy was his devotion to it.

Tony Mauro, a longtime Supreme Court reporter for *USA Today*, wrote an op-ed for that newspaper on January 16, 2001, actually insisting that Ashcroft's Christianity was a disqualifier for a cabinet position. Ashcroft once stated that America has "no king but Jesus," and Mauro warned that this vision "counts out millions of Americans of other faiths or no faith. . . . If Ashcroft's view leads him to think that ours is a Christian nation, or that only Christians have the right answers to the nation's problems, then indeed his vision is too narrow to take the job of Attorney General." Mauro also asked the Senate to probe Ashcroft's religious beliefs before allowing his appointment. Were Ashcroft Jewish, or a Muslim, or a Buddhist, Mauro would look like a bigot for making that suggestion. But Ashcroft is a Christian. Different rules apply for conservative Christians.

Not surprisingly, the *Washington Post*—the same paper that famously described the religious Right as "poor, uneducated and easy to command"—also carped about Ashcroft's Christian faith. This treatment continued even after he was confirmed as attorney general. On May 14, 2001, the *Post* featured this "scoop" on its front page: the attorney general had a prayer group. Stop the presses!

Post reporter Dan Eggen breathlessly reported that the easily commanded, uneducated masses were now staining the nation's halls of justice with their religion. "Bible Sessions with Staffers Draw Questions and Criticism," the subhead declared. It turns out that the critics within the Justice Department were, as Eggen acknowledged, "unwilling to be identified by name." Hiding behind the shield of anonymity, one Justice attorney complained that Ashcroft should "do the business of the government, not establish a religion," while another "career Justice lawyer" called the devotionals "totally outrageous." Eggen explained that Ashcroft's prayer group was an issue as a result of this warning put in a federal government manual issued in 1997: "Because supervisors have the power to hire, fire, or promote, employees may reasonably perceive their supervisors' religious expression as coercive, even if it was not intended as such. Therefore, supervisors should be careful to ensure that their statements and actions are such that employees do not perceive any coercion."

Eggen did allow the attorney general's aides to explain that Ashcroft had done these half-hour devotionals for years, that no one was forced to join in, and that his top aides didn't participate and felt no pressure to participate. So why was this news, let alone *front-page* news? The message the *Post* was sending was that prayer should be seen as a dangerous practice at the highest levels of government. The First Amendment's pledge to prevent a state-established religion had been ruthlessly twisted into a warning for top officials to avoid the appearance of personal religious belief anywhere near a government building.

While many people of faith would admire the attorney general's attempts at daily meditation and prayer, the media often portrayed Ashcroft's faith as a problem, even a menace. Perhaps reporters would prefer that the inner sanctums of Washington be preserved for more appropriate personal and nonreligious behavior, like recreational sex with interns.

8

Gay Rights: A Cause, Not a Story

"The [GOP] platform is, again, very strongly pro-life and rejects abortion rights, and the platform specifically comes out against gay unions, and against legal protections based on sexual preferences. So is this really an open, compassionate, tolerant party?"

—Charles Gibson to Lynne Cheney, ABC's GOOD MORNING AMERICA, *August 2, 2000*

"Why are so many politicians finding it so attractive to attack homosexuality?"

—Charles Gibson, ABC's WORLD NEWS TONIGHT, *June 16, 1998*

"Gays and lesbians are beaten to death in the streets with increasing frequency—in part due to irrational fear of AIDS but also because hatemongers, from comedians to the worst of the Christian right, send the message that homosexuals have no value in our society. Sometimes that message has a major-party affiliation and a request for a campaign contribution. In the post–cold war era gays have been drafted to replace communists as the new menace to the American Way: We're told gays corrupt youth and commandeer art and entertainment to win converts."

—Dan Rather, THE NATION, *April 11, 1994*

W HILE HOMOSEXUALITY AND gay rights have been significant topics in our national dialogue for years, the mainstream media seize on breaking news stories to promote the agenda of the small but vocal (and powerful) gay rights activist community. And in the summer of 2003 the media saw a new opportunity to support the militant homosexual movement, which in typical news coverage is rendered mainstream.

On June 26, 2003, the Supreme Court, by a vote of 6–3, struck down a Texas law that forbade gay sex. The Big Three television networks read from the same script in reporting the decision as a great victory. ABC's Cynthia McFadden proclaimed, "Those in favor of gay rights considered the opinion a triumph," while CBS's Richard Schlesinger said that "gay rights activists . . . are ecstatic with the decision" and NBC's Pete Williams reported, "Gay rights groups were jubilant over today's sweeping decision." But how did the networks characterize those who opposed the court's decision? As extremists, of course. And those extremists were summed up simply: as "conservatives."

ABC's McFadden, after tagging the liberals who supported the court's decision with the noncontroversial label of "those in favor of gay rights," declared that "on talk radio, conservatives called the decision a travesty." CBS's Schlesinger and NBC's Williams took the same approach, each reporting that "conservative groups" had condemned the court's decision. But McFadden went further. Wrapping up her report, she told anchor Peter Jennings, "Gays and lesbians are clearly encouraged, but given some of the ferocious language on the other side, full equality may be a good ways off." *Ferocious?* McFadden had swiftly characterized those who opposed the Supreme Court's ruling as hateful, even though she had quoted only two opponents, both of whom objected to the court's legal reasoning only.

In another NBC report, Roger O'Neill tried to offer viewers some perspective, saying the decision had left "regular Americans with plenty to ponder." But it seemed he wanted to guide "regular Americans" to the correct thinking on the subject, warning them away from "extremes." O'Neill declared, "On the extremes, talk show host Rush

Limbaugh [was] lambasting the court, agreeing with Justice Antonin Scalia's dissenting opinion that the court has taken sides with gays in America's cultural wars." Citing a Supreme Court justice's dissenting opinion is, apparently, an "extreme" action. As the Media Research Center's Brent Baker pointed out, by O'Neill's logic the three Supreme Court justices who dissented in the case were also "extremists," as were the majority that upheld state sodomy laws back in a 1986 decision.

It was the old media tactic: Make your liberal friends seem mainstream—indeed, don't ever use the term "liberal" when describing them—but ensure that everyone knows that conservatives are extremists. The media apply this double standard time and again when reporting on gay rights issues, as a major Media Research Center study revealed. From 1995 to mid-1998 the center reviewed 411 national newspaper stories on five gay left-wing groups, and out of all those stories, the label of "liberal" was used only five times, or a mere 1.2 percent of the time. So skewed was the labeling that in two stories the Human Rights Campaign, a prominent gay rights group that Democratic presidential hopefuls pander to, was described as "nonpartisan" or "bipartisan."

Just as the pro-abortion lobby assigns the "extremist" label to its opponents, so too does the gay-Left movement use that term to describe anyone who opposes its militant agenda. The Human Rights Campaign has taken many shots at its opponents over the years. When Jerry Thacker was appointed to the Presidential Advisory Commission on HIV and AIDS in January 2003, a spokesman for the gay rights group called Thacker "an extremist ideologue who persecutes and demeans an entire class of people impacted by this disease." Thacker himself was HIV-positive, but the Human Rights Campaign spokesman insisted that he "has no business advising the president of the United States on how the government should address the epidemic." In January 2002, another Human Rights Campaign official wrote an op-ed in which he claimed that "attacks from the extreme right wing have not abated as the barbaric warlords from smaller organizations compete for [Pat] Robertson's coveted throne." Back in 1998, the *New York Times* quoted Human Rights Campaign officials talking about House Republicans "throwing bones to the extreme right wing of the party," about "the extreme right wing" having "a stranglehold on the leadership" of Congress, and about legislation that represented "a capitulation to political religious extremists." *Times* reporters challenged none of those assertions about the right-wing "extreme" from the "nonpartisan" Human Rights Campaign. And that is the real problem: The liberal media don't question the labels used by a militant movement pushing a radical agenda. To the media, the only "extremists" are on the right; everyone else, no matter how militant, is the mainstream.

Going After the Next Goal

As soon as the Supreme Court overturned the Texas law banning homosexual sex, gay rights groups looked ahead to their next goal, and the national media were happy to support them in their campaign. Cynthia McFadden of ABC News indicated that the gay rights campaign was only beginning when she said, glumly, that "full equality may be a good ways off." *Newsweek* was more direct, putting this question on its July 7 cover: "Is Gay Marriage Next?" Similarly, the day after the court handed down its verdict, the *Washington Post* offered this front-page headline: "A Debate on Marriage, and More, Now Looms."

Legalizing gay marriage was, of course, the goal of gay rights activist groups. In 2002, James Zogby and the GLCensus Partners surveyed more than 1,500 self-identified homosexuals, bisexuals, and transsexuals and found that by far the top goal of the gay movement was the legal recognition of same-sex unions: 47 percent of respondents listed it as their top goal, and 83 percent selected it as one of their top three goals. Because of that, the powerful gay lobby had been pushing hard for gay marriage, even before the Supreme Court's decision in the Texas sodomy case. In August 2002 gay rights groups achieved a symbolic but nonetheless important victory when they convinced the always sympathetic *New York Times* to include gay unions as part of its "Weddings" announcements in the Sunday paper.

The media deemed the goal of legalizing gay marriage perfectly mainstream, opposed only by—you guessed it—"conservatives." At the end of July 2003, ABC's *World News Tonight* ran a piece on gay couples who wanted to marry but were forbidden by law from doing so. Reporter John McKenzie sympathetically portrayed the plight of one gay couple he interviewed for the story, featuring this statement from one of the men: "I think that anything short of marriage is treating us as second-class citizens." McKenzie was quick to add, "But many conservatives adamantly disagree." The statement was partially true but terribly misleading. Yes, many conservatives were not in favor of gay marriage. But conservatives were not alone. In fact a *majority* of all Americans opposed gay marriage, as a CBS News/*New York Times* poll from earlier that month had revealed. According to the poll, 55 percent of Americans said they opposed a law allowing homosexual couples to marry. Even among Democrats and Independents, more people were against gay marriage than were in favor of it.

These facts, however, complicated the media's simplistic account of extreme conservatives versus mainstream America.

While downplaying those complicating factors, the media seized on developments that furthered the gay rights cause. In July 2003 another "Far Right" institution offered its position on the subject of gay marriage: the Catholic Church. The Vatican issued a statement condemning gay marriage and calling on Roman Catholic lawmakers to vote against legalizing marriage between homosexuals. ABC's *World News Tonight* was quick to signal this statement as controversial, with reporter Bill Blakemore declaring, "Catholics are split on the issue." To support that claim, he interviewed Cheryl Jacques, a Massachusetts state senator who was Catholic but disagreed with the Vatican's position. Jacques stated, "We will keep our principles about what's good for our country and our constituencies separate from our individual religious principles." Perfectly reasonable for Blakemore to quote Jacques, right? Sure, but why didn't he inform viewers that the state senator was openly gay? Certainly that information was relevant to this Catholic politician's assessment of the Vatican's decree.

To ABC, Cheryl Jacques was making a noncontroversial statement about her "individual religious principles." As we saw in the previous chapter, however, certain "individual religious principles" are highly controversial in the media's eyes. They become particularly controversial when they seem to threaten the liberal orthodoxy about gay rights. Senator Rick Santorum, Republican of Pennsylvania, learned this in April of 2003, when his comments to the Associated Press created a firestorm. "I have no problem with homosexuality," Santorum said in the interview. "I have a problem with homosexual acts. . . . It's not the person, it's the person's actions. And you have to separate the person from their actions." The AP, shocked, reported that Santorum had even been "given a chance to clarify his comments before the story was published" but that he had refused. According to the story, Santorum said, "I can't deny that I said it, and I can't deny that's how I feel."

Gay rights groups were outraged by the comments, and the media gave in-depth coverage to the "controversy" Santorum had created. But why were his remarks so outrageous? To be sure, some Americans disagreed with Santorum. Still, his comments were entirely consistent with the teachings of the Catholic Church, and by all accounts Santorum is a devout Catholic, a man of deep faith. But that was part of the issue: In the media's eyes, Catholicism itself is controversial. And no matter how sincere a person might be in his faith, his views are measured only against a liberal orthodoxy that commands moral relativism. Cheryl Jacques of Massachusetts was treated respectfully as a Catholic politician even though—or *because*—she publicly denounced Church doctrine, while Rick Santorum was castigated for acknowledging that his Catholic faith was central to his life and views. Indeed, while many Americans admired Santorum as a man of principle even if they disagreed with him on homosexuality, the Associated Press could only express befuddlement that he would turn down an opportunity to "clarify" (read: deny) his comments.

"Ignored for Political Reasons"

Long before the Supreme Court took up the subject of Texas's sodomy law, the national media were offering spin control for gay rights groups. We've seen how the October 1998 murder of Matthew Shepard, a homosexual, became a huge national news story, with the cover of *Time* magazine proclaiming, "The War Over Gays." The liberal media predictably used the occasion to blame religious conservatives, calling for hate-crime laws and other items on the gay-Left agenda. But why did the national media ignore a murder that occurred less than a year later, a murder that was just as shocking as Shepard's?

On September 26, 1999, thirteen-year-old Jesse Dirkhising died from suffocation after being bound, gagged with underwear in his mouth, blindfolded, drugged, taped to the bed, and raped with objects by one gay man while another gay man watched. In this modern media age, ratings-obsessed news programs rush to report on lurid murders of children (can you say JonBenet Ramsey?). But in this case it seems the liberal media did not dare incur the wrath of the militant gay movement by reporting a grisly murder story that had as its villains two homosexuals. Had Dirkhising been openly gay and his attackers heterosexual, you can bet the mortgage the crime would have led every network's evening news broadcast.

The primary offender in this tale of politically correct self-censorship had to be the Associated Press. While the AP had put the story of the Shepard beating on its national wire, it sent out only local dispatches about the Dirkhising murder. Even these stories were but two-hundred-word pieces of colorless court reporting, which suggested to editors that the story could be buried deep inside the paper. Amazingly, although Dirkhising's killers implied that the boy had died because of a "sex game" gone awry, the Associated Press never described them as gay men.

The *Washington Times* told the story of this horrific murder, but, all too predictably, only two other national outlets—the *New York Post* and Fox News Channel—picked up on the story. Fox News filed a series of reports and made the Dirkhising murder a major topic on its talk shows, but still the established media refused to touch the story. Amazingly, the liberal media saw no news in this statement from a spokesman for the Human Rights Campaign, the gay rights group: "This has nothing to do with gay people." The statement was demonstrably false, but it was more shocking coming from the Human Rights Campaign, which was the same group that had led the media to the story of how "hatred" from the "Far Right" and Christian conservatives had resulted in the murder of Matthew Shepard. That propaganda campaign—which was central to the organization's fund-raising efforts—was marked by poisonous incivility, reckless guilt by association, and ugly rhetorical excess. And yet conservatives are the extremists.

When a mainstream outlet finally deigned to cover the Dirkhising story, it was merely to defend the media's indefensible double standard. On the Time.com website, reporter Jonathan Gregg acknowledged that the Dirkhising story "received relatively little coverage"—actually, it had at that point received *no* coverage on the networks, in the newsmagazines, or in the biggest newspapers—"while Shepard leaves a story that will probably endure for years to come as a symbol of intolerance and lowest-common-denominator conformity." But he quickly dismissed the notion that "we in the media elite were unwilling to publicize crimes committed by homosexuals because it didn't suit our agenda." Gregg argued that, "essentially, Shepard was lynched—taken from a bar, beaten and left to die because he was the vilified 'other,' whom society has often cast as an acceptable target of abuse; Dirkhiser [*sic*] was just 'another' to a pair of deviants." In other words, he was saying that the victim of a "hate crime" matters much more than someone who doesn't fit a politicized category. Then Gregg repeated the reckless claim that Shepard's killers "dramatically reflected some of society's darkest influences—an acceptance of the persecution of gays" and that "many in our society think that beating up gays is justifiable." Really? Just who had suggested that the violence against gays was acceptable? Just who were these "darkest influences" he cited?

Jonathan Gregg might have wanted to bury the Dirkhising story, but alternative news outlets would not let that happen so easily. In March 2001, the key figure responsible for Jesse Dirkhising's death was convicted of first-degree murder. At that point, writing in the *New Republic,* Andrew Sullivan pointed out the clear double standard that Gregg and others had so adamantly denied. Sullivan, an openly gay journalist, wrote, "Difficult as it may be to admit, some of the gay-baiting right's argument about media bias holds up. Consider the following statistics. In the month after [Matthew] Shepard's murder, Nexis recorded 3,007 stories about his death. In the month after Dirkhising's murder, Nexis recorded 46 stories about his. In all of last year, only one article about Dirkhising appeared in a major mainstream newspaper, the *Boston Globe*. The *New York Times* and the *Los Angeles Times* ignored the incident completely. In the same period, the *New York Times* published 45 stories about Shepard, and the *Washington Post* published 28. This discrepancy isn't just real. It's staggering." So why, Sullivan asked, were the media so obsessed with Shepard and indifferent to Dirkhising? "The answer is politics," he concluded. "The Shepard case was hyped for political reasons: to build support for inclusion of homosexuals in a federal hate-crimes law. The Dirkhising case was ignored for political reasons: squeamishness about reporting a story that could feed anti-gay prejudice, and the lack of any pending interest-group legislation to hang a story on."

"There Is No Other Side"

The media have made it clear that they intend to cover gay rights not as a controversial issue but as a cause to be advanced. And the gay movement is relentless, pressuring an already sympathetic media at every turn. For example, Cathy Renna of the Gay and Lesbian Alliance Against Defamation (GLAAD) told an October 1999 gathering, "One of the most important things you can do is have those tough conversations with journalists about when it is completely inappropriate to run to some radical group like the Family Research Council because of misguided notions of 'balance.' We have to offer them some more moderate voices, or convince them that there is no other side to these issues. . . . We are now in the position of being able to say, we have the high ground, we have the facts, and we don't have to go one-on-one with these people." Renna was shamelessly imploring the gay movement to spin the media, to get journalists to abandon any notion of balance whatsoever (though she didn't explain why the idea of balance in news reporting is so "misguided"). Using the familiar tactic, she labeled anyone who opposed gay rights groups as "radical."

With the gay movement exerting such pressure on the mainstream media, it is no surprise that newsrooms shied away from stories like the Jesse Dirkhising murder. The gay Left has been so successful that it now exerts its influence inside the newsroom as well as outside. Richard Berke, an openly gay *New York Times* reporter, was promoted to the paper's number two slot at the *Times*'s Washington, D.C., bureau in the summer of 2002. In 2000, the same Berke announced in a speech before the National Lesbian and Gay Journalists Association (NLGJA) that homosexuals were gaining power in the news business. "There are times when you look at the front-page meeting [at the *Times*]," Berke crowed, "and . . . literally three-quarters of the people deciding what's on the front page are not-so-closeted homosexuals."

This is no accident. Nearly every national media outlet financially sponsors the NLGJA's annual convention and sets up a recruiting booth at the conference every year. The 2003 convention attracted the usual list of media powerhouses as sponsors, recruiters, and speakers. According to the NLGJA's website, the *Los Angeles Times* paid $35,000 to be a sponsor at the "Groundbreaker Level"; CBS News paid $15,000 to be a sponsor at the "Editorial Level"; NBC News, Knight-Ridder, NPR Online (which is taxpayer-funded), the *Washington Post*, *Newsweek*, CBS2/KCAL9, and CNN each paid $10,000; and ABC News, Bloomberg, Comcast, Fox News, Hearst Newspapers, the *San Francisco Chronicle*, and Time Inc. paid $5,000 apiece. Many media organizations also participated in the Career and Community Expo: ABC News, the American Federation of Radio and Television Artists, the Associated Press, the *Atlanta Journal-Constitution*, CBS News, CBS2/KCAL9, CNN, Hearst Newspapers, Knight-Ridder, the *Los Angeles Times*, the National Association of Hispanic Journalists, National Public Radio, the National Writers Union, NBC News, *Newsweek*, the Project for Excellence in Journalism, Fox News, the Gannett Company, HBO, the *San Francisco Chronicle*, the *San Jose Mercury News*, the *South Florida Sun-Sentinel*, the *Boston Globe*, the

New York Times, the *Washington Post,* Time Inc., the Tribune Company, and U.S. Newswire/Media Link. Among the speakers and participants were CNN's Judy Woodruff, *Los Angeles Times* publisher John Puerner, Fox News's Rita Cosby, PBS's Richard Rodriguez, and ABC's Jeffrey Kofman. And all this was just at one convention.

In short, mainstream news organizations see homosexuals as a group to be actively courted. The gay movement has become such a favored party that news coverage of gay rights has become a joke. No matter how extreme the agenda of gay rights groups, no matter how reckless their rhetoric, no matter how militant their actions, they get favorable coverage from the fawning press. Just as important, the media do important work for these groups, vilifying their opponents and spiking stories that might reflect unfavorably on the gay community.

Andrew Sullivan was right. It's staggering.

9

Guns: Why Cover the
Neanderthal Perspective?

*"Why are you only focusing on licensing and registration [of guns]?
Why aren't you going for more than that? Why aren't you going, for
example, for a total ban?"*

—Bryant Gumbel *to Million Mom March organizer Gail Powers,
on CBS's* Early Show, *May 12, 2000*

*"Who are we? We are the mothers of America. We are the people who
ate protein during our pregnancies. . . . Don't dare tell us that we
don't have the right to keep those children safe. We are the people who
put latches on the kitchen cabinets, baby gates on the stairs, car seats in
the back of a minivan. . . . Don't dare tell us that we don't have the
right to keep our children safe. But that is exactly what we've been told
every time commonsense gun legislation has been defeated by the Congress of the United States."*

—Anna Quindlen *of* Newsweek, *speaking from the podium at the
Million Mom March, May 14, 2000*

*"Get rid of the guns. We had the Second Amendment that said you
have the right to bear arms. I haven't seen the British really coming by*

my house looking for it. And besides, the right to bear arms is not an
absolute right anyway. . . . But I think if you took away the guns, and
I mean really take away the guns, not what Congress is doing now,
you would see that violent society diminish considerably."

—*Roger Rosenblatt, PBS's* NEWSHOUR, *May 20, 1999*

Y COLLEAGUE Tim Jones recounts a story about a deer-hunting trip he took back in his small Kentucky hometown. Great excitement occurred on the second day of the trip when word spread through the small community that his hunting buddy's great-aunt, seventy-seven years old, had shot and wounded an out-of-town intruder who had broken into her rural home. After the badly wounded man was taken into custody, the county sheriff asked the lady if she had been afraid.

"Yes," she answered, "afraid I'd run out of bullets."

The elite media simply cannot comprehend this kind of people, people they would describe only as backward McCoys. They are to be ridiculed, or feared.

In the mind of the elites in Washington and Manhattan, these people should definitely not have guns, the Second Amendment be damned. And the mainstream media simply ignore the fact that guns are the most effective deterrent to violence. In 1997, criminologist Gary Kleck estimated that people used guns to defend themselves against an assailant or a burglar as many as 2.5 million times a year—which, according to Kleck's estimate, was approximately three times as often as criminals used guns to commit crimes. But the national media didn't make much of this startling and important statistic, for it interfered with the message they wanted to convey about guns, a message that was, needless to say, far from balanced. Media Research Center senior analyst Geoffrey Dickens reviewed all gun-policy stories on ABC, CBS, CNN, and NBC in the two years after Kleck issued his estimate. Out of a total of 653 gun-policy stories on the networks, only

12 times were there mentions of Americans defending themselves against crime by exercising their constitutional right to bear arms. These "news" stories presented a very misleading picture to the average viewer in order to make the case that firearms should be limited or even banned.

In many cases reporters barely conceal that they are public policy advocates. Dickens's study revealed that of the 393 network news stories advocating a position on gun control, 357—or 91 percent—advocated increased federal gun control. In other words, there was an astounding 10-to-1 ratio of news segments advocating more gun control compared to those opposing increased gun control. ABC was the worst offender, with its news programs voicing the pro–gun control position 135 times but the anti–gun control position just 4 times. This is hardly what an objective observer would consider balance.

Exploiting Tragedies

Just as natural disasters provide the media the opportunity to push the radical environmentalists' agenda, violent tragedies of any sort offer the press new openings to lobby for stricter gun control. In October 2002, Nina Totenberg seized on the war on terrorism to make the case, once again, for gun control in the United States. On *Inside Washington*, she argued, "If we think we're going to fight the war on terrorism without some sort of significant gun control, we are crazy." But fellow panelist Charles Krauthammer quickly pointed out that this was a tendentious argument: "Let me assure you of one thing: Terrorists will find guns whether they're legal or not."

The exchange between Totenberg and Krauthammer occurred right at the time when snipers were killing innocent civilians in the Washington, D.C., area. Not surprisingly, some media figures exploited the tragedies—and the wall-to-wall news coverage the snipers were receiving—to advance the gun-control cause.

CNN's Judy Woodruff was probably the leading gun-control advocate at the time. Woodruff acted as if her interview with Sarah Brady were an infomercial for the Brady Campaign to Prevent Gun Violence, asking the gun-control lobbyist, "I mean, how do you keep going" in the face of a gun-rights lobby "so strong and so powerful and so relentless" that "it's hard to make a difference?" Wrapping up another interview, this one with Lieutenant Governor Kathleen Kennedy Townsend of Maryland—a pro–gun control Democrat who was running for governor—Woodruff spoke these words over video of Charlton Heston holding up a rifle: "Is this the right picture for NRA president Charlton Heston to be starring in as the sniper case plays out?" In her interview with Townsend, Woodruff did not ask the lieutenant governor about a *Washington Post* report that the State of Maryland had failed to comply with FBI requests for background information on potential gun buyers. But two weeks earlier, in an interview with Republican gubernatorial candidate Robert Ehrlich—an interview in which she pressed the Republican on how he must be "on the defensive" on the gun issue—Woodruff *had* quoted from a *Post* story to challenge Ehrlich: "[A voter] looked at you and said, 'Why can't you take a position to keep people from getting rifles and other guns?' What do you say?"

Of course, probably the most infamous and incomprehensible act of home-grown violence in recent memory was the Columbine High School tragedy, which predictably spawned biased coverage of the gun issue. On April 20, 1999, in Littleton, Colorado, Columbine students Dylan Klebold and Eric Harris killed twelve fellow students and a teacher before turning their guns on themselves. The horrific killing spree dominated the news for more than a week. What could have made two teenage boys so hateful, so murderous? Was it their access to guns? Was it a popular culture that glorified violence without consequences in a hundred video games and a thousand movies? Were the two youngsters simply sick? Or were they evil beyond belief?

In the eyes of the judgmental media there was only one explanation: guns. And the lobbying group the media most despise, the National Rifle Association (NRA), became the focus of attacks. It didn't help that, by unfortunate coincidence, the NRA's long-planned annual convention was set to begin just days after the Columbine massacre—and in Denver, right up the road from Littleton. What to do to contain the imminent public-relations nightmare? Cognizant that the national media always shower blame on the NRA after a high-profile shooting, the organization canceled its plans for a large gun exhibition, announcing that it would retain only its core "meeting of members" and an awards dinner on May Day. This seemed to satisfy no one within the media, which reacted with blind fury.

ABC's Peter Jennings introduced his network's attack piece the day after the slaughter: "The gun lobby scaled its plans down, but it may not have been enough." A night later, CBS reporter Sandra Hughes showed a billboard of Charlton Heston holding a rifle (a familiar target for the liberal media): "The National Rifle Association billboard is a cruel reminder for those still grieving over the events in Littleton that next week the NRA is coming to Denver, even though Mayor Wellington Webb asked the NRA to go away." *Newsweek*'s "Conventional Wisdom" box sniped: "Fifteen die and they 'scale down' their convention. How many would it take to cancel it?"

Was this fair? Was there even an attempt at balance here? Ask this question: Is there any use of armed force that would *not* be interpreted by the media as an embarrassment to the NRA? Or reverse the process: Have you ever read or heard a report about a violent incident that the networks portrayed as embarrassing to Handgun Control Incorporated or the Violence Policy Center because the victim had been cowed into not purchasing a weapon to defend himself?

The Columbine massacre proved one thing: The gun-control crowd, not the gun-rights lobby, should have been embarrassed. Legislation to keep guns away from youngsters had done nothing to prevent the tragedy. As CNSNews.com reported, the two teen assassins broke eighteen—yes, *eighteen*—separate federal and state gun laws. Didn't that at least merit consideration in the media's endless stream of stories? Perhaps not, because it might have reinforced the NRA's belief that criminals will get guns and use them no matter how many laws are passed.

The Media's Bully Pulpit

Although tragedies like the Columbine massacre should raise important questions about gun control, the media focus on what to them is a moral certainty: Guns should be banned. No matter what the evidence might indicate, more gun control is an absolute necessity. Many journalists even acknowledge that gun-control laws aren't doing the job but call for guns to be outlawed anyway. On the May 1, 1999, edition of *Inside Washington, Newsweek* editor Evan Thomas said he didn't think gun control would have much impact, "but I think we ought to do it anyway just to make a statement as a society. Even if you save a couple of lives then it's worth it." *Time* correspondent Jack E. White one-upped Thomas. "Whatever is being proposed is way too namby-pamby," he claimed. "I mean, for example, we're talking about limiting people to one gun purchase, or handgun purchase, a month. Why not just ban the ownership of handguns when nobody needs one? Why not just ban semiautomatic rifles? Nobody needs one."

It has become a mantra for the gun-control lobby as well as for members of the media: Guns are evil instruments that no one needs and that ought to be removed from society. One needn't even own a gun to see the authoritarian mind-set at work here. Imagine the government declaring that no one "needs" unhealthy cigarettes, or fat-loaded fast food, or SUVs. On the gun-control issue the media have abandoned any notion of objectivity.

Abandoning objectivity often means giving gun-control proponents bully pulpits for their views, no matter how poorly informed they are. A year after Columbine, the antigun Million Mom March was held in Washington, D.C., and Donna Dees-Thomases, the march organizer, quickly became a regular on network television. Dees-Thomases was interviewed on ABC's *Good Morning America* a full month before the march, and Diane Sawyer introduced the segment with this tribute: "Well, one month from today, tens of thousands of women are expected to converge on the nation's capital, showing support for what they call commonsense gun legislation. It's being called the Million Mom March, and even though the number may not quite reach a million, it's still pretty impressive so far, especially, as we said, when you consider that the organizer, Donna Dees-Thomases, says that she's never really organized anything larger than a carpool before that." That wasn't even the first *Good Morning America* appearance for Dees-Thomases. On March 23, ABC's Elizabeth Vargas had interviewed her, posing "questions" such as this: "You have actually taken great pains with this march not to politicize it. I understand you've been telling some candidates for different offices, perhaps even Hillary Clinton, that 'We'd like your support, but from the sidelines, thank you. We don't want to politicize this.' " To Vargas, Dees-Thomases was "a typical mom" who "has made it her mission to stop the bloodshed." NBC's Lisa Myers saw it the same way, describing Dees-Thomases as "a suburban mom [who was] too busy with her two daughters and a part-time job to pay much attention to politics."

The media loved this image of the nonpolitical suburban housewife turned grassroots activist. But the truth was more complicated. As Brit Hume of Fox News reported on May 10, "Donna Dees-Thomases, the New Jersey woman who's leading the so-called Million Mom March on Washington to promote gun control, has been characterized in nearly all media accounts as a housewife and mother who was moved to act by TV footage of a shooting at a day camp. It turns out, however, that she's also a professional public relations specialist who most recently worked for Dan Rather at CBS News. And she's the sister-in-law of Susan Thomases, Hillary Clinton's longtime close friend and political adviser." Hume could have added that Dees-Thomases had worked for Democratic senators on Capitol Hill and was a contributor to Hillary Clinton's Senate campaign.

For the most part, Dees-Thomases offered little more than treacly sentiment in her interviews. Typical of her comments in interviews was this statement made on the *CBS Evening News:* "Look what the Mothers Against Drunk Driving did. They banned the irresponsible use of alcohol. That's all. We're trying to do the same with guns." With the media leading the cheers for her Million Mom March, Dees-Thomases didn't have to worry about the details of her antigun position. That was fortunate for her, because when an interviewer finally did press her, she revealed her sophomoric grasp of gun facts.

In his interview with Dees-Thomases, Bill O'Reilly of the Fox News Channel asked reasonable questions about her objectives. Even while stating clearly that "I'm for strict regulation of handguns," O'Reilly quite properly challenged her to explain the march and also what new federal gun laws could achieve. *What precisely were the aims of the march? How would gun laws keep handguns out of the reach of gang members? Should law-abiding Americans who wanted to buy handguns be able to do so?* But when O'Reilly asked her to cut through the propaganda and address specifically what gun-control measures could accomplish, Dees-Thomases snapped, "I didn't come out here, you know, spilling statistics, Bill." When he asked about one of the march's more humorous claims—that gun control was needed to stop tragedies like the April 2000 shootings at Washington's National Zoo, even though the District of Columbia had banned handgun ownership years earlier—she dodged again: "I don't come here to talk about whether these specific laws would have cured that." She and her message were both fluff.

Still, the media fawned over the Million Mom March. (Incidentally, it's always interesting to observe how the media cover Washington marches, of which there are many every year. While the Million Mom March becomes the focus of the national media, the seventy-five thousand pro-lifers who annually march on Washington get ignored.) My favorite commentary came from *Newsweek*'s resident oddball feminist, Susan Faludi, who saw cosmic messages coming out of the rally: "The Million Mom March's rhetoric strikes a blow at the psychological solar plexus of the pro-gun movement, the alliance between pro-gun and anti-abortion sentiments." And there was more: "Reproductive control and lack of gun control are inseparable halves of what feminists once dubbed the 'male protection racket': If women have no control over their wombs, then they are helpless dependents in need of men's protection. But if women can make their own choices, they no longer need the paternal guardianship either. That is why gun ownership and anti-abortion advocacy go together: each props up the other."

Faludi didn't try to hide her agenda, but then neither do the rest of the liberal media, even those news outlets that are supposed to be objective. As Geoffrey Dickens of the Media Research Center convincingly demonstrated with his two-year study of the networks' coverage of gun issues, the news media's reporting on the gun-control debate is shockingly biased. And this is not an unconscious bias. The media have an explicit agenda that they undertake with messianic zeal. Gun-rights advocates may have their own stories to tell and their own arguments to make (remember Gary Kleck's estimate that guns are used as many as 2.5 million times annually to defend against assailants and burglars?). But in the mainstream media, where decent folks congregate, these Neanderthals are simply not going to get a fair hearing.

PART THREE

ACTORS, NOT OBSERVERS

How the Media Try to Influence Events

10

The Year the News Media Died

W E HAVE SEEN how the news media apply their liberal world-view to a variety of important issues and use their platform to advocate for liberal policy. They do this as a matter of course; indeed, the media provide a daily diet of bias. But the bias becomes even more pronounced with certain major news stories. When these special events arise, the media don't simply apply a liberal spin to the news they are reporting; they actually attempt to influence the course of events. As we will see, sometimes the media are successful in their attempts, sometimes not. No matter the result, however, the fact remains that journalists are not disinterested observers of the national scene, as one might hope and expect—and as they insist they are.

One of the biggest news stories in recent memory began in January 1998, when the American public first learned that President Bill Clinton might have had a sexual relationship with a White House intern named Monica Lewinsky. For the next year, this story dominated the news. In fact, those who deny the existence of liberal media bias often point to that news coverage as evidence that the press did not go easy on Clinton; in fact, many on the Left argue that the media were unduly harsh on the president.

That is absurd. As a careful examination of news coverage during the Clinton presidency reveals, the media had a love affair with Bill Clinton. And in fact, no year better illustrated this point than 1998.

How does one describe that year? Was it the "Year of the Intern"? Was it the "Year the Law Died"? Or could it be labeled the "Year the News Media Died"? In hindsight, maybe it was all three.

Love at First Sight

The media were on Bill Clinton's side long before the American people heard the name Monica Lewinsky. A myth holds that Clinton endured negative coverage even when he was just another Democratic candidate for president. In truth, his popularity with the press corps was evident as early as the New Hampshire primary in 1992, and it endured after he pardoned his last felon and walked out of the White House door with the "W" keyboard letters in January 2001. From the start, the media saw Clinton as one of them, an antiwar baby boomer who had come of age in the 1960s. It helped immensely that his wife, Hillary, a Yale Law School graduate and political activist herself, was a kindred spirit. The couple—they were both so smart and hip—had liberal views on government and a myriad of social issues. In March of 1992, *New Republic* senior editor Hendrik Hertzberg—no rightwinger—observed the spell Clinton had cast on the press corps: "The group of people I'll call The Press—by which I mean several dozen political journalists of my acquaintance, many of whom the Buchanan Administration may someday round up on suspicion of having Democratic or even liberal sympathies—was of one mind as the season's first primary campaign shuddered toward its finish. I asked each of them, one after another, this question: If you were a New Hampshire Democrat, whom would you vote for? The answer was always the same; and the answer was always Clinton. In this group, in my experience, such unanimity is unprecedented." Hertzberg went on to explain why: "Almost none is due to calculations about Clinton being electable . . . and none at all is due to belief in Clinton's denials in the [Gennifer] Flowers business, because no one believes these denials. No, the real reason members of The Press like Clinton is simple, and surprisingly uncynical: they think he would make a very good, perhaps a great,

President. Several told me they were convinced that Clinton is the most talented presidential candidate they have ever encountered, JFK included."

The press not only supported Clinton, they voted for him in a near-unanimous manner, as *Chicago Tribune* reporter Elaine Povich revealed in her 1996 book *Partners and Adversaries: The Contentious Connection Between Congress and the Media.* Of 139 Washington, D.C., bureau chiefs and correspondents surveyed, 89 percent said they had voted for Clinton in 1992. Fifty percent of the group identified themselves as Democrats and only 4 percent as Republicans. Furthermore, 61 percent of the supposedly objective press identified themselves as "liberal" while only 2 percent labeled themselves "conservative" or "liberal to moderate."

The favorable coverage continued into Clinton's presidency despite so many actions that warranted serious investigation from a watchdog press. If there are three journalistic stages to scandal stories—allegation, investigation, and resolution—the media's record covering the Clinton administration was sad. At times they simply refused to touch an allegation, even after some legal body had resolved the story for them. Take Judge Royce Lamberth's decision on December 19, 1997, to fine the White House $285,000 for baldly lying about the composition of the Clinton health-care task force, which had planned to socialize one-seventh of the American economy. The American Association of Physicians and Surgeons had sued to open to the public Hillary Clinton's task force meetings, as required by law. Ira Magaziner, the meetings organizer, had claimed in a court memo that closed deliberations were legal because all members of this task force were full-time government employees doing their jobs. But Judge Lamberth ruled that it was clear that many of the 650 persons involved in the task force were not federal employees. In his decision, Lamberth declared, "It is clear that the decisions here were made at the highest levels of government." Were the subject a Republican, such a statement most certainly would have let loose the what-did-he-know-and-when-did-he-know-it hounds. But this was Clinton. The media virtually ignored it.

On other occasions, a Clinton scandal might start with a small burst but would lose impetus as the White House pressed its liberal friends to resist being tools of the right-wing hatemongers. Take Hillary Clinton's $100,000 commodities bonanza. James Blair, the legal counsel for the giant Tyson's Food Corporation and a longtime friend of the Clintons, had helped Mrs. Clinton invest $1,000 in commodities in October 1978, and this investment somehow ballooned into a $99,537 windfall by July 1979. I say "somehow" because Mrs. Clinton never offered a sound explanation for this extraordinary return. Still, all this prompted from the media were their softball questions in the famous Pink Lady press conference, when the first lady offered pointless answers that left everyone cooing about her "performance." What Mrs. Clinton said was of no importance; it was how she said it and how she behaved that had the press aflutter.

Time reporter Michael Duffy described Hillary's press conference as "a riveting hour and 12 minutes in which the First Lady appeared to be open, candid, but above all unflappable. While she provided little new information on the tangled Arkansas land deal or her controversial commodity trades, the real message was her attitude and her poise." Helen Thomas, then with UPI, was just as effusive in her praise. "She kept her cool, it was a tour de force. I think that everyone was truly enchanted with how remarkable her performance was." NBC anchor Tom Brokaw told viewers that Hillary "was cool, articulate, and for the most part very responsive to all questions." Peter Jennings saw Hillary as she saw herself—in historical terms—and felt compelled to tell ABC viewers what they should find important. "Women around this country will find this undoubtedly important: 'We have had some difficulty adjusting, we're transitional figures.' She points out, that in her view, the country is having some difficulty adjusting to a working woman in the role of First Lady. . . . I think most people will regard this certainly as an enormous effort by Mrs. Clinton to set the record straight as she can."

So how did Hillary make that hundred grand? We'll never know. The media dropped the commodities issue.

And so it went through scandal after scandal. Then came the Monica Lewinsky story. This scandal *was* different, but not for the reasons that liberal defenders of the media put forward. What made this Clinton scandal unique was that the media *had* to take it to the finish line—from allegation through investigation to resolution. They could ignore neither the federal investigation nor the impeachment process.

But reporting the story through to the end did not mean giving Clinton harsh coverage—quite the contrary. The Clinton-Lewinsky scandal, in the eyes of the national media, was never a case of truth and lies, and certainly not a matter of right and wrong. For the press, it was a potent combination of sexual allegations and perjury charges that captured the attention of the usually apolitical public still feeding on the table scraps of O. J. Simpson and JonBenet Ramsey updates. The scandal offered a grand setting and powerful protagonists and antagonists, as well as sex, lies, and . . . well, audiotape. It wasn't history in the making; it was living drama. It wasn't a constitutional crisis; it was entertainment. It was water cooler dynamite. Finally, this was a Clinton scandal the media could enjoy. But in the end, falsehood, obfuscation, and lust for power triumphed over truth, clarity, and law. And Clinton's media supporters played a powerful role in that.

The media's focus on the Lewinsky scandal actually *helped* Clinton in another way: It diverted attention from other, more serious scandals that the press should have thoroughly investigated. Consider, for example, the "Chinagate" story, which involved one Johnny Chung, Chinese government money being funneled to the Democratic National Committee, and U.S. missile technology being provided to China. The allegations in this case were extremely serious, but the story was an afterthought to the national media, who were preoccupied with sex and with proving that perjury didn't matter. In fact, none of the Clinton administration illegalities mattered. As NBC's Claire Shipman explained in February of 1998, "Who's thinking about Buddhist nuns when the issue is illicit sex in the White House?"

So the Lewinsky saga became the big story. And in covering this story, the media defended the Clinton administration even as the president of the United States continued to disgrace himself. To be fair, some members of the Washington press corps reported the scandal with professionalism. *Newsweek*'s Michael Isikoff, for example, deserves credit for exposing this depraved president. Also, ABC's Sam Donaldson, who returned to serve a second stint as ABC's chief White House correspondent when the Lewinsky story broke, refused to be fooled by the double-talk, constantly challenging the administration on one issue after another.

But those were exceptions. On the whole, the media were blatant in their support of Clinton, even when he went on television to shake his finger in the nation's face and declare angrily (and falsely), "I did not have sexual relations with that woman, Miss Lewinsky," and even when, seven long months later, he confessed to what had really happened, conceding what Americans already knew—he was a liar. The media also played along when Hillary Clinton, appearing on friendly ground at NBC's *Today* on January 27, 1998, unabashedly claimed that the infidelity charges would not be "proven true" and deliberately created a smoke screen with her now famous statement that a "vast right-wing conspiracy" was plotting to get her husband. It would be an epic struggle, the Clintons and their media acolytes assured us, with the hateful, extremist, "vast right-wing conspiracy" arrayed against a caring and concerned, if somewhat mischievous, president—the "lovable rogue" as Geraldo Rivera once called him. The liberal media would do anything for their great president, as *Time* contributor Nina Burleigh graphically illustrated in the summer of 1998 when, writing in the *New York Observer,* she said, "I would be happy to give [Clinton] a blow job just to thank him for keeping abortion legal. I think American women should be lining up with their presidential kneepads on to show their gratitude for keeping the theocracy off our backs."

For the most ardent Clinton defenders, those unfortunate surrogate family members, the whole ordeal was thoroughly humiliating. What are we to make of poor Eleanor Clift and Bryant Gumbel? They lost whatever shred of credibility they hoped to retain as a result of their constant obfuscation during Clinton's tenure. The day the Lewinsky story broke, Clift tried this silly defense of Clinton on MSNBC: "Well, he's been elected twice with people knowing that he has had affairs. Now is the fact that this woman is twenty-one, I mean she's still of age I suppose." Besides, Clift argued, "libido and leadership is [*sic*] often linked." One almost feels sorry for her.

On his Nielsen-challenged CBS show *Public Eye,* Gumbel was even more partisan, more embarrassing: "These allegations have been spawned by a series of secretly recorded audiotapes. Behind the tapes and the charges: Special Prosecutor Kenneth Starr, the same Republican partisan who has unsuccessfully dogged Mr. Clinton for three and one-half years." Gumbel asked reporter Scott Pelley, "Scott, as you and I both know, a popular move these days is to make a titillating charge and then have the media create the frenzy. Given Kenneth Starr's track record, should we suspect that he's trying to do with innuendo that which he has been unable to do with evidence?"

Within days of the nation's introduction to Monica Lewinsky, some in the media were already tired of the story. Nancy Gibbs of *Time* employed her overripe prose in portraying Clinton's what-me-worry State of the Union address as a glorious respite from the crimes at hand: "He invited his exhausted audience to take a holiday from Lewinsky and spend a refreshing hour and 12 minutes feeling like a country again. . . . He had become all human nature, the best and the worst, standing there naked in a sharp, dark suit, behind the Teleprompter. That which does not kill him only makes him stronger, and his poll numbers went through the roof. . . . That may have been a miracle, but it was no accident: Americans are less puritanical and more forgiving than the cartoon version, and this President is never better than in his worst moments."

The media also revealed their support for the Clinton administration with the terms they used to frame the debate. For example, the national media happily used the word "war" to characterize the conflicts between Independent Counsel Kenneth Starr and the White House. The cover of *Time* read "Starr at War," and *Newsweek* promised the latest on "The Secret Sex Wars." Tom Brokaw began a NBC newscast by dramatically declaring, "Tonight, the war between the White House and Whitewater prosecutor Kenneth Starr went to a new level."

Where did this terminology come from? From none other than Hillary Clinton. In the famous "vast right-wing conspiracy" interview, the *Today* show's Matt Lauer pointed out that Democratic spinmeister James Carville had called the administration's political struggles a "war," and Mrs. Clinton took to the theme. "I do believe that this is a battle," she said, before railing against that unnamed group "that has been conspiring against my husband since the day he announced for president." This language was quintessentially Clintonian, designed to demonize Starr and raise doubts about the investigation. And it worked. When the media picked up the war metaphor, it took away the moral high ground of an independent counsel. The disinterested prosecutor investigating criminal targets degenerated into a partisan political aggressor. The Clintonites didn't dare strive for moral superiority in those days, but they could settle for moral equivalence and confusion.

Beyond announcing a "war," the Clintonistas accused the prosecutor of partisan political persecution. Obediently, and quite predictably, the national media fell in line, digging deep into Starr's past and, through innuendo, maligning his motives. CNN pursued this angle, which was not a shock, given that the network was then headed by longtime Clinton friend and adviser Rick Kaplan. Kaplan had known Clinton for twenty years, had prepared him for the famous Gennifer Flowers interview on *60 Minutes,* had advised him on media strategy during the 1992 New York primaries, and was later rewarded with an overnight stay at the Clinton White House. On January 28, this "Friend of Bill" produced a roundtable seminar on "media madness" against Clinton. Another beaut came the next week: "Investigating the Investigator," where one reporter announced that Starr's "conservative connections—his links with the president's political opponents—have made him suspect." Another reporter suggested, "Even if Starr's critics overlooked his connections to the Right, they'd probably still find ammunition by focusing in on his tactics."

The press filed one report after another looking at Starr as a politically partisan prosecutor. Media polls revealed the effectiveness of the story line, dutifully "confirming" that a majority of Americans believed that Starr was waging an unnecessary war against Clinton. NBC reported that 64 percent of the public thought the independent counsel's investigation was "partisan and political" while only 22 percent characterized it as "fair and impartial." But after years of unchallenged James Carville and Co. attacks and Dan Rather's constant references to

Starr as a "Republican prosecutor," how could the results have been otherwise?

Let's be honest. Did the American people really know enough about Starr's investigation to be able to judge its fairness? For that matter, did the press? At the time, no one outside of the investigation knew where Starr was heading, let alone the fine legal points he and his team were addressing. The entire process was shrouded in grand jury secrecy. Consequently, any talk of partisan vendettas was pure speculation, and the media fed that speculation by reporting rumors and unsubstantiated leaks emanating from who knows where.

What a difference a decade made. Ten years earlier, Lawrence Walsh, who spent $40 million prosecuting the Reagan administration, enjoyed every benefit of the doubt from the press. The media—in so many cases, the very same reporters who crucified Starr—never described the Iran-Contra prosecution as a "war." Oh, they did refer to, and constantly condemned, the "dirty little war," but that was the distasteful Contra resistance in Nicaragua. But a "war" between Walsh and the Reaganites? I challenge anyone to find a single major media reference to it.

Lawrence Walsh's decision to reindict Caspar Weinberger and leak documents sullying George H. W. Bush a mere four days before the 1992 election reeked of abuse. So where was the talk of "persecution"? Where were the stories about partisanship, and where were the subsequent polls confirming the public's annoyance? The *Time* headline "A Mystery Without an Ending" could have been used a dozen times throughout the Clinton presidency to focus on a dozen separate unsolved Clinton scandals. But no headline of that sort ever materialized.

Tributes to the First Couple

A constant refrain from the Clinton administration, and one the media were more than happy to repeat, was that the Clinton union was a model marriage. To many married Americans, the Clinton union looked like a grisly car accident, especially after the revelations about Lewinsky. But no "bimbo eruption" ever stopped the spin doctors in the White House and their allies in the media from cooing about the Clintons' marital bliss.

Selling the Clinton marriage was much easier in the early days, when the adultery, even when acknowledged, was conveniently . . . distant. Beginning his career as a Clinton courtier during the 1992 campaign, Sidney Blumenthal boldly spun the Gennifer Flowers allegations in the *New Republic*: "While George Bush—all whiteness— talks about 'family values,' the Clintons demonstrate them by confessing to adultery." The following year, Margaret Carlson of *Time* rapturously described the Clintons' loving marriage: "Valentine's Day at the Red Sage restaurant. Even at a romantic outing, the President can be the date from hell, talking to everyone but the girl he brung. . . . Finally alone, they have 'painted soup' and the lamb baked in herbed bread. They exchange gifts and touch each other more in two hours than the Bushes did in four years." Those repressed Bushes, they were really the problem, it seems. It couldn't get better than this for the Clintons: a media demanding that the president's infidelities be ignored while gushing over the Clintons' marital fidelities.

When the Lewinsky scandal broke, a majority of Americans believed that the president was lying about sex with a twenty-one-year-old intern. A *Time*/CNN poll in January 1998 found that 54 percent of the public believed he had had an affair with Lewinsky while 38 percent thought he hadn't. A February 23 survey by CBS News and the *New York Times* found that 59 percent of the public felt the charges of an affair with Lewinsky were "probably true" while 31 percent thought otherwise. A Fox News/Opinion Dynamics poll that month found that 53 percent thought Clinton had had a sexual relationship with the intern while 26 percent believed the president's denial. Another February survey, this one from the Pew Research Center, found that 56 percent of the public believed it was definitely or probably true that Clinton had lied under oath about Lewinsky while 35 percent thought it was probably or definitely not true. Clearly—

overwhelmingly—the public believed the president had committed perjury and was lying about sex.

And yet the liberal media were unmoved. Some in the press continued to proclaim that white was black. "There is no 'arrangement' about tolerating infidelity," Gloria Borger wrote in the February 2, 1998, *U.S. News & World Report.* "They are passionate about each other, for better and worse. More than one staffer reports being 'embarrassed' when in the room with the first couple as they openly touched each other." That was simply misleading, and deliberately so. There had been repeated infidelity. Not only had Hillary chosen to stay and tolerate it, but she was now running the scandal-scuttling effort (and much of the rest of the White House). As for embarrassed staffers seeing open touching between the Clintons, they'd also seen open verbal warfare, allegedly with flying furniture as props. But for the news media to report that would be a violation of privacy, I suppose.

Newsweek's Karen Breslau and Matt Cooper (cooperative husband of Clinton spin controller Mandy Grunwald) offered an absurd and embarrassing account of the Clintons' marriage in February 1998. After repeating Hillary's mantra that "the only people who count in any marriage are the two that are in it," Breslau and Cooper proclaimed, "There is a simple alchemy to their relationship: She's goofy, flat-out in love with him and he with her. 'They don't kiss. They devour each other,' says one aide. He needs her—for intellectual solace, political guidance and spiritual sustenance." And the intrepid "reporters" weren't done: "Clinton haters"—how easily that phrase came to supposedly objective journalists—"and even some supporters wonder whether their marriage will end with the presidency. That seems wildly unlikely. Neither Clinton plans to trade in a public career for shuffleboard. As long as they're in the limelight, their turbulent partnership seems certain to endure—for better or worse. That's because they see themselves in almost Messianic terms, as great leaders who have a mission to fulfill."

Such tributes drew out the distinctions between these "great leaders"—leaders who wanted only to "go back to work for the American people"—and the "partisan and political" independent counsel who was out to bring them down. And the media did not let up on Kenneth Starr. In June, a brand-new magazine published by liberal activist and Clinton-Gore campaign contributor Steven Brill prompted another barrage of "news" stories when it took the independent counsel's investigation to task for alleged leaks to the press. (What? Government officials leak stories? *No!*) The important point was the one Starr himself made: The independent counsel's office was simply pursuing its mandate and had not violated any laws or Justice Department regulations. But legal issues didn't seem to matter to the media—and they certainly didn't matter when the president's law-breaking was under discussion.

Brill's story also made the ridiculous claim that "the press seems to have become an enabler of Starr's abuse of power. . . . Almost everyone in the press eagerly let the man in power [Starr] write the story." Unfortunately for Brill, the statistics disproved this claim. Dr. Robert Lichter's Center for Media and Public Affairs released a study of the networks' coverage of Starr in the first four months of 1998; the study showed that an astounding 89 percent of network comments evaluating Starr (that didn't come from Starr or his staff) were negative. Once again, however, the media were less interested in the facts than in the story they wanted to convey, and they used the Brill piece to launch another round of attacks on the independent counsel.

What about Brill himself? Did his partisan background matter? Take it from me: A conservative media critic discussing press coverage of the Clinton administration couldn't complete his first sentence without the establishment press questioning his agenda, his biases, and the color of his shoes. So why didn't the media question Brill's agenda? He was a major donor to the Clinton-Gore campaign, not to mention numerous other liberal Democrats. A 1997 Brill essay in a Yale alumni publication recalling his college days said it all: "I knew I was a good, progressive liberal who sympathized with everyone who wanted to drive back the Nixonian forces of evil. I'd been a Timothy Dwight organizer of the campus-wide toilet flush timed for the moment of President Nixon's inauguration." But in the eyes of the media, Brill was just another objective observer.

Defending the Indefensible

On Monday, August 17, 1998, Bill Clinton went before a grand jury and finally admitted to an adulterous relationship with Monica Lewinsky, and that night he made the same admission in a nationally televised address. In other words, the president had lied through his teeth to his country. That was something even the most loyal Clintonite could not deny.

Immediately the Defend Hillary spin machine went into overdrive. We were told to believe that the poor woman, who up until this time had been portrayed as tough, intelligent, and capable, had discovered the truth about her husband's latest tryst with his (most recent) paramour only days before the August 17 deposition. Suddenly this fierce woman—who had resorted to clever legal wordsmithing when the Lewinsky story broke, claiming that the allegations against her husband would not be "proven true"—was now stunned, shocked, and saddened. That's what the White House was saying, and what many prominent journalists wanted us—and themselves?—to believe. It stretched the bounds of logic to the breaking point.

On the talk show *Inside Washington, Newsweek* editor Evan Thomas claimed, "I couldn't believe it when I first read that she didn't hear about it till Thursday. It seemed improbable to me because she's so smart and because she's been here before. But I am beginning to believe it now. I mean, our reporting indicates that it sounds implausible, but marriages are complicated things—she may have just willfully decided she didn't need to hear it straight from Clinton, and Clinton may have held out to the last minute before telling her."

Hillary just couldn't lose with the press. Even those journalists who thought she was lying about what she knew found ways to praise her. On August 14, the Friday before President Clinton testified, NBC's Andrea Mitchell tossed bouquets in her defense of the first lady: "[Hillary is a] politician, strategist, lawyer, protector—in a marriage that friends say is based on brutal honesty and unconditional love. . . . Close friends say she knew everything from Day One and still went on

NBC in January to deny all." But instead of denouncing a lying first lady, Mitchell equivocated: "So how does she cope? What other wife would tolerate so much embarrassment? Two clues to Hillary Clinton's character: Friends say she is deeply religious and incredibly angry, blaming Ken Starr, not her husband." When you're a Clinton, it's a "deeply religious" trait to lie to millions of Americans and blame an innocent person.

Yet on Monday, August 17, after Bill Clinton gave his deposition, Mitchell revised her account: "Friends say the Clintons had a difficult, frosty, private talk over the weekend when she learned the real details of his relationship with Monica Lewinsky. . . . Friends say she's known all along something happened, but no details, so she chose to believe her husband's early denials." So much for a marriage based on "brutal honesty and unconditional love." The details had changed, but Mitchell's thrust was the same: Hillary Clinton was to be admired for her bravery and loyalty.

While Mrs. Clinton was to be admired, Starr was to be pilloried. Bill Clinton had admitted he had lied, and it was clear to most that he had lied *under oath*. Clinton would not be forced to plead guilty to a charge of perjury, but he would avoid criminal charges only through a plea agreement that stripped him of his ability to practice law in Arkansas. All this should have vindicated Starr, but instead the media attacked the independent counsel even more fiercely. The day after Clinton's confession, MSNBC's Keith Olbermann, the much-traveled news and sports broadcaster, cast aside any pretense of objectivity, displaying outright contempt for Ken Starr. Olbermann asked the *Chicago Tribune*'s Washington bureau chief, James Warren, "Can Ken Starr ignore the apparent breadth of the sympathetic response to the president's speech? Facially, it finally dawned on me, that the person Ken Starr reminded me of facially all this time was Heinrich Himmler, including the glasses. If he now pursues the president of the United States, who, however flawed the apology was, came out and invoked God, family, his daughter, a political conspiracy, and everything but the kitchen sink—would not there be some sort of comparison to a persecutor as opposed to a prosecutor for Mr. Starr?" After a wave of viewer outrage, Olbermann did apologize for his statement. But it is never-theless shocking that a news broadcaster would compare Starr in any way to the Nazi leader who implemented Hitler's Final Solution.

And the attacks on Starr were only part of the media's pro-Clinton spin. Olbermann's colleague at MSNBC, anchor Brian Williams, reg-ularly took sides. "These are days of almost McCarthyistic charges and countercharges in the nation's capital," he began one show. "With a president vowing to stay and fight, and others nakedly embarking on a campaign to get him, the president's poll numbers are softening, the party lines are hardening." This was precisely the kind of language being employed by David Kendall, James Carville, and the rest of the Clinton attack machine.

MSNBC's afternoon host, Edie Magnus, revealed similar pro-Clinton bias. When the House Judiciary Committee voted to release the videotape of Clinton's testimony, Magnus commented, "The Republicans of course are coming out and saying, 'This was serious, bipartisan, collegial, cooperative, respectful conversation,' and the Democrats are coming out and saying, 'They rammed it down our throats. There was never any discussion. This is a rush to judgment purely to embarrass this president.'" A perfectly legitimate account of the situation, right? Well, Magnus quickly abandoned her balanced approach by following up with this: "My question at the get-go is: Already it smells. It's the weightiest thing they do, to remove a presi-dent from office, and already it smells." Some "question"!

The media's determination to support the Clinton spin was never more evident than in the few months leading up to the Clinton impeachment proceedings. They were committed to the mantra that the scandal was about sex, nothing more, and that the Republicans were conducting a witch hunt. The constitutional crisis was reduced to politics, to bickering. By the time the House of Representatives took up the impeachment question, it was the Republicans who were on trial.

On October 5, the day after the party-line Judiciary Committee vote to approve articles of impeachment, Katie Couric of NBC's *Today* asked Representative Asa Hutchinson, the Republican from Arkansas,

"I'm sure, Congressman, you are aware of the polls and most people in this country, according to the polls, do not believe impeachment hearings should go forward. Are you afraid of a backlash against the GOP?" Hutchinson's reply reflected the defensive posture a battered GOP had assumed from the media assault: "Well, the greatest concern for a backlash would be that the American people perceive that we're being unfair, overly partisan in this battle and trying to be vindictive." Couric smelled blood. "Don't you think they perceive that right now?" she retorted.

Meanwhile, on the same morning that Couric was grilling a Republican, ABC's *Good Morning America* was dutifully providing the Clinton spin. Cohost Lisa McRee asked Representative Zoe Lofgren, Democrat from California, "But with regard to this report that new charges will be added, is there any doubt in your mind that this is about inflicting political damage, and is there anything you can do about it?"

Some journalists were so militant in their support of Clinton and their disdain of Republicans that they jettisoned even the appearance of objectivity. When the president's impeachment trial began, members of the establishment media were willing to report virtually any attack on Republicans and the impeachment process, no matter how intellectually and ethically dishonest the charge might be. The low point came when the House impeachment managers were blasted for being white. And male. And Christian.

CBS Evening News reporter Phil Jones relayed that line on January 6, 1999. "Democrats believe House managers are conservative zealots," Jones said, "and some Republicans agree." To validate the slam, Jones turned to one of the most liberal Republican members of the House (but naturally not labeled as such), Representative Peter King of New York, who described the House managers as "a very hard-core group. Some of them I have a lot of respect for, but I think on balance you're talking about a group of individuals who are very hard-nosed and determined to get Bill Clinton." If liberal Democrats had impeached a Republican president, how likely would it be that CBS News would spotlight a conservative Democrat to tag his party's majority as extremists? But before viewers had a chance to think about that, Jones was driving the point home: "Indeed, the impeachment managers are strikingly alike. All thirteen are white, all thirteen males, all thirteen Christians, all thirteen lawyers. Eight have been prosecutors. Average age: fifty-two." Just *shocking*, wasn't it? Well, another key player in the impeachment was also a white male Christian who had been trained as a lawyer and who was exactly fifty-two years old: Bill Clinton. But Jones didn't mention that.

NBC's Lisa Myers felt the same need to conduct a Caucasian check when she examined the Senate jury. "It's one of the most unusual juries ever assembled," she reported. "One that looks nothing like America: 91 percent male, 97 percent white. The only minorities: Senators [Ben Nighthorse] Campbell, a Native American; [Daniel] Akaka, native Hawaiian; and [Daniel] Inouye, Asian-American." Since this jury was popularly elected, should we assume America's voters are racists?

On *The McLaughlin Group*, Eleanor Clift lost control. "That herd of managers from the House, I mean, frankly all they were missing was white sheets!" she screamed. "They're like nightriders going over! This is bigger than Bill Clinton!" The House managers, she added, "put a right-wing, zealous face on the Republican Party which does not serve the party well in the future." It was no longer enough for the GOP to be the party of religious-right zealots, according to the likes of Clift. The Republican Party was now the Ku Klux Klan.

Why was race or gender or religion relevant anyway? (Remember, Clinton himself was a white male Christian—was that wrong, too?) Reporters couldn't defend Bill Clinton, but they could destroy the credibility of his opposition. Race, sex, and religion were just convenient weapons. The liberalism that many of these journalists espoused was supposed to be about diversity and harmony, but the attacks on the House impeachment managers revealed that political needs would triumph over any ideals to which liberals might pay lip service.

Personal attacks were a major part of the pro-Clinton media's approach to the story. These were particularly useful because they obscured the facts of the case. A familiar charge was that the president's opponents were tyrannical Puritans out to get Clinton simply because he had had sex. Diane Sawyer's *20/20* interview with Kenneth

Starr on November 25, 1998, was probably the clearest example of this tactic. From the outset, the ABC anchor made Kenneth Starr, not Bill Clinton, the issue in the impeachment. Remarkably, she suggested that Starr could be unfit to lead the Monicagate probe because of his personal opposition to adultery. "Tonight, an exclusive interview with independent counsel Kenneth Starr," she began, "a man accused of trying to impose his personal beliefs on everyone else." The screen then flipped to Sawyer asking Starr: "So to the people who say you're a prude, you're a puritan, you're the sex police—you say what?" Sawyer continued labeling Starr: "The man who has held a country captive finally speaks. . . . When is this going to be over?"

All this came in the first few seconds of the piece. Surely Sawyer knew better. She *knew* Mr. Starr was "imposing" nothing. He was following the law that says that perjury is an offense against the judicial process. She *knew* Mr. Starr was not "holding a country captive." Bill Clinton had dragged out the investigation for months, constantly delaying Starr's probe with spurious claims of Secret Service and government attorney-client privilege. She *knew* all these things, yet it made no difference. Mr. Starr, just like that, was to be the man "accused."

Sawyer pounded the soft-spoken officer of the law throughout the interview. She tried to make an issue of what she felt was Starr's uptight religious upbringing. "What was the most rebellious thing you did?" she asked him. Starr's reply: "I'd have to stop and think. I was not rebellious. I really was not. Sorry. I kind of played by the rules, and that's the way I lived my life." A pretty fair answer, don't you think? But in the editing process Sawyer taped this voice-over, signaling to her viewers that Starr's response should be an immediate disqualifier: "So what happens when this man becomes independent counsel and begins investigating a president charged with covering up, lying under oath about a sexual relationship?" There could be no doubt where Sawyer was headed. She asked Starr if he thought he was "in that sense . . . out of touch with the political judgment of the American people, who say everyone was covering up sex. There was gambling in the casino in Casablanca and you are the only one who is shocked. We are not shocked."

Blammo. Starr's integrity now disqualified him from judging Clinton's lack of the same. This was disingenuous. Sawyer knew full well that it was not Starr's job to be in touch with the "political judgment" of the people. It was his job to investigate and prosecute alleged crimes committed by Clinton or his intimates, period. To suggest otherwise was a prime example of Clintonian obfuscation combined with sensationalism.

Unfortunately, Sawyer wasn't finished. She suggested that the American people were shocked not by the president's wild life but rather because Ken Starr had, in his referral to Congress, included the tabloid details—the evidence—of Clinton's outrageous encounters. "I think there were sixty-two mentions of the word 'breast,' twenty-three of 'cigar,' nineteen of 'semen,' " she complained. "This has been called demented pornography, pornography for Puritans. Were there mistakes made in including some of this?"

The mind reels. What was she talking about, this "demented pornography . . . for Puritans"? This feigned outrage was once again designed to obscure the facts: The president had specifically denied in a sworn deposition—and to the American people—that he had had sex with Monica Lewinsky, and he had done so even after being shown a detailed definition of sex that included contact with Lewinsky's breasts or genitals. To prove the perjury, Starr had to provide the intimate details. Yet, by Sawyer's logic, Starr was therefore to blame for "mistakes made"? When Starr defended the explicit nature of his referral, Sawyer would have none of it. "It seems to me, listening to you, that you have no doubt that what you did in the referral was the right thing. You have no doubt that proceeding against the president in the way you have proceeded is the right thing. There is something about certainty that scares a lot of people." At another point she declared, "As you know, you have been cast in the role of a moral crusader in an ambiguous world, that you are self-righteous, sanctimonious, that you have moral certainty into areas where other people have doubt and humanity." Now, Sawyer didn't say who had cast him in this role. She didn't have to provide evidence to support this broadside. The point was to portray Kenneth Starr as the villain.

Was Starr's "certainty" the real problem in the Clinton-Lewinsky case? Why weren't the facts of the case relevant to Sawyer? Why didn't she pay more attention to the credible charges of perjury that Starr's team had meticulously documented in its voluminous report to Congress? Sawyer's bluster was nothing more than politically convenient situational ethics.

In the mainstream media's twisted worldview, insisting that a president abide by something called the truth and that the law somehow matters became a much greater offense than lying under oath.

The Legacy

When the Senate acquitted President Bill Clinton of impeachment charges on February 12, 1999, that was *that*. Monicagate might have made good copy for all those months, but Clinton's liberal defenders in the media weren't going to let it obscure his legacy. Would the Lewinsky affair be the first thing remembered about the president in the years to come? Almost immediately this was the topic of many news segments, and predictably, only the most liberal of professors were invited for interviews to answer the question.

Hours after the vote, CNN viewers were treated to Robert Dallek, who had recently been seen trashing Ronald Reagan on the PBS series *The American Experience*, and Douglas Brinkley, whose book about Jimmy Carter tried to rehabilitate the image of one of the biggest presidential failures of the century. On CNN, Professor Brinkley did the same refurbishing routine for Bill Clinton as he had done for Carter: "Hopefully, we'll have a fuller view and also understand that he's had a great many important strengths. He is the first post–cold war president, he had to put America into—he signed a lot—over two hundred trade pacts around the world, NATO expansion, at least attempts at peace in places like Bosnia and Northern Ireland and the Middle East."

On CNBC, Tim Russert spoke with Clinton biographer David Maraniss and the ubiquitous Doris Kearns Goodwin about the Clinton legacy. Maraniss's biography, it should be noted, was far more balanced than his syrupy 1992 Clinton campaign dispatches. But Goodwin, then a regular on PBS's *NewsHour with Jim Lehrer* and on NBC and its cable outlets, was anything but objective. PBS and NBC would occasionally note that she had worked for Lyndon Johnson, but they never mentioned that she was a Friend of Bill and Hillary. (The Clintons loved her book on Eleanor and Franklin Roosevelt so much that she was awarded one of those hundreds of Lincoln Bedroom sleepover slots.) Sure enough, Goodwin's only complaint about Clinton was that he had not given us another LBJ Great Society: "If he had allied with these Democrats earlier, in 1992, in 1994, even 1996, if he'd given them a mandate when he ran again, things might have been different. In this extraordinary time of prosperity, suppose he'd been able to incite the country to care about the people who weren't really benefiting, the one in four kids in poverty, to care about doing something big about education, not just these minor things, we could have had another idealistic era, maybe . . . but that's the thing I'll always be sad about. At a time of prosperity, we could have mobilized the country to bring out that idealistic moment." At another point in the conversation, Goodwin revealed why it was absurd for the networks to present her as an objective chronicler of the historical record. Speaking excitedly about Hillary Clinton's plans to run for the Senate, Goodwin said that she hoped the first lady would run for the Senate in New York as a liberal: "I'm always imagining these people are more liberal than they are because I want them to be."

Katie Couric and *Today* also had Brinkley and Goodwin on to discuss Clinton's place in history. Brinkley was worried. "I think the serious scholars looking at the Clinton presidency will be able to pick and choose the best part," he suggested. "But unfortunately, like Nixon— we don't realize Nixon is the father of the Endangered Species Act or the Environmental Protection Agency. We think of Nixon as Watergate. And I think Clinton will be remembered predominantly for impeachment even though many other good things occurred on his watch."

Actually, many other *bad* things occurred in the Clinton administration. But thanks to the media's biased and wholly inadequate coverage of the Clinton presidency, many Americans never learned the full extent of Bill Clinton's misdeeds and corruption. Even when it came to the impeachment, which liberal historians like Brinkley worried would overshadow Clinton's legacy, the media had successfully obscured the key issues by focusing on only one aspect of the story—sex—and attacking the independent counsel whose job was simply to investigate whether the president of the United States or his intimates had committed any crimes.

Sure, Americans might remember Bill Clinton as an adulterer, but as reprehensible as his adultery was, it was not the true scandal of his presidency. The Clinton spin controllers and a cooperative media had allowed Bill Clinton's worst offenses to fade to the background.

11

The *Real* Story of Election 2000

I N *Lies and the Lying Liars Who Tell Them,* his bestseller from the late summer of 2003, liberal comedian Al Franken tries to refute the notion that the media have a liberal bias. Just look at the 2000 presidential election, he proclaims. Vice President Al Gore got it much worse from the media than George W. Bush did. Franken's evidence? A study by the Pew Charitable Trusts Project for Excellence in Journalism claiming that Gore was the subject of more negative stories and fewer positive stories than was Bush.

Aha! says Franken. (Well, actually he says, "Holy *shit!*") From this study about the 2000 election he concludes, "There is no liberal bias when it comes to politics."

Simple enough.

Or is it?

First of all, if one is going to prove definitively that the media have no liberal bias, it might be a good idea to look at the news coverage of more than *one* event. As we have seen in this book, the media's liberal bias affects how they cover a host of different issues.

But even if we do take the 2000 presidential election as our case study, is the best way to assess whether the media exhibit a bias to look only at their coverage of the candidates themselves? Of course not. To be sure, whether candidates are portrayed favorably or unfavorably is a critical issue. But liberal political partisanship goes beyond a favorable treatment of one candidate over the other. To take just one example, the media can give in-depth coverage to pet liberal issues while ignoring issues of concern to conservatives or, perhaps worse, disparaging those concerns. The way the media choose to cover issues can actually dictate the terms of debate, by forcing candidates to focus on particular issues.

Look at the 2000 Bush campaign. Because of the way the liberal media have traditionally hammered conservatives for campaigning as, well . . . conservatives, the Bush team adopted a new approach. To avoid looking insensitive to the common man in the eyes of the press, Bush and his advisers chose the touchy-feely "compassionate conservatism" theme. They focused almost all their advertisements on the Left's issues, like health care and education. They kept almost every congressional conservative from the speaker's podium at the Republican convention in Philadelphia. They offered almost no bold conservative policy prescriptions. And what good did it do? We'll see.

Franken is really no different from the others on the Left who deny that liberal media bias exists. Paul Begala, the former Clinton spin man who took his act to CNN, tried this trick on me on February 5, 2003, when I went on *Crossfire* to debate Eric Alterman of the *Nation*, who was peddling his book *What Liberal Media?* Begala, in an effort to support the Alterman view that the vast right-wing conspiracy was alive and well and being run out of Roger Ailes's office at Fox News, tried to blindside me with evidence "proving" the news media's conservative bias. Announcing that Alterman's book had "inspired" him, Begala said he had asked "this very able research man on our staff" to "punch up a couple of stories to just look at the 2000 campaign and how the media covered Mr. Bush and Mr. Gore. And we contrasted different negative stories about the two men. . . . There were 1,282 stories about Al Gore going to a Buddhist temple. Bad story for Gore. There were 10 stories about Dick Cheney selling oil field equipment to Saddam Hussein in Iraq, to Moammar Gadhafi in Libya, and to the Ayatollah in Iran. There were 817 stories about Al Gore claiming he invented the Internet. . . . Which he never claimed. Fourteen stories about George W. Bush avoiding service in the National Guard. There were 263 stories about Al Gore wearing earth-tone clothes. Not the most important thing in the world. But only 12 about George W. Bush allegedly committing insider trading at his oil company." Begala concluded triumphantly, "Tell me again about the liberal media, because it cracks me up, man!" His supporters in the studio audience laughed and enthusiastically applauded.

It was the quintessential Begala moment. In the machine-gun format of *Crossfire,* I had about 3.2 seconds to respond.

In retrospect, I realize I was too kind when I replied that I didn't believe him or his researcher. What I could have said—and probably should have said—was that Begala was being purposely deceitful. The simple reality is that in a couple hours' time one afternoon no single staff researcher can put together an empirical and authoritative study. It simply cannot be done. Begala's researcher had played with the Nexis computer system and asked it to show all the mentions of Gore and various issues, and of Bush and certain issues, and had simply counted them. The researcher did not analyze any of the stories that appeared. Were they news stories? Were they editorials? Were they op-eds? Were they in a newspaper's style section? Were they actual stories or just simple mentions? Were they reporters' words or quotations from politicos? On and on it goes. In short, what Begala was putting on national television was a farce of a study—and he knew it. This is the kind of thing one puts up with when dealing with liberals on national TV. Like Al Franken, Paul Begala was going for that simple "Aha!" moment, when in reality it's not so easy to dismiss the mountains of evidence of liberal media bias that the Media Research Center and other groups have documented over a period of many years.

Franken's book is a reminder of the flimsy evidence liberals use to make their bizarre case that the media do not display a liberal bias. Even if we assume that the numbers in the study Franken gives us are correct, there are important questions to be asked. If he's basing his entire case on the 2000 presidential election, the Pew study he cites at least covers the whole thing, right? Well, no. It doesn't even cover the whole campaign. The study, according to its overview, "examined the weeks of September 23–29, October 7–13, and October 14–20"—or *three weeks* out of the whole campaign. Oh yeah, and as you might recall, a few things happened *after* the election that were kind of important. How did the media cover the lengthy postelection stand-off? Franken doesn't say.

So, to address the misleading arguments put forward by Al Franken, Paul Begala, et al., let's look carefully at the 2000 presidential election, including what happened after Election Day, since that was a critical part of the story. If, as Franken maintains, "the media just *hated* Gore," they sure had a strange way of showing it.

Who Are the Real Liars, Mr. Franken?

Imagine we're back in 1988, during a presidential campaign. A local Texas television station has just reported that the Republican candidate, Vice President George H. W. Bush, is a slumlord. A poor family that lives off government handouts, with a father who can't work and five children (two of them disabled), can't get Bush to fix their broken toilets and other household problems. The house they've rented from Bush is within sight of Bush's home, and they say that, though they've waved at his limousine, he has never noticed them. They say they've been complaining for months to Bush Realty. Ultimately, according to this local report, Bush Realty didn't send a plumber; it sent an eviction notice.

How would the national media react to that story? It is safe to say that the family would be plastered across *60 Minutes* and *20/20*, on the front page of every newspaper, and on the cover of *Time*. Ted Koppel would begin *Nightline* with a sermon about hypocrisy: "In his long political career, Vice President Bush has claimed to serve the people, but clearly there are two kinds of people: those with whom he plays, and the kind to which he hands his coat and tells to go pound sand." In this scenario, Bush would not be able to get off a plane without being hounded by drooling attack dogs. "Mr. Vice President," would come the bellowing cry, "is this how you propose to treat the poor and downtrodden in America?" The story, in short, would validate the media's conventional wisdom that conservatives are haters who wake up in the morning looking for poor families to throw out on the streets. This scandal never occurred with Vice President Bush, of course. But it did happen with Al Gore in 2000. Tracy Mayberry, whose troubled, poor family lived within sight of Gore's home in Carthage, Tennessee, couldn't get Gore Realty to fix her broken, smelly toilets and other household disasters. Amazingly, when Gore Realty did respond, it responded with an eviction notice. Mrs. Mayberry took her story to Nashville CBS affiliate WTVF-TV and called Gore a "slumlord." Alerted to the story, a suddenly contrite Gore tried to minimize the damage and promised to put the Mayberry family up in another house while their home was repaired.

There is no way this didn't qualify as news. Al Gore had made a career parading around as the defender of poor government dependents against the rapacious rich. For the *Washington Times,* the story led off the front page. It was a major story for the Fox News Channel. It was all over the *New York Post.* But that's to be expected. For the rest of the so-called news media it was ho-hum time. Mr. Gore was a liberal Democrat running for president, so there was a different rule book.

The story broke on a Saturday morning, June 3, with an Associated Press dispatch. The *Washington Post* and the *New York Times* buried the AP story deep inside their Sunday papers. NBC's Sunday *Today* aired a few seconds and CNN's *Inside Politics* spent thirty-eight seconds on it Monday afternoon. (Unlike Fox, neither bothered to show video of the crumbling rental house.) There was no other national television coverage. ABC's *Good Morning America* interviewed Gore days later but didn't ask a single landlord question. Major newspapers and the newsmagazines were no better, as a Nexis search revealed. Searching Nexis's "major newspaper" category from June 1 to June 30, 2000, yielded an anemic twenty-five stories about the Gore slumlord saga. Searches of *Time, U.S. News & World Report,* and *Newsweek* produced no stories. There was only one passing mention, in a June 26 *U.S. News* column by Michael Barone.

So Gore got the equivalent of a free pass for his slumlord ways, but he had other problems. His proclivity for prevarication was starting to manifest itself, so much so that the media couldn't always avoid the story. For example, addressing the Teamsters national convention in September, Gore came up with another invention, this time a story about how his mother used to sing him to sleep with union songs. "You know," he told the union delegates, "I still remember the lullabies that I heard as a child, [such as] 'Look for the union label.' " *USA Today* reported the tall tale two days later, noting that the song was written for union TV commercials in 1975—when Gore was twenty-seven. The cable networks covered the lie, which caused Gore aides to scurry about in damage-control mode, claiming that he had really meant a 1901 song with the lyrics "Remember the union label." One night later, NBC discussed the whopper, though ABC and CBS simply hummed and whistled past the story.

Over time, Gore's problems with the truth would become so pronounced that even the ultraliberal, pro-Gore *New York Times* would have to run a story that examined its candidate's many lies. It appeared deep inside the paper, on page A26, on October 6, far later than it should have. Still, the *Times* piece was interesting. It showed how Gore's lying was, if nothing else, incredibly dumb. "This predilection of Mr. Gore's is all the more surprising because it often involves trivial matters—ones that could easily be checked—such as how Mr. Gore recalled a childhood lullaby that did not exist," *Times* reporter Richard Berke wrote. "Even as he tried to defend Mr. Gore, Art Torres, chairman of the California Democratic Party, could not come up with an explanation for the misstatements. 'I have no idea,' he said. 'I'm not a psychiatrist.' "

Not all of Gore's lies involved "trivial matters," however. In a June 15 interview with PBS anchorman Jim Lehrer, Gore denied that an economic recovery had ever taken place in the 1980s, which spoke volumes about the economic policy he would pursue as president. Lehrer said to Gore, "Let me read you what Governor Bush said about [the booming economy]: 'The momentum of today's prosperity began in the 1980s with sound money, deregulation, the opening of global trade, and a 25 percent tax cut.' Has he got it wrong?" To hear Gore's response was to be amazed at the degree to which the vice president, like his boss, would shamelessly distort the historical record, would lie to boost his own cause. "Oh yeah, of course," said Gore. "Because we had a miserable economic performance in the 1980s, and you don't have to take my word for that. Ask anybody on the street who went through it. We had the worst recession since the Great Depression of the 1930s."

How on earth could anyone say we had a "miserable economic performance" on a national scale in the 1980s? Unlike Gore, economic data don't lie. A Cato Institute report by William Niskanen and Stephen Moore told the story. During the Reagan years, which came on the heels of the disastrous Carter administration, inflation shrank from 13.5 percent to 4.1 percent; unemployment, from 9.7 percent to 5.5 percent; and the thirty-year mortgage rate, from 18.9 percent to 8.2 percent. At the same time, more than seventeen million jobs were created, and real median household income grew by four thousand dollars during the Reagan era after experiencing no growth from 1973 to 1980. In short, it was until that point the greatest peacetime expansion in U.S. history, and as Bush said, it laid the groundwork for the boom of the 1990s. As for Gore's claim that "anybody on the street" (presumably this included his almost-evicted tenants?) would agree with him about the 1980s, how does one explain those allegedly despairing Americans reelecting Ronald Reagan in a landslide victory and then electing his handpicked successor four years later?

Gore continued to tell whoppers and, for the most part, the media continued giving him a pass. The situation was so bad that even some reporters started wondering if the media were being fair. Credit *Washington Post* media reporter Howard Kurtz for putting the media bias issue on the front page, even if the story contained the usual *Post* skepticism. Kurtz's September 25 story described media bias as "the elephant in the room" and "the shadow that some believe is hovering over the presidential race." As Kurtz wrote, "Even as nonpartisan an observer as political analyst Charlie Cook felt compelled to declare in the *National Journal* that reporters are 'larding their stories with their own ideological biases' in favor of Gore." Some liberals, in fact, were beginning to see that the media bias charge was not a figment of conservative imaginations. Why else would former *Newsweek* scribe Mickey Kaus ask, "Was a Democratic operative right when she told me, before the Dem convention, that 'as long as Gore reaches a certain level, the press will help us win it'?"

The Kurtz story, by the way, was published during the first week covered by the Pew Charitable Trusts study that Al Franken cites—in other words, at a time when the media were supposedly more favorable to Bush than to Gore.

Taking Care of Gore

The Democrats could safely rely on the Big Three TV networks to downplay, or even spike, stories that might hurt their hold on the voters. On September 18, the *Boston Globe* reported that at a seniors event in August, "Gore, the master of many policy details, mangled the facts" by suggesting that his mother-in-law paid three times as much for her arthritis medicine as the Gores did for their elderly dog's. According to the *Globe* article, Gore had claimed the dog's bill was $37.80 while his mother-in-law's was $108. "The Gore campaign admitted that he lifted those costs not from his family's bills, but from a House Democratic study, and that Gore misused even those numbers," the *Globe* stated. In other words, he lied.

Just imagine what would have happened had this come from Bush. But it was Gore, so the dynamics were different. The story broke on a Monday morning, but CBS didn't get to it until Wednesday night, and NBC handed in its overdue homework the next night; ABC got an F for no effort at all.

The *Boston Globe* story wasn't Gore's only problem on September 18. At an event in Las Vegas that day, the man who saw himself as an expert on health-care issues stumbled all over the word that described breast-cancer detection technology. Gore declared that potential breast-cancer victims faced "a long waiting line before they could get a biopsy or, uh, or a uh, another kind of, what am I looking for, a sonogram or. . . ." People in the crowd had to help him out: "Mammogram!" they shouted. Not a major issue, right? Wrong, and credit one anchor for explaining the importance. "There was the campaign event where Gore forgot the word mammogram, called it a sonogram, before asking some nurses in the audience for help," Brian Williams noted on MSNBC on September 21. "No big deal, mind you, but had that happened to Bush the news media would have used it to further the theme that the Texas governor has a troubled relationship with the English language."

And that night, Gore only dug his hole deeper, when he told his whopper to the Teamsters about the union songs his mother used to sing to him as a child. It seemed that, in pandering to favored special-interest groups, Gore had no problem lying if it would win him votes.

Despite the damage Gore was doing to himself, the media were still taking care of him. This is where the liberal media's favorable treatment of pet issues was a boon to the Democrat. After all, when the liberal candidate champions a liberal issue blessed by the media, he knows to expect favorable treatment. And in the fall of 2000, the hot issue was a universal prescription drug subsidy to Medicare. This was a liberal cause that the media were eager to support, but they knew it wasn't an easy sell. A wonkish policy prescription presentation doesn't make for headlines or scintillating TV. The media thrive on "personalized" stories; that is why candidates put a human face on the issues.

The Democrats—and the media—needed a victim, a juicy story around which to build a simpleminded socialist homily. Enter Winifred Skinner.

Mrs. Skinner, a seventy-nine-year-old widow, stood up at a September 27 Gore town meeting in Altoona, Iowa, to explain how her prescription medication was so expensive that she couldn't afford to eat. So "to put food on the table" and still pay her $250 a month in prescriptions, she said, she walked the highway, picking up cans for recycling. "I walk an hour and a half to two and a half, sometimes three hours, seven days a week, and I pick up cans, and that's what puts the food on my table," she told Gore.

Al Gore dutifully kissed Mrs. Skinner no less than five times and signed her up as a debate adviser. And, like a grand orchestra picking up their violins en masse as the Democrats conducted, the networks rushed to the story.

"This is the way campaigns are supposed to work!" ABC's Terry Moran exclaimed. "A candidate, a voter, and a big issue—the high cost of prescription drugs." On CBS, Dan Rather claimed that Skinner was "no child, but she belongs on a poster about high drug costs." MSNBC's Chip Reid was positively tingling as he explained that the Gore campaign had been hunting for an effective victim of Big Pharmaceuticals. "This one was spontaneous," he gushed, "and wow, is it resonating!" The message was not subliminal: The media were bowled over by this charming oldster and her can-collecting plight.

The next morning, the rhapsody began anew. NBC's Jim Avila found the tender story of a senior citizen who lives, well, can to mouth, to be "a simple, sweet story, driving home what for seniors is shaping up as a cornerstone issue." Mrs. Skinner was, he said, "a woman of dignity, walking her Midwest town to survive." ABC's *Good Morning America* did its part to make this a cornerstone issue. "Outrage over the cost of prescription drugs in America has a new face today," Charles Gibson reported. The following segment carried the most unsubtle of graphics: "Prescription Drug Outrage."

Yes, there should have been plenty of outrage, but for different reasons.

As the Winifred Symphony played on, those silly things called facts began to poke through the network propaganda line. CNSNews.com executive editor Scott Hogenson took the initiative to do what was seemingly so difficult for others: He called Mrs. Skinner. And he found that this was by no means a desperate woman itching for a new entitlement. Quite the opposite. Mrs. Skinner made it clear she wasn't interested in federal assistance. "No, no, I don't want the taxpayers to pay for my medicine," Skinner insisted to Hogenson. "I'm a proud person and I want to earn it and I want to do it on my own. I don't accept charity and I don't get food stamps. I qualify, but I don't get them because I don't want the taxpayers to support me."

There was more. Skinner's children were financially comfortable, but she wouldn't accept any help from them—and this included taking money from her wealthy son or living in the open apartment on his eighty-five-acre horse farm. The *Washington Post* noticed something else. Mrs. Skinner had attended the Gore meeting, and spoken at it, after some helpful union prompting; it turns out that Mrs. Skinner was a retired autoworker who at one time was president of her United Auto Workers local. So where was her union pension? She was receiving a paltry $129 every month from the union. Given that the unions were lavishing yet another $40 million on political activism in that election, wasn't there a story in *that*?

This spectacle reveals what happens when a press eager to boost liberal causes finds a "human" story that is too good to check out. To be sure, the media also have a strong competitive streak; everyone wants to be the first with a story, and that can prevent thorough reporting. And emotion counts for so much in the media today that facts are ignored if they get in the way of drama—especially drama that underscores the importance of liberal causes. In this case, the networks were so busy practicing victimology that they ignored—or were in denial about—reality. The reality was that most seniors already had prescription drug coverage, as *Investor's Business Daily* reported. Over the years, insurance coverage of prescription drug costs for Americans had improved dramatically, and out-of-pocket costs had fallen from 66 percent in 1980 to just 27 percent in 1998. These trends occurred without a big federal program, which perhaps explained why they just didn't register with the media. All that was important was that the Left wanted a new universal Medicare benefit, one that would pay for every prescription no matter how rich the elderly people were, at the expense of younger taxpayers already buried in tax bills.

Piling on Gore? Not Really

Democrats were starting to look and act desperate by the fall of 2000. The reality that their nominee for president had a compulsive tendency to make things up was sinking in. The image was sealed with the first presidential debate, on October 3, in which he told tall tales in front of forty-six million Americans. Gore couldn't resist a tall tale when he tried to put a human face on the issue of public education. He told the dramatic story of a fifteen-year-old student in Sarasota High School in Florida who had to stand during class because "they can't squeeze another desk in for her."

Dramatic, yes; true, no. The school's principal, Daniel Kennedy, said that Gore's information was "simply misleading," and he explained why to CNSNews.com: "I would not permit any students to stand. We have 2,480 students on a practically brand-new campus. In my opinion, it's one of the top high schools in the nation right now. We don't have any portable classrooms. All of our students are in regular classes and we have 900 computers, 600 Internet sites. We'd never allow a student to have to stand up during class." It took one phone call from CNSNews.com to learn the truth, but that was one phone call the news media were unwilling to make.

Gore's other tall tale that night actually got a fair amount of mainstream media attention—though not at first. During the debate, responding to Bush's praise of James Lee Witt, the Federal Emergency Management Agency director under Clinton, Gore tried to tie himself to the praiseworthy Witt by claiming, "I accompanied James Lee Witt down to Texas" in 1998 when it was ravaged by fires. But the next morning, Gore was forced to concede that "I got that wrong"—he hadn't toured the site with Witt. In fact, though his comment had implied that he had gone to Texas specifically to survey the devastation, he had actually gone down to give a speech at a Democratic Party fund-raiser. While the debate was front-page news for the next couple of days, the Witt fib wasn't part of the story. Brief mentions of it were buried deep inside the major newspapers and came only after Gore had been forced to acknowledge his tall tale. The *New York Times* and the *Washington Post* ran its first mentions on October 5, on pages A30 and A18, respectively. *USA Today*'s first mention came on October 6, three full days after the debate, and it appeared on page A4.

Soon enough, however, the story couldn't be ignored, and a furor ultimately erupted. The Witt story received coverage on the networks, in the newsmagazines, and in major newspapers. Gore's poll numbers suffered. *See,* people like Al Franken and *Time's* Margaret Carlson declare, *the media loved to pick on Al Gore, so they can't be biased.*

But the aftermath of Al Gore's James Lee Witt story did *not* prove that the media were no longer biased (or that, as some argue, the media never were biased). Actually, it demonstrated something quite different: that liberal media spin does not always win the day. With the rise of alternative media outlets, from talk radio to the Internet to cable television to conservative newspaper columnists, the liberal media can no longer spin any issue as they choose. They no longer dominate, unchallenged and unchallengeable. To be sure, for all the attention paid to these alternative news outlets, the mainstream media still enjoy far more viewers and readers, and therefore have far more power, than these other news sources. But the 2000 presidential election did reflect profound changes that have been occurring.

Indeed, while liberals like to talk about the attention given to Gore's lies and exaggerations in the 2000 campaign, nearly every Gore gaffe that would become part of the campaign talking points was originally ignored by the major media. Only after Gore's misleading statements gained some degree of traction through the alternative media's relentless coverage did the mainstream news outlets acquiesce and cover the stories—sometimes. And Gore's people usually made matters worse for themselves by huffing that their candidate's gaffes weren't really gaffes.

One blunder that haunted Gore occurred on March 9, 1999, when he boasted to CNN's Wolf Blitzer about having been a founding father of the Internet. By the 2000 campaign, the claim of creating the Internet had become a symbol of Gore's troubling habit of grossly exaggerating. Gore's flacks tried to explain it away, saying that he had never claimed to have "invented the Internet" and pointing out that he actually said, "I took the initiative in creating the Internet." So what? No matter the phrasing, it was a preposterous claim.

If one had to name a point at which the Internet was "created"— the Internet is an extraordinarily complex system with a long, complicated history—it would probably be in 1969, when the Pentagon started a program out of which what we now know as the Internet grew. Sure, when he was in Congress, Gore supported some legislation that helped develop technology that ended up helping the Internet's development. But does that modest record justify such an exaggerated claim about his role in "creating the Internet"? Certainly not. But Wolf Blitzer didn't challenge Gore on his outrageous statement; he didn't even blink. Blitzer's colleagues were no different. The statement went completely unreported on television for ten days. It was the same pattern of media apathy and omission that would follow almost every other Gore boast and flub.

The Same Old Double Standard

In late October 2000, just one week before Election Day, the media gave us one more outrageous example of their double standard. When Aretino Industries, an independent conservative group from Texas, ran an ad in a handful of markets claiming that the Chinese espionage that had occurred during the Clinton-Gore administration might lead to a nuclear war, the media echoed the Gore camp's message by savaging the Bush campaign for this last-minute negative advertising. The Aretino Industries spot was a strange reproduction of Lyndon Johnson's infamous "Daisy" ad from 1964, which suggested that Barry Goldwater would lead America into nuclear war. To its credit, the Bush campaign immediately demanded that the producers of the "Daisy" ad pull their spot. In any case, the ad buy was tiny—just $60,000—while the media gave it millions of dollars worth of airplay.

The Associated Press reflected the media's urgency to highlight this controversy, promoting the story as "top news" on October 27. And the AP story read like a DNC press release, beginning this way: "The Gore campaign said a new Republican attack advertisement modeled after the infamous 'Daisy' commercial . . . is a 'desperate tactic' by conservatives to help George W. Bush." Interestingly, the networks did not jump on the controversy right away: That night, ABC's *World News Tonight* didn't mention the ad at all, while the *CBS Evening News* and NBC's *Nightly News* actually offered pretty balanced stories, both noting that the Bush campaign had called for the ad to be pulled. The next morning, however, the spin was on. On CBS's *Early Show,* Bryant Gumbel asked Vice President Gore, "Speaking of attacks, I don't know if you've seen it or not, but on behalf of Governor Bush, the GOP has taken to running the infamous 'Daisy' commercial of Goldwater days and substituting the language and using you, and suggesting that your dealings with China have threatened national security. What's your reaction to that?" Gumbel's premise was dishonest—the GOP had nothing to do with that ad— but Gumbel had never displayed much interest in the truth when he was attacking conservatives. Over on ABC's *Good Morning America,* reporter Antonio Mora referred to the ad as an "example of nastiness" and concluded by saying, ominously, "It's not known who put up the money for the ad." Mora did not deem it necessary to inform viewers that neither the Republican Party nor the Bush campaign had anything to do with the ad.

Now compare this to the media's reaction to what was clearly the most vicious, exploitative attack ad of 2000, this one a *$2 million* television campaign paid for by the National Association for the Advancement of Colored People (NAACP). The NAACP's ad attempted to tie Bush to the horrific 1998 murder of James Byrd, a black man who was walking home from a family gathering in Jasper, Texas, when he was attacked, beaten, chained to the bumper of a truck, and dragged to death by three murderous white supremacists. Over black-and-white video of a pickup truck dragging a chain, the daughter of the victim declared, "So when Governor George W. Bush refused to sign hate crimes legislation, it was like my father was killed all over again." There were no two ways around it: The NAACP was linking Bush directly to a vicious racist lynching.

When this heinous commercial was released, there was barely a peep from Brokaw, Jennings, Rather, Shaw, and Company. ABC didn't devote a single story to it. NBC mentioned it on *Meet the Press* but didn't do a story. CBS coverage? Zippo. CNN gave it the most coverage, but that coverage was mostly in the form of a question here or there during a talk segment. It did just one full story on the scandal. Even Fox News devoted only two stories to it.

Pressed to defend his ad on Fox News's *Hannity and Colmes*, NAACP chairman Julian Bond made the preposterous claim that it was a nonpartisan act of education. This was the same "nonpartisan" Julian Bond who thought Republicans in the Reagan years acted like "crazed locusts" waging "an assault on the rule of law." For good measure, James Byrd's daughter added disingenuously that her comments weren't intended to hurt Bush. Yet none of this merited comment from the networks.

Both the "Daisy" ad and the NAACP's spot were reckless and uncivil. But whereas the Bush campaign demanded that the "Daisy" ad be pulled, the Gore campaign said it found nothing wrong with the NAACP's attack ad. Gore running mate Joe Lieberman, in yet another blow to his personal integrity that year, said he thought it was just fine on *Meet the Press*. Gore spinmeister Mark Fabiani, playing Pontius Pilate, told CNN, "That's not any of our business, and we haven't weighed in one way or the other on it." So while the "Daisy" producers took the ad off the air, the NAACP was free to brag about spending $2 million on the spot.

Objectivity Goes Out the Window

Finally, Election Day arrived. Millions of Americans went to the polls in what would be the closest election in years. The networks, energized by the horse-race nature of the campaign, brought out all the stops for their election night coverage—and blew it.

On Election Night 2000, the nation's television media provided perhaps the worst election night coverage in history.

In the mad rush to be first with the story, a few networks were reporting early in the night that Al Gore had won the state of Florida, which essentially would have clinched the election for the Democrat. But as more votes came in and it became evident that the Florida numbers weren't following the projections of the networks' exit polls (which would turn out to be flawed), the state was moved out of the Gore category and placed in the toss-up category. Eventually, long after night had passed into morning, the networks moved Florida into the Bush column and declared him the president-elect. Then the fun really started. For more than a month, through repeated recounts and debates over hanging chads, pregnant chads, voters' intent, and voters' certification, attorneys for both sides argued back and forth while county election commissioners developed their own very personal standards for what constituted a legal ballot. The squabble went into the courts. And it was throughout this long ordeal that the national media abandoned any pretense of objectivity and joined the Gore team's repeated efforts to overturn the results of the election. Ultimately they didn't succeed, but that wasn't due to a wanting of effort.

The "news" coverage of the long postelection standoff was nakedly partisan. Anyone who thinks that it didn't matter to the media that Gore was the one challenging the election results should consider the comment of *Newsweek*'s Howard Fineman. When radio host Don Imus asked the *Newsweek* reporter if the media would have acted the same if Bush had finished several hundred votes short and challenged the results, Fineman responded, "Are you kidding?" The media, he said, would have claimed "that George Bush was a crybaby, that he was the spoiled son of a failed president. You know, you could just hear, the personal attacks on Bush would be just absolutely vicious."

Al Gore, however, was portrayed as fighting for the bedrock principle that "every vote matters," even as recount after recount showed that George W. Bush was the winner. And Gore's allies in his partisan crusade were not just in the media. In a startling display of judicial activism, the Florida Supreme Court—six justices were appointed by Democrats and the seventh was a coappointment—would make no fewer than four separate rulings on the case. The Florida court's activist nature became apparent early in the squabble, on November 17, when it acted on its *own* motion to bar the state from certifying election results. The court made the motion in response to a circuit court decision earlier that day that upheld Florida secretary of state Katherine Harris's refusal to consider hand recounts.

On the night of November 21, the Florida Supreme Court issued another ruling, this one causing utter chaos. Despite the lack of a clear, uniform standard for counting votes, the court ruled that counties could continue their hand recount. The only condition was that the counties had to have their amended totals to the secretary of state's office by 5 P.M. the following Sunday, November 26—although that provision, we were to learn, was subject to interpretation.

The court also criticized Florida's duly elected secretary of state, Katherine Harris, in its opinion, claiming that she had attempted "to summarily disenfranchise innocent electors in an effort to punish dilatory board members" who filed late recounts. The right to recounts, the court said, superseded a "hyper technical reliance upon statutory provision." (Harris, of course, had maintained that those "hyper technical" statutory provisions represented the law, which she had sworn an oath to uphold.)

But the national media saw nothing political in all this. Instead, the Florida Supreme Court decision was hailed as a "momentous" victory for Al Gore. On NBC, legal reporter Dan Abrams duly noted the court's "very harsh" language about Katherine Harris, but at no point in his story did he even question whether an activist court had leapfrogged the written law. Tim Russert took out his board and started doing the math for a Gore victory, skipping over the fact that a state law would need to be ignored to achieve that victory. On ABC, Diane Sawyer applied a flashlight to a dimpled ballot and, since she couldn't see a vote, pronounced the Florida hand recounters to be "phenomenal" because somehow they had.

Media figures packaged the November 21 decision with the preposterous notion that the Florida high court really wasn't liberal. "There are seven justices," ABC's Peter Jennings told viewers. "Six were appointed by Democratic governors. Our legal analyst in Florida tells us that only one of the judges is considered to be a liberal. The rest are regarded as moderate to conservative." Of the Big Three networks, only NBC noted what Jennings had conveniently left out: Two of the justices (including the chief justice) were "active contributors" to the Democratic Party, making them as political as can be.

But what to do about the reality that Bush won the initial count in Florida and recount after mandatory recount thereafter? The media had to present black as white. Amazingly, those who insisted on following the letter of the law were cast as the arbitrary and partisan abusers of the public trust, while those who insisted on arbitrarily and capriciously changing the rules in order to alter the results were presented as the forces of fairness and deliberation.

The media portrayed Gore's certification-suppressing lawyers as the heroes of this democratic uprising. Tom Brokaw called Gore lawyer David Boies "a legend in his own time." *Newsweek* was equally impressed, writing, "Ever since the election, the Bush forces had seemed outgunned and outsmarted by the Gore campaign." The magazine described Gore's legal team as "the vice president's flying squad of super lawyers—including Microsoft slayer David Boies and media-friendly constitutionalist Laurence Tribe." They were "crafty" yet down-to-earth: "Breakfasting on Krispy Kreme donuts and doing their own typing and Xeroxing, these expert hired guns were trying to extract a Gore victory from the bewildering chaos of Florida's anarchic election system."

Those who created "chaos" and benefited from "anarchic" conditions were charming heroes. Those who tried to create new legal precedents out of thin air were the guardians of democracy. No legislature or elected official in Florida could stand in the way of a judicial branch run amok, but this wasn't wrong, dishonest, or an abuse of justice. And if Bush were "outgunned and outsmarted" out of the presidency in a process where the political end justified the means, so be it.

When the counties were unable to meet the Florida Supreme Court–mandated November 26 deadline, Secretary of State Katherine Harris officially certified Bush the winner by 537 votes, giving Bush the state's twenty-five electors. Together with the Texas governor's other 246 electoral votes, these gave Bush the presidency.

But the certification meant nothing, not to the Gore lawyers and not to the media covering them. Harris, like the laws she was following, was just an annoying bump in the road. So meaningless did NBC consider the certification of the next president of the United States that it refused to interrupt the network's airing of *Titanic* for Harris's certification. The network lamely tried to excuse its behavior by stating it had aired a couple of minutes of coverage during a commercial break. And yet the very next night, when Gore spoke to the nation, NBC showed the Undead Candidate's *entire* desperate address live. On the afternoon of Tuesday, November 28, when Gore addressed the country again, NBC *again* interrupted its programming to air Gore live. NBC couldn't compare with CBS and Dan Rather, however. In his November 26 report on the certification, Rather strained to pin the "Republican" warning label on Harris—not once, but at least six times. For good measure, he questioned the finality of her decision at least ten times. And to deconstruct the meaning of certification, he used his bizarre Muhammad Ali–like poetry, saying Harris would announce the winner "as she sees it and she decrees it." Evidently, in Rather's eyes, the duly elected Harris had somehow anointed herself the Queen of Florida. Introducing Bush's remarks later that night, Rather took a subtle shot at Bush, stating that the Texas governor was "convinced more than ever that he is the next president of the United States."

Over at ABC, a sleepy-eyed Peter Jennings also telegraphed his unhappiness with this seemingly final result. On November 26, as Harris and her two fellow certifiers signed the documents sealing Gore's doom, Jennings rebutted, "Let's reassert what we said at the beginning. This is not over by any means, as formal as it looks." To Jennings, this was more Argentina than America, not a disputed election but a war. "So, another phase in the presidential war," Jennings told his viewers, "and it is still very much a war, as you will see when you get up tomorrow and see the election challenges filed in Florida and a variety of other places as well. But there it is, speaking as president-elect tonight, which he is, technically. . . . It may yet change."

Like John Belushi's Bluto in *Animal House*, the anchors were declaring that it wasn't over until they decided it was over.

The legal wrangle continued as the Gore camp went back to court, with Gore partisans charging that Republicans were subverting democracy in their shameful attempt to stop the counting and insisting that Gore had every right to insist on endless recounts, even when those attempts were thrown out of court. In short, to try to steal the election, the Gore camp was willing to try any gambit, play any trick, promote any distortion. And, in a shocking display of partisanship energized by fear, the media cheered the Gore team on. The "news" coverage became a farce.

On November 27, the day after certification, Dan Rather suggested to Republican lawyer Ben Ginsberg the liberal argument that the GOP, despite having met every legal challenge and received formal certification, was in grave danger of losing the election. "The proof," according to Rather, was in "how hard you and others are fighting on behalf of George Bush to stop the counting." That same night, CBS reporter Byron Pitts whipped out a blackboard to present Gore's recount fantasy math. "By the Democrats' math, Al Gore should have finished at least 1,288 votes ahead of George W. Bush." Pitts arrived at this number by meticulously detailing the Gore lawyer claims, but by the time he finished he had apparently run out of time—not a single Republican counterargument was presented.

Some in the press all but brought out the pom-poms. On the afternoon of the 27th, waiting to air a conference call between Al Gore and Joe Lieberman and Democratic leaders Dick Gephardt and Tom Daschle—a staged public relations event if ever there was one—MSNBC afternoon anchor Ashleigh Banfield thoroughly embarrassed herself. "The last time I was this excited about a two-minute warning for a telephone call," she intoned breathlessly, "was when I was waiting for my prom date to call and invite me to the prom."

On November 28, the day after the Gore team asked the Leon County, Florida, Circuit Court to force Miami-Dade and Palm Beach counties to finish their hand recounts, the networks crackled with excitement at the news that the circuit court judge would examine Gore's challenges. Judge N. Sanders Sauls ordered fourteen thousand disputed ballots from Palm Beach and Miami brought to his court in Tallahassee. But on December 4, after the ballots were collected, loaded in a truck, hauled to Sauls's courtroom in northern Florida, and carefully examined, the judge threw out every single Gore complaint for lack of evidence. On the same day, the United States Supreme Court vacated the Florida Supreme Court's original November 21 decision ordering the hand recount to continue, instructing the lower court to put its ruling on hold until it could explain exactly what it was trying to accomplish.

But despite these clear refutations of the Gore team's case, the media continued with the story line that the process was not over. On MSNBC on the night of December 4, James Warren, the Washington Bureau chief of the *Chicago Tribune,* explicitly told viewers that the media's true objective was to convince Americans it wasn't over. "It's going to be the job of papers like us and news outlets like yourself," Warren said, "to remind them that Wednesday, there's a significant trial in Seminole County; that last Friday, there was an interesting suit filed in Martin County; and this may not end with possibly the Florida Supreme Court [reversing] in some fashion."

The media also did not object when the Democrats made a shocking about-face on their demands that "every ballot must be counted" (which the Gore team had uttered time and again). But "objective" journalists didn't make much of the fact that the Democrats moved to have the courts void twenty-five thousand absentee ballots, many of them military ballots from Seminole and Martin counties. At best, this was a political double standard; at worst, blatant hypocrisy. But the mainstream media ignored the interesting development that Gore was trying to have it both ways.

Despite the media's undying support, Gore couldn't seem to win. On December 8, Gore's challenges to the Martin and Seminole county absentee ballots were thrown out of court. But that same day, the Gore team finally got a victory the Democrats (and the national media) had been praying for. No surprise, the favorable decision came from the Florida Supreme Court that the networks had tried to portray as non-partisan. Not only did the court overturn Judge Sauls's verdict about the Palm Beach and Miami county ballots, but it also ordered manual recounts to restart *and* that 383 votes from an earlier recount be *added* to Gore's total.

The media, of course, hailed the Florida Supreme Court decision as a great victory. Dan Rather's CBS report on the night of December 8 was typical: "The Florida Supreme Court significantly revived Gore's chances of overtaking Texas governor Bush." But the networks went on the offensive again when, after Bush's appeal, the U.S. Eleventh Circuit Court of Appeals ordered Florida officials not to change Bush's previously certified 537-vote lead and then when the U.S. Supreme Court ordered the manual recounts stopped until December 12, when it could hear the case.

The mainstream media reflected their biased approach in how they treated the different court decisions. When the Florida Supreme Court voted in Gore's favor in a split decision, ABC, CBS, and NBC did not once mention the ideology of the four judges in the majority. But the following afternoon, when the U.S. Supreme Court halted recounts with a stay, you could hear explosions in newsrooms coast to coast. Suddenly the same media found wild-eyed partisanship, deep division, and public-relations damage. A scandal, by God! An outrage! Time and again, network reporters made sure viewers knew of the "conservative/liberal split" on the court so they could realize "conservatives" were behind the stay order. So, too, did the papers: Neither the *Washington Post* nor the *New York Times* made mention of division in their headlines on the Florida Supreme Court decision, but both found a "split" or "divided" court in the U.S. Supreme Court decision.

CBS, as usual, was even more outrageous. In the same December 8 report in which he reported that "the Florida Supreme Court significantly revived Gore's chances of overtaking Texas governor Bush"—without mentioning anything about the ideology of the Florida justices—Rather explained the GOP options: "Bush will appeal to the U.S. Supreme Court, which has a majority of Republican-appointed justices. The Republican-controlled Florida legislature is now almost certain to choose its own slate of Bush electors, setting up a possible constitutional and political showdown." In the event that viewers had missed Rather's relentless—and by now quite unconscionable—emphasis that the U.S. Supreme Court was as Republican as Katherine Harris or Kenneth Starr, he loaded his musket with grapeshot and pulled the trigger with this question to law professor Jonathan Turley: "Since the U.S. Supreme Court has seven of nine justices appointed by Republican presidents, why should one not believe that they're going to overturn this Florida State Supreme Court decision today and pretty quickly?"

On the afternoon the Florida Supreme Court handed down its decision, Sam Donaldson went so far as to warn Republicans not to highlight the liberal Democrat judges in the state. "If the Republicans complain that this was a Democratic court in Florida, that's a little dangerous ground," Donaldson claimed. "Seven of the nine justices of the United States Supreme Court were appointed by Republican presidents."

Lost in this politically loaded "news" analysis was any mention of the difference between the U.S. Supreme Court majority's defense of judicial restraint against the Florida court's wildly inventive judicial activism. Throughout five weeks of the electoral mess, the networks had followed one unmistakable pattern: Every court, politician, or activist who supported Al Gore was not to be labeled a "liberal," or even a "Democrat." But conservatives and Republicans were to be labeled early and often as partisan and therefore controversial, non-credible. Anyone relying exclusively on the "objective" media could be forgiven for thinking that on one side sat the public interest, democracy, and nonpartisanship; while on the other, vicious, partisan, and bullying hard-right ideologues.

On December 12, the U.S. Supreme Court put an end to the charade. The court remanded the case to Florida but rejected any further recounts. Bush officially had 2,912,790 votes to Gore's 2,912,636. Bush had won by 154 votes—a razor-thin margin to be sure, but final. Bush had Florida, and with it, the Electoral College victory. After more than a month of recounts and court decisions, the 2000 election was over.

But the Battle Goes On

Of course, for the media, whose candidate had lost, the election couldn't be over. Early on, several media outlets let it be known they would be conducting their own examination of the hanging chads and disqualified ballots to determine who *really* won Florida. It would take time, the media sleuths explained, but *they* would get to the bottom of it.

Sure enough, after months of sifting through the most confused ballots of the most confused voters in Florida, the media announced that the recount was complete. And the dramatic conclusion? Bush had won. Again.

After wasting millions of dollars to document for the *n*th time what we already knew, the Bush victory was somehow "news" because the major media had deemed it so. And yet there are those who didn't, haven't, and won't ever accept the Bush victory. They are thoroughly convinced that Gore was the winner, and nothing will change their minds.

Even on the week of September 11, 2001, almost a full year after the elections, the cover story of *Newsweek* was still at it, this time arguing that Bush was an "accidental president" selected by jurists, not elected by the people. In partisan language, reporter David Kaplan suggested that Chief Justice William Rehnquist, along with Justices Antonin Scalia and Clarence Thomas, "had long ago become part of the Dark Side. [Sandra Day] O'Connor appeared beyond compromise." Only mushy Anthony Kennedy could have saved America from President Bush, but he caved in. *Newsweek* was treading on turf it could share only with the left-wing *Nation* magazine.

The day before Halloween, ABC's legal expert Jeffrey Toobin appeared on NBC's *Today* show to promote his book on the Florida battle. Katie Couric read from his opus: "The wrong man was inaugurated on January 20, 2001, and this is no small thing in our nation's history. The bell of this election can never be unrung and the sound will haunt us for some time." Toobin helpfully added, "This was a process that I don't think led to the democratic will of the electorate being vindicated." But given ABC's track record covering the election, who the hell cared what ABC's legal expert thought? And there's a better question: What was ABC thinking, employing a "legal expert" who insisted that his utterly partisan interpretation of the "democratic will" superseded all the election laws? One also wonders why ABC didn't let Toobin promote his partisan book on its own airwaves, since Toobin's interpretation was no more twisted to the left than what had been presented by virtually everyone else in the national media.

The Real Scandal

As we have seen, probably the most disturbing aspect of liberal media bias is that the news media actually attempt to dictate the national agenda, to influence the course of events rather than simply report on what happens. And although virtually no one in the leftist press acknowledges this, the media directly influenced what happened in Florida. Indeed, *they* caused the Florida imbroglio. The entire mess would have been avoided had it not been for the direct, unquestionable irresponsibility of the national television networks.

This is the real story of Election 2000. The television networks—not the Democrats, not the labor unions, not anyone but the television networks—almost stole the national election from George W. Bush. Here's how.

Rewind the tape back to October 30, a week before the election. On that day, Florida's secretary of state, Katherine Harris, issued a formal statement to the press. Her purpose was to remind the media of a key but often overlooked geographic fact: Florida's "Panhandle" region falls in the Central time zone, and as such polls there would remain open one hour later, until 8 P.M., Eastern Standard Time (EST). "The last thing we need," she wrote, "is to have our citizens in the Central time zone think their vote doesn't count—because it certainly does." She explained the imperative of holding off an early call on the election: "Waiting until 8 P.M. EST allows all Floridians the opportunity to decide the outcome of races within Florida."

Simple enough. Still, on election night every major TV network ignored her. At 7 P.M. EST, ABC, CBS, CNN, Fox, and NBC all announced that the polls had just closed in nine states when in fact they were still open in Florida. With the exception of Fox, the networks repeated this statement again and again throughout the hour. For purposes of illustration, between 7 P.M. and 8 P.M. CBS made thirteen explicit statements citing poll closures in Florida and another fifteen implicit ones.

To what effect? Having heard from the networks that the polls were closed, a sizable number of voters, a solid majority in that region being pro-Bush, stopped voting.

The highly respected, and historically deadly accurate, polling firm of John McLaughlin and Associates commissioned a survey of Panhandle voters to determine what the networks' irresponsible call cost the candidates. Its conclusion, released on December 6, 2000: "If the Panhandle turnout had not been depressed by the media call and had stayed consistent with the statewide turnout rate of 68%, as the Eastern Time Zone region did, roughly another 15,000 voters would have come to the polls. Our survey indicates that these registered voters who were discouraged from voting by the media's premature call would have voted for George Bush by 2-to-1, and would have widened his lead by about 5,000 votes. This expanded margin would have rendered much of the current litigation and manual recounting unnecessary."

Daniel B. Perrin, the executive director of the Committee for Honest Politics, filed a second report. In testimony before the United States Senate Governmental Committee in May 2001 he reported, "Our own preliminary findings, issued two weeks after the election, concluded that approximately 19,133 Florida voters were disenfranchised. . . . Given the 2:1 vote advantage enjoyed by Bush over Gore in the Panhandle counties, the minimum effect was a loss of 12,761 votes for the Bush campaign."

Perrin buttressed the empirical with the anecdotal, submitting to the Senate excerpts from affidavits taken of election officials in Florida. Their statements are devastating.

> POLL WORKER, BAY COUNTY, PRECINCT NO. 23: "I have been a poll worker since the 1970s. Voting was steady all day until 6:00 P.M. Between 6:00–7:00 P.M. it was very different from past elections. It was very empty. The poll workers thought it was odd. It was like 'the lights went out.' We joked with the deputy on duty because there was no one in line for the deputy to be placed behind when the polls closed."

CLERK FOR ELECTIONS, OKALOOSA COUNTY, PRECINCT No. 37: "We had over 1,300 people turn out with an average of about 100 voters per hour until the last hour. . . . Soon after 6:00, I noticed that the volume dropped to almost zero. In past elections, there was usually a rush of people coming from work, trying to get to vote before the polls closed."

CLERK OF ELECTIONS, OKALOOSA COUNTY, PRECINCT No. 34: "I began to get my workers to take their dinner breaks before 6:00, anticipating people coming before the polls closed. Between 6:15 and 6:20, I looked around and asked, 'Where is everybody?' My poll workers were just as perplexed as I was. I don't think we had more than five people from 6:15 until we closed at 7:00. We had an average 80 voters per hour until the last hour."

DEPUTY FOR ELECTIONS, SANTA ROSA COUNTY, PRECINCT No. 34: "We have the second largest precinct in the county with 4,678 voters. . . . There was a steady flow all day. By the last hour, there was a dramatic decline in voters. It is the deputy's job to stand behind the last voter in line at 7:00 P.M. Eight years ago in the presidential election, there were so many people in line that the last voter did not vote until nearly 10:30 P.M. When I went outside at the end of the day to tell people to hurry along, there was no one in the parking lot."

POLL INSPECTOR, ESCAMBIA COUNTY, PRECINCT No. 8: "We had the usual rush in the early morning, at noon and right after work. There was a significant drop in voters after 6:00. The last 40 minutes was almost empty. The poll workers were wondering if there had been a national disaster they didn't know about. . . . The last 30 minutes was particularly empty. There is usually a line after the poll closes. In this election there was no one."

We watched and read seemingly thousands of media stories discussing those hanging chads and dimpled ballots, the counts and recounts. But how many journalists acknowledged that there should never have been a recount at all? That the networks' sloppiness on poll closures in the Florida Panhandle—even after they had been alerted specifically to the issue—had caused tens of thousands to believe a falsehood and consequently not vote? That George W. Bush would have won this state, perhaps not handily but certainly decisively, had it not been for the networks' botched announcement? In short, how willing were the media to report that the networks' deplorable performance had ultimately triggered a constitutional crisis that should never have happened and that almost cost George W. Bush the presidency?

A Nexis search of all broadcast network news stories from November 7 through December 31, 2000, tells a chilling tale of cowardice. On NBC, *Today* host Katie Couric asked one question regarding the Panhandle controversy of Chris Matthews, who suggested that the Republicans go get legal counsel; on the evening news Tom Brokaw made one mention—not a story, just a mention—and that was that. Meanwhile, neither ABC nor CBS filed a single report on the Panhandle debacle.

The print media were no different. *U.S. News & World Report* and *Time* each gave the controversy a mention; an entire story, apparently, was out of the question. *Newsweek* also made a mention, but with a leftist, pro-Gore twist: Reporter Jonathan Alter (surprise!) simply dismissed the media scandal as irrelevant. The *Washington Post* devoted one story to the issue. The *New York Times* logged an anemic three reports.

On cable television the news was better, but still not pronounced. Fox News featured an interview with Representative Billy Tauzin, Republican of Louisiana, who accused the media of a pro-Gore bias; a short discussion of the issue during an *O'Reilly Factor* interview with Representative Chris Cox, Republican of California; a discussion between *Beltway Boys* Morton Kondracke and Fred Barnes; a Brit Hume "Grapevine" segment; and a lead item on Tony Snow's *Fox News Sunday*. CNN devoted more attention to the issue than any other network did, with its fourteen stories or segments discussing or mentioning the networks' early call. Though the total far exceeded any other network's, it was still paltry given the cable network's twenty-four-hour-news cycle. Moreover, five of the fourteen hits actually turn out to have been one story repeated four times.

Writing in the November 15, 2000, *Atlantic Monthly,* Stuart Taylor put the media's shameful performance in its proper perspective with this devastating analysis: "What about the thousands of Bush backers in the Florida Panhandle who are said to have gone home without voting rather than standing in lines at the polls, because they had been misled by the confident network reports that Gore had already won Florida? Is there a legal remedy for them? Perhaps not, because they were misled by the media rather than confused by an officially approved ballot form. But legalisms aside, it's hard to see why a voter who chose not to spend two minutes deciphering a somewhat confused ballot form has been 'disenfranchised,' but a voter who chose not to spend an hour in line after being told by the media that Bush had already lost was just unlucky."

12

A Story Too Important to Forget

T HE PRESIDENTIAL ELECTION in 2000, and the lengthy postelection standoff, made for the biggest news story of that year. This
truly historic election was indeed a major story, but it was such an
all-consuming episode that it seems to have blurred our memory of
another story from that year, one that likewise received wall-to-wall
news coverage. This is unfortunate, for the story I have in mind is far
too important for it to fade away so easily. It involved a six-year-old
boy whose mother lost her own life while trying to ensure that he
would not have to suffer under the yoke of communism.

The American Left, and its supporters in the mainstream news
media, would be content to have us forget this ugly episode in our
nation's history. The U.S. government seized a child at gunpoint and
sent him back to live in the communist hell that is Fidel Castro's Cuba.
But liberals do their best to deny, or obscure, this truth. It has always
been this way. The moral equivalence of the Left had them sneer at
President Ronald Reagan when he stated flatly that communism was
an evil enterprise. Even at the end of the cold war, in 1990, Strobe
Talbott—who would become Bill Clinton's deputy secretary of
state—could argue in *Time* magazine "that the Soviet threat isn't what
it used to be—and what's more, that it never was." As much as liberals
attempt to rewrite history, however, we must remember that President
Reagan was right, that the communist system of the Soviet Union was

a true, dangerous evil—and what's more, that this communist evil still exists, be it in China, North Korea, or Cuba.

As one who has witnessed firsthand what communism has wrought, I can assure you that this is a brutal system that must be opposed, which makes the story of Elián Gonzalez—and how the American news media reported it—all the more horrifying.

Las Madres de Los Desaparecidos

In July of 1987 I ventured down to Daniel Ortega's Sandinista Nicaragua to gather some film footage for a series of television commercials advancing Ronald Reagan's efforts to overthrow the communist regime. No cameramen wanted to accompany me to a war zone unless I paid them astronomical fees, so I called longtime friend Mark Barnes, a California political consultant, and asked him if he was up for an adventure. He accepted immediately and within a day had his crew together: Larry Cushman would do the filming, John Carvelli would handle sound, and Barnes would make the arrangements and ultimately produce the spots.

Right off the bat we knew we had a problem: How to get in? The communist Sandinistas had imposed rigorous limitations on the foreign press: The media had to apply for official credentials before being allowed to enter the country with their equipment. We weren't the news media, of course, and we couldn't exactly state we were there to support the effort to oust Ortega's dictatorship. We would just have to pose as journalists and wing it once we landed in Managua. With some creative use of passport photos and lamination materials, Mark's wife, Mary, was able to create official-looking press passes for our mythical TV show, *Newswatch*. When we arrived in steamy Managua we were able to convince security officials, after much pleading, that we hadn't known the rules; they let us out of the airport with our camera equipment intact.

Our mission was to circulate first around Managua gathering footage of the communist squalor in this once relatively prosperous capital. Then we would travel north to the capital of Honduras, Tegucigalpa, where we'd link up with our contacts within the Contra movement and travel by jeep back into Nicaragua, through the dense jungles, and to the Contra base camp to interview the freedom fighters.

The days we spent in Managua were memorable for the sheer incompetence of the Sandinista security operation, truly Keystone Kops material. The Hotel Intercontinental, the major—no, only—gathering place for foreigners, was crawling with Sandinista agents monitoring the guests. We took cabs our first two times out—rental cars being impossible given the decrepit condition of the city's streets—but both times it was immediately apparent that our drivers were government agents: They extolled the virtues of Daniel Ortega and broke into cold sweats when we asked them to take us to locations we knew were prohibited to the public. Ditching them and the idea of taxis altogether, we contacted the U.S. Embassy and through them procured a driver for the remainder of the visit.

Then there were the soldiers—everywhere the soldiers. As we neared the infamous, and totally off-limits, El Chipote prison in downtown Managua, they drew their rifles on us, demanding that we turn off our camera. Once persuaded that the camera was off, the soldiers, still training their rifles on us, badgered us with questions—while Cushman surreptitiously filmed the whole thing and Carvelli slipped into the brush to snap photos of the prison. The soldiers finally let us go when we convinced them we were an advance team for NBC News, gathering footage for a special tribute to El Presidente.

And then there were the security agents. At the hotel's reception desk the morning we checked out, they grabbed our passports and demanded a $60 "exit fee." Amazed by such brazen extortion, I jokingly asked if we could get receipts. "Of course," replied one of them, and he quickly handed some out. As we went out the door, however, we were met by two more agents. "Receipts!" they demanded; they dutifully confiscated the evidence of the government extortion.

Moments like this were somewhat comical, but there was nothing humorous about this experience. Everywhere we turned we saw the misery, both physical and spiritual, of a nation ravaged by a communist "utopia." In the supermarkets (we were thrown out for filming there, too) we saw row after row of communist propaganda—leaflets, newspapers, books, and the like—but virtually no food. Few could afford to drive cars, and the only vehicles on the road had dented sides, cracked windshields, and engines cobbled together (it was impossible to find spare parts). A walk down the streets, which were filled with the nauseating stench of raw sewage, lead to the ragged beggar trying to peddle an old shoe, a rusted belt buckle, a broken door hinge—anything to generate a handful of *cordobas* to feed his family.

But nothing could have prepared us for a meeting with *Las Madres de Los Desaparecidos* (the Mothers of the Disappeared Ones), the organization of women whose husbands and sons had vanished at the hands of communist "justice" and were presumably dead or rotting in the underground dungeons of El Chipote. Las Madres was founded by a once-prominent Nicaraguan lawyer who, for his efforts, had seen his offices burned down and then had been beaten and had his life threatened. This courageous old man ushered us into his makeshift offices— a shack, really—and showed us the stacks upon stacks of legal petitions seeking due process he had filed, all worthless in the eyes of the communist government. We interviewed him, and then asked to meet some of the mothers personally. "Give me a couple of days," he said, in Spanish. "I will send for you."

Two days later we were given a time and a location. We drove down a dingy street and entered a nondescript, unlit, two-room shack with dirt floors and a tin roof. Wooden benches and old chairs had been set up around the two rooms, and some two dozen peasant women, most with little children sitting on the floor around them, sat silently waiting for us in the near dark. We would learn later that some of them had traveled on foot for two days to have the opportunity to tell their stories.

We set up our cameras, the sound, and what lighting we could, and began. We gringos were suffocating from the sweltering heat in the shed, and yet these proud women sat straight, refusing to lose their dignity even after a violent thunderstorm erupted and a massive rat fell through the tin slats above us. One of the women silently picked up a stick and beat the rat to death while another two picked up the carcass and threw it out the door. They quietly returned to their seats while I stared at the ceiling, wondering what other animals might come raining down.

One by one they told their tales, each one more harrowing than the last. Their younger children, unaware of what was happening, played with one another, while the older ones sat in eerie silence, staring. Near the end of the interviews, I felt a tug at my leg and looked down. A little boy, maybe six years old, was trying to get my attention. *"Hola, muchacho!"* I greeted the tyke, rather amused by the interruption. But he just looked up silently with the most beautiful blue eyes I've ever seen, wide open in childhood innocence—and hope. Finally he spoke. "Are you bringing my daddy home?" the lad asked softly, his voice pleading.

The very moment he uttered those words, my heart broke. I can't recall how I answered, or even if I answered, as I knelt down and hugged him. What could I say to a child whose father was probably already dead? Here was the ultimate victim of the totalitarian state. While I had always opposed communism, now I despised it with every fiber of my being.

Thus it was that some twelve years later I could understand immediately why another mother from another country suffering under a communist regime would sacrifice her own life to bring her young son to America. Elián Gonzalez's mother did not want her son to have to endure the wretched misery of communism any longer, and she would pay any price for her son's freedom.

The Elián story became a bitter one, however. At its core, the issue was a custody battle over a small child. But by calculated design, the American Left and its sympathizers in the media expanded the Elián saga into an attack on Miami's anticommunist Cuban American community, which was depicted as rigid and intolerant, standing in the way of reuniting a boy with his father. To support this twisted account, media apologists consistently portrayed communist Cuba as a humane, socialist paradise. Because of this moral equivalence, the Clinton administration, and the national press corps that so enthusiastically cheered it on, sent Elián Gonzalez back to hell.

"Why Did She Do It?"

The Elián saga began just before Thanksgiving 1999, when his mother, Elisabeth Brotons, left Cardenas, Cuba, a seaport on the island nation's northwest coast; she and her young son crammed into a sixteen-foot motorboat with eleven other Cubans. The boat capsized off the Florida coast, and Brotons and at least ten others drowned. Elián, tired, cold, and frightened, was found floating in an inner tube three miles off Fort Lauderdale on November 25 and taken to a local hospital.

The child recovered quickly and was allowed to leave the hospital the next day in the custody of his great-uncle, Lazaro Gonzalez, until the Immigration and Naturalization Service (INS) could determine his status. Almost immediately, Juan Miguel Gonzalez, the boy's father, demanded his return to Cuba. Let it be clear, though: This was not simply a matter of a father's trying to reunite with his son. As NBC's Andrea Mitchell reported on December 15, "Castro is personally micromanaging the Elián case." Indeed, on December 5 Castro had accused the United States of the "flagrant crime of kidnapping" and declared, "We are going to move heaven and earth" to get the boy back. "It will be a war, an international battle."

In response to the demands for Elián's return to Cuba, on December 10 Lazaro Gonzalez submitted an asylum application to the INS on the boy's behalf. By the New Year of 2000, Fidel Castro's friends in the United States had rallied to the cause. Representatives of the left-wing National Council of Churches (NCC), an old enabler of Castro's brutality, went to Cuba and met with Elián's father on January 3. The NCC reps promised the boy's father that they would fight to return the boy to totalitarian Cuba.

Two days later, the INS officially decided that Elián belonged with his father and must be returned to Cuba. A petition to Attorney General Janet Reno to overturn the decision was denied, so Lazaro Gonzalez went to court in mid-January to stop the INS action. Over the next three months, the Clinton administration repeatedly evidenced its spinelessness, and the liberal news media continually evidenced its pro-Castro tendencies by hiding the horrible realities of Cuban life and attacking the Cuban-American community.

Hillary Rodham Clinton epitomized the Clinton administration stance. Once the chair of the board of the Children's Defense Fund, the liberal group that for many years had featured as a sort of logo a child's drawing with the scrawled-out words, "Dear Lord, be good to me, the sea is so wide, and my boat is so small." But the little boat and the big sea meant nothing to Mrs. Clinton in 2000. The former children's advocate had nothing to say about six-year-old Elián and his plight at sea. Typical of the Clinton White House spin, spokesman Howard Wolfson excused this curious abdication of Mrs. Clinton's self-proclaimed passion for children by saying, "Hillary Clinton knows that we must take politics out of this decision." This clashed mightily with what Hillary had written in the 1970s, when she complained that "the pretense that children's issues are somehow above or beyond politics endures and is reinforced by the belief that families are private, non-political units whose interests subsume those of children."

Mrs. Clinton was not alone. Indeed, Elián's plight betrayed the Left's real priorities. For all the liberal talk of "compassion" and "the children," the Elián Gonzalez situation revealed those to be empty phrases. Even if it meant looking hypocritical, leftists spat out phrases they abjured, like "family values," to justify how they could show no concern for the welfare of this small child and could be so willing—even eager—to dishonor the mother's dying wish. They continued having their warm, fuzzy feelings for Castro and his revolution and continued rejecting the idea that America somehow offered a child a better life than did dehumanizing Cuba. It was shocking: Imagine the Left's reaction years ago if Chile's Pinochet or South Africa's Botha had demanded the return of a child to his country.

And the liberal media let them get away with this. Amazingly, almost no one in the news media found Hillary Clinton's about-face on the issue of children's rights to be particularly newsworthy; Mrs. Clinton, a candidate for the U.S. Senate, was not pressed hard to explain her position on Elián Gonzalez or her feelings about administration policy. Principles did not matter, for in pretending to be "objective," the liberal news media adopted a pose of moral equivalence.

In fact, some reporters made themselves vehicles for ludicrous Cuban propaganda. NBC's Jim Avila was arguably the worst. On April 4, 2000, not long before the Elián situation came to a head, Avila filed a *Nightly News* piece suggesting that if Elián did go back to Cuba, he would become a "a four-foot-tall deity in a country that officially does not believe in God." The NBC reporter said that the boy's holy status would entitle him to live the "Cuban good life," which Avila defined as—I kid you not—receiving monthly perks like five free gallons of gas and an extra fifteen dollars' worth of rice, beans, and shaving cream. Seems like low-balling it a bit for a demigod.

On March 30, Avila insisted that "Cubans point to the good things about their country," one of which was "an education system that is the envy of Latin America." But another reporter, even while trying to celebrate Cuba, had inadvertently revealed the truth that Avila's Cuban propaganda obscured. On December 31, 1999, ABC's Cynthia McFadden had praised Cuba, and taken a jab at America, by reporting that Cuban children's "role models are engineers and teachers and librarians," not "the baseball players or Madonna or pop stars." Still, reporting on her visit to Havana elementary schools, McFadden had admitted that "in the classrooms we visited yesterday there was [*sic*] certainly no computers and almost no paper that we could see." There's no paper in the classroom, but never mind, Cuba is still somehow the educational marvel of Latin America.

Eventually Avila made clear why he was burnishing the image of the communist island nation: because he thought that was where Elián belonged. On April 8, he expressed puzzlement as to why Elián's mother, a maid, would leave Cuba and her "prestigious" job: "Why did she do it? What was she escaping? By all accounts this quiet, serious young woman, who loved to dance the salsa, was living the good life, as good as it gets for a citizen in Cuba." Avila concluded that she had made a terrible mistake in leaving: "An extended family destroyed by a mother's decision to start a new life in a new country, a decision that now leaves a little boy estranged from his father and forever separated from her."

A mother's desire for freedom for her child had "destroyed" her family. Thus declared NBC.

Avila's series of reports reflected the moral equivalence of the liberal media, and of the American Left in general. Avila and many others simply couldn't understand that America represents something far more important than financial opportunity. As my colleague Tim Graham of the Media Research Center wrote, "What made Elián's mother escape? Perhaps it's what makes America different from Cuba, which isn't just a glut of consumer goods. It's the right to your own life, your own opinions, your own freedom. It's not something most Americans would give away for a $15 bag of rice, beans, and shaving cream." To someone under the yoke of communism, "living the good life" has nothing to do with take-home pay; this is why Elián's mother risked everything, including her life, to reach America with her young son.

Jim Avila was not the only journalist trying to cast Cuba in the best light possible. In the April 17 *Time* magazine, Nancy Gibbs fell into the Avila trap of looking purely at the creature comforts available to Elián in Cuba: "Altogether, in wages, tips and bonuses, he [Elián's father] earns more than 10 times Cuba's $15 average monthly salary— enough to afford to buy Elián imported Power Ranger toys and birthday piñatas fat with Italian hard candy and German chocolates. . . . Elián enjoyed that rarest of Cuban luxuries: his own air-conditioned bedroom."

Also on April 17, *Newsweek*'s Brook Larmer and John Leland declared that "Elián might expect a nurturing life in Cuba, sheltered from the crime and social breakdown that would be part of his upbringing in Miami. . . . The education and health-care systems, both built since the revolution, are among the best in the Americas, despite chronic shortages of supplies. . . . The boy will nestle again in a more peaceable society that treasures its children."

On the April 8 edition of the *McLaughlin Group*, *Newsweek*'s

Eleanor Clift made this astonishing claim: "To be a poor child in Cuba may in many instances be better than being a poor child in Miami and I'm not going to condemn their lifestyle so gratuitously."

Dan Rather even defended the communist dictator himself. On April 22, Rather commented, "While Fidel Castro, and certainly justified on his record, is widely criticized for a lot of things, there is no question that Castro feels a very deep and abiding connection to those Cubans who are still in Cuba. And, I recognize this might be controversial, but there's little doubt in my mind that Fidel Castro was sincere when he said, 'Listen, we really want this child back here.' " Not only did Elián Gonzalez have the Cuban good life awaiting him, but the loving, caring Castro had the boy's best interests at heart.

According to the spin from the liberal news media, we would all be so lucky as to live in this island paradise with its cuddly communist dictator.

Zealots

The media were not content merely to portray Cuba as a lovely spot to raise a family. They had to demonize the staunchly anticommunist Cuban exiles who so vocally supported Elián's right to remain in America. These exiles rallied around Elián Gonzalez for the simple reason that they had lived under Castro's communist regime and thus they knew the reality that the liberal news media tried so hard to obscure.

Time magazine's Tim Padgett declared, "In the end, the drama may reveal how fed up both societies are with the 'Dr. Strangelove' hysteria of U.S.-Cuba relations." To Padgett—and many other reporters—the main source of that "hysteria" were the anticommunist Cuban Americans, who were, said a sociologist quoted by Padgett, "damaging their cause in most Americans' eyes."

Cuban Americans—ardently anti-Castro, pro-Reagan, patriotic, Catholic, pro-life—must be the media's least favorite minority. Throughout the controversy, they were regularly described as "hard-line," "militant," "dysfunctional," "opportunists," and "zealots" running a "jihad." An MSNBC graphic on Cuban exiles in Miami pledging to surround the Gonzalez home to protect the boy boldly declared, "Captors or Saviors?" Anchors like the *Today* show's Katie Couric wondered endlessly if these "zealots" were going too far.

What other minority in America gets this kind of media treatment? These disparaging words—accusations, really—would simply never be leveled at blacks, Latinos, Native Americans, homosexuals, or any other "oppressed" minority group.

But the Cuban exiles had incurred the wrath of the liberal news media because they so vocally opposed the Clinton administration's policy to return young Elián to Cuba. Miami's Cuban American population organized protests—most notably, a daily vigil around Elián's adopted home. Liberals love protests, but only when the rallies are in line with the liberal orthodoxy—against war, against fossil fuels, against gun rights, and so forth. Since the Cuban exiles' anticommunist protests did not support the Left's "progressive" agenda, they were ripped in the liberal media.

On December 20, 1999, *Newsweek*'s Joseph Contreras and Russell Watson signaled that the Cuban exiles were "extremists" by recycling the communist spin: "Castro claimed that the boy's father, Juan Miguel Gonzalez, had been offered $2 million by the 'extremist Cuban American mafia' if he would move to Miami and live there with Elián." On January 6, 2000, CBS reporter Byron Pitts blamed the Cuban American community for harming Elián: "Six weeks ago this community embraced a boy who had watched his mother die at sea. Tonight there is fear that embrace has become a choke hold."

As time went on, the media made Cuban Americans seem even more extreme. On April 3, Katie Couric championed the spin control of "some" people who suggested that Miami was as tyrannical as Cuba: "Some suggested over the weekend that it's wrong to expect Elián Gonzalez to live in a place that tolerates no dissent or freedom of political expression. They were talking about Miami." The next day, on ABC's *World News Tonight*, John Quinones repeated this argument: "In Miami it's impossible to overestimate how everything here is colored by a hatred of communism and Fidel Castro. It's a community with very little tolerance for those who might disagree." Over on CBS's *Early Show* on April 14, Bryant Gumbel offered the sort of loaded question for which he had become famous: "Cuban Americans, Ms. Falk, have been quick to point fingers at Castro for exploiting the little boy. Are their actions any less reprehensible?"

On April 17, *Time's* Tim Padgett, the magazine's Miami correspondent, summed up the media's attitude toward the "hard-line" anticommunists surrounding the six-year-old survivor: "The 'banana republic' label sticking to Miami in the final throes of the Elián Gonzalez crisis is a source of snide humor for most Americans. But many younger Cuban-Americans are getting tired of the hard-line anti-Castro operatives who have helped manufacture that stereotype."

This was the public-relations line of the day: Anticommunist protesters were a source of snide humor and shame. When they weren't portrayed as embarrassing their fellow Cuban Americans, they were packaged as dangerous, authoritarian, antidemocratic opponents of the First Amendment. Padgett warned about the prospect of civil disobedience against Clinton administration efforts to send the boy packing to Cuba. "The U.S.'s Cuba policy," he wrote, "has indulged the notion that Miami, because of its special anti-Castro mission, sometimes gets a pass on the democratic rules that the rest of country observes." One sociologist told Padgett that because Cuban exiles are perhaps the most privileged refugee group in the United States, "most Americans refuse to believe that their civil disobedience over Elián is legitimate." Padgett then proclaimed, "Viewed from that perspective, shutting down freeways is no longer protest, merely petulance."

This was yet another example of the double standards the liberal news media observe. While shutting down traffic to protest communism was petulance, shutdowns involving "global capitalism" were another matter altogether. In the very same issue of *Time* in which Tim Padgett denounced the Cuban exiles' protests, Adam Zagorin examined planned protests for the upcoming World Bank and International Monetary Fund meetings in Washington, D.C. Zagorin quoted one leftist leader saying, "It's going to be a festival of resistance. We want to stop the current model of globalism that helps giant corporations at the expense of virtually everyone else." This "festival" was to be saluted, according to Zagorin: "The protests will surely raise the temperature of debates on global-trade and economic issues. For demonstrators, their appetites whetted by Seattle, the agenda includes the U.S. political conventions this summer."

Appetites whetted by Seattle? That's where gangs of anarchists in December 1999 broke windows and smashed businesses, costing downtown merchants $12 million, according to the *Seattle Times*. But *Time* couldn't find anyone to be embarrassed by these "hard-liners" or by their wanton destruction of public and personal property. Zagorin did not argue, as Padgett did of the Cuban American protesters, that they had a "desperate craving for geopolitical attention in this post–cold war world."

Others followed this same double standard. As conservative columnist Rich Galen pointed out, Kathleen Schalch of National Public Radio (NPR) found it newsworthy to report on the "pageantry"—the Left can be delicious in its descriptions—that the capitalist haters would bring to Washington: "Workshop leader Nadine Block gently helped the group focus on images that might say something about the IMF and the World Bank and re-create some of the pageantry of the demonstrations in Seattle." But regarding the Cubans in Miami, Schalch's NPR colleague Philip Davis warned of an explosion of hate: "Miami residents braced for an explosion of disruptive protests from the Cuban American community," in what was "the biggest and perhaps last chance for Miami's Cuban community to spotlight their hatred of the communist regime in Cuba."

What, no pageantry?

Dénouement

After months of protests, and months of relentless news coverage in which the liberal media made clear that Elián Gonzalez should be returned to communist Cuba, the situation abruptly came to a head on

April 22, 2000. It is a day that I wish I could forget but never will. Like millions of Americans following the Elián saga, I had gone to bed the night before watching news reports about the frantic negotiations taking place to resolve the impasse. Optimism was in the air; negotiators claimed real progress was being made.

It was false hope. By three o'clock that morning, Janet Reno's Justice Department had decided that negotiations had failed and that the time had come to use force. The raid was temporarily halted when it appeared negotiations might start again, but by 4 A.M. the negotiations were off and the raid was back on. Just over an hour later, U.S. marshals wearing visored helmets and bulletproof vests and carrying automatic weapons stormed the modest home of Lazaro Gonzalez, where Elián was staying. Several members of the Gonzalez family were present, as was Donato Dalrymple, the fisherman who had pulled the frightened boy from the ocean nearly five months earlier.

The marshals worked with grim efficiency. They busted down the door and quickly separated the family from Elián. One marshal leveled his weapon at Dalrymple and a terrified Elián, pulling the child from his rescuer's arms. An Associated Press photographer who had accompanied the marshals into the house caught this moment on camera: The image provided a disturbing ending to this sad story. The marshals quickly threw a blanket over the boy's head and dragged him to a waiting van that whisked him away. Ultimately he was taken to a military base just miles from the White House, where the president a day later would be rolling Easter eggs with children to show us that all's well that ends well.

I've been disappointed in my country before, angry too. But I'd never been ashamed. This day, I was ashamed to call myself an American.

Certainly much of that shame had to do with the spineless behavior of our government. We had a president, as cowardly as he was corrupt, who sent his attorney general to do his dirty work while he extolled the "rule of law" (which he personally broke constantly). We had an attorney general who had learned absolutely nothing from the bloody Ruby Ridge incident and who used Gestapo tactics that were indistinguishable from Fidel Castro's. And we had an opposition party, the GOP, that did nothing to stop the rogue Justice Department.

But most shocking of all was how so many members of the news media attempted to justify this barbaric action in the name of objective news analysis. Now that it was all over, it was time for damage control, and the liberal media tried to spin, spin, spin the Clinton administration's horrific capitulation to Castro. We heard on ABC's *Good Morning America* how an emotional Reno had "wept" because "she did not want this to happen." NBC trotted out a professor from Tufts University to hammer the Cuban American community once more: "I think the [Miami] family has really abused this child," he charged. Katie Couric concurred: "We forget the impact all these protesters treating him like some kind of saint is having as well. That must be confusing for a little boy." Over on CBS, Bryant Gumbel declared that "the Miami relatives never, never, ever recognized the right of the father to have custody of the boy," a line flatly contradicted by one of the official negotiators, who maintained that the Miami family had done precisely that hours before the raid. Back at NBC, reporter Jim Avila was at it again, shamelessly carrying Castro's water as he filed one report after another, including a feature on the boy's grandparents. "They started the fight for Elián," he began. "Energized an island. Went to the United States in a failed mission to bring him back. And now that father and son have been reunited, they walk triumphantly through the Gonzalez family home town." Avila reported that one grandparent "says Elián finally sounds happy."

It was—and apparently still is—inconceivable to the Avilas of the national press corps that hundreds of thousands of people would want to flee that hell called Cuba. It meant little, if anything, that their families have been imprisoned on that island, or machine-gunned if they attempted to flee. It meant nothing to them that Elián's mother sacrificed her own life and risked her son's to escape this island paradise. This little boy was returned to hell, gift-wrapped by our government, with the media's blessings.

13

The Other Clinton

O N JANUARY 20, 2001, when George W. Bush stood on the Capitol steps and took the oath of office as the forty-third president of the United States, the Clinton era ended.

Or did it?

Just as her husband vacated the Oval Office, Hillary Clinton assumed a spot in the United States Senate. Though she was only the junior senator from New York, there was no doubt that Mrs. Clinton was a rising star in the Democratic Party. Sure enough, it soon became an open secret that the former first lady had her eyes on the presidency. And within a couple of years speculation was rampant that she wouldn't wait until 2008 to try to grab her husband's old job. Not bad for someone who was serving in her first elective office.

The national media, acting as de facto Clinton campaign manager, fed the speculation, portraying Mrs. Clinton as the savior the Democratic Party was looking for. The publication of Hillary's White House memoir, *Living History*, in the summer of 2003 gave the fawning media yet another chance to act as publicity agents for the ambitious politician. Of course, such favorable treatment came as no surprise to anyone who had been observing the media coverage of Mrs. Clinton over the years.

The We-Love-Hillary Brigade

When, in the late winter of 1999, first lady Hillary Clinton let it be known that she might run for the United States Senate, the media applause was immediate, loud, and sustained. Indeed, long before she formally announced her candidacy for the Senate seat in New York, Hillary was the subject of countless media stories, with reporters speculating breathlessly about her upcoming race. There was an almost perverse element to it all.

Mrs. Clinton's record didn't matter to the media. They didn't care that Hillary Clinton had been the architect of a failed national healthcare proposal. That it was Hillary who had invented the "vast rightwing conspiracy." That it was Hillary, not Bill, who had been the White House Stonewaller-in-Chief. That it was Hillary's Rose Law Firm that couldn't find and reportedly destroyed key documents. That it was in Hillary's own bedroom in the White House, no less, where other Rose Law Firm billing records mysteriously reappeared. That it was Hillary who had been the force behind firing the White House Travel Office staff, or that the charges of fraud used to justify the firing were so dishonest that a jury needed a whopping two hours to acquit Travel Office chief Billy Dale. That it was Hillary who had given one fanciful explanation after another about how she came to make $100,000 from a $1,000 investment in the commodities market. That it was reportedly Hillary who had hired Craig Livingstone, the former bar bouncer who collected hundreds of raw FBI files on the Clintons' political opponents. That it was Hillary, supposedly a feminist leader, who had first denied the charges of adultery against her husband and then, when the truth could no longer be denied, refused to acknowledge the seriousness of what he'd done.

The record established Hillary Clinton as a liar and a relentless character assassin. But the media were not going to question Hillary about any of these things, and just as important, they were going to challenge anyone who had the audacity to do so. In a move that would make James Carville proud, the media conducted a preemptive strike against "the New York tabloids" that might reinvestigate her scandal record now that she was considering the race. *Newsweek's* Jonathan Alter wrote, "Sure, the *New York Post* would carp about billing records and cattle futures. So what? Hillary can handle that." The mainstream media would be too busy praising Mrs. Clinton to bother investigating not-fully-explored scandals that they considered "old news." Hillary's media supporters also wanted it known that her record must be off-limits for her opponents as well. Alter again: "If [presumptive opponent Rudolph] Giuliani hits her with old scandal stuff, it will backfire."

And Alter was writing in late February 1999, some *twenty months* before the 2000 election. From the start, the left-wing press was signaling not that it was out to cover Hillary Clinton, but that it was out to coronate her.

Media enthusiasm for a Hillary Senate campaign only grew stronger as time went on. Mrs. Clinton hadn't formally announced whether she was running, and already her campaign for Senate was generating much more publicity than the campaigns of those who were seeking the suddenly pedestrian office of president. The Center for Media and Public Affairs studied the network evening news shows for the first five-and-a-half-months of 1999 and discovered that presidential candidate George Bush had attracted twenty network stories; presidential candidate Elizabeth Dole, fourteen stories; and presidential candidate Al Gore, fourteen stories. But Hillary Clinton trounced them all, attracting thirty-three stories, or almost as many as Bush and Gore *combined.* Sure, a first lady running for federal office while her husband was still in the White House was unprecedented. But what did it say about the networks that they would find her yet-to-be-launched campaign more interesting and more important than an existing presidential race?

Some journalists, like CNN's Jeff Greenfield, were quick to point out that studies like this deal only with numbers, and not content. The point was correct, in theory. For example, a numerical study from 1992 showed Dan Quayle getting a tremendous amount of press, but a content analysis of that coverage showed it to be overwhelmingly negative—so much so that it derailed his political career, permanently. On the other hand, the many stories on Hillary were downright rapturous. In one "interview" with Mrs. Clinton, on May 14, 1999, CNN's Christiane Amanpour proclaimed, "A lot of the women that I meet from traveling overseas are very impressed by you and admire your dignity. A lot of the people you meet are people who suffered, people you saw today, and who believe that they identify with you because they have seen you suffer. And in a speech in Africa last year, you spoke about living for hope and reconciliation, living for forgiveness and reconstruction, and living for a new life." After that tribute, Amanpour finally got around to these oh-so-probing questions: "Have you been able to apply that to your own circumstances? Have you been able to forgive your husband?" Now, really, does it get any sappier than that?

Well, yes, it does. On March 12, 1999, Diane Sawyer gushed about the first lady on ABC's *Good Morning America*: "Finally, last November 1998, Hillary Clinton showed the world what she could do on the campaign trail without Bill. Political mastery, every bit as dazzling as his, the thoughtful speech, unapologetically strong, emboldening Democrats, electing senators. So her friends say she has really earned this campaign, this moment, if she chooses, earned it by changing herself, searching, stumbling, and at the end, by standing, not by her man, but by herself."

On May 26, Dan Rather put it more succinctly: "Once a political lightning rod, today she is political lightning. A crowd pleaser and first-class fund-raiser, a person under enormous pressure to step into the arena . . . polls show she is one of the most admired women in America."

The encomiums weren't limited to television, either. On April 1, *Washington Post* reporter Peter Baker made an April Fool of himself as he reported from North Africa, where the first lady was touring. "How does a woman who eagerly told an audience this morning about education and economics in Guatemala and Uganda turn her attention to the pork-and-potholes issues that arise in places like Utica and Ithaca?" he asked. "How does a woman whose international profile is so high that bystanders in Africa two years ago referred to her as 'the queen of the world' adjust to becoming a low-ranking member of the seniority-conscious Senate?" Yes, that was a "news" report.

Since the media were backing her so strongly, the only real threat to Mrs. Clinton's campaign came from the (undeclared) candidate herself. In a *Talk* magazine interview published in August 1999, Hillary shot herself in the foot, offering the preposterous excuse that her husband's perpetual philandering was caused by his traumatic childhood. She also wanted the world—i.e., the voters in New York—to know she found it amazing that Bill became this tremendous leader of our country after all the "abuse" he had suffered.

To offset the ensuing ridicule, the Clinton White House went into immediate spin mode (when was the White House ever *not* in spin mode?), but it was unnecessary. Hillary's apologists, including *Talk* editor Tina Brown, were there already. On August 2, ABC put Brown and *Talk* interviewer Lucinda Franks on *Good Morning America* to make Hillary's bizarre case that a marriage full of adultery is true love. Brown said the interview proved the depth of the Clintons' bond: "What you feel is this is a couple who share the passion for the world, for doing good for politics, for making life better for other people. This is their great bond, and it really has brought them together with almost a sort of spiritual intensity." For her part, Franks claimed the marriage "is quite wonderful in its, you know, in its interdependence of conversation, of ideas, of excitement, of chemistry, sexual chemistry." Franks went further, with this most unfeminist defense of the philandering president: "I also feel that many of these encounters . . . began way back in Arkansas, when women would throw themselves at him, even at Yale. I mean, he's a very handsome man, and he looked like a Beatle back in Yale. You can see pictures of him. I mean, he was gorgeous."

Almost everyone in the press missed—or ignored—the biggest headline of the *Talk* interview. Fox News Channel's Jim Angle didn't. He pointed out Hillary's dishonesty: "The first lady is now admitting a history of infidelity by Mr. Clinton, something that both of them have sought so often to deny."

Castigating the Bullies

When the New York Senate campaign began in earnest, Hillary finally had to answer a few real questions, but not many. NBC's Tim Russert was one of the few who wouldn't be rolled. While moderating a debate between the first lady and her Republican opponent, Representative Rick Lazio of Long Island, Russert asked the question that would have haunted this woman from beginning to end had she been a conservative. Would Mrs. Clinton, he asked, apologize for misleading the country with her "vast right-wing conspiracy" comment and her claim that the Lewinsky affair would not be "proven true"?

Woe to Russert for daring to ask that (perfectly reasonable) question! *Washington Post* columnist Richard Cohen promptly savaged Russert's inquiry: "Not since the old Saturday night fights has TV seen such a low blow." Continuing the poor-Hillary line, Gail Collins wrote in the *New York Times,* "All of us have moments in our lives that we prefer not to recall even while cowering in a darkened closet. Mrs. Clinton's just happens to be stored in the files of every news bureau on the planet."

These arguments didn't deserve rebuttal; they deserved a laugh track. Russert's question was both fair and long overdue. Mrs. Clinton's infamous *Today* show appearance raised serious questions about her integrity. What did it say about the first lady that she would invent a story about a "vast right-wing conspiracy" designed deliberately to ruin the personal reputations of her political opponents and then would sit back while her allies used the story to do just that? More important, what did it say about her integrity that when Russert gave her the opportunity to apologize for her character assassination she refused to do so? The first lady, it seems, was never interested in the truth; for months she had urged the same old strategy: stonewall, lie, and rain hellfire on Kenneth Starr. But no, she wouldn't apologize, wouldn't even acknowledge misleading anyone.

Russert was right to bring up Mrs. Clinton's *Today* show performance for another reason. Even if one bought Hillary's line that she didn't know her husband had been guilty of infidelity (again) when she railed about the vast right-wing conspiracy—*did* anyone buy that line?—the question remained: Why did she resort to Clintonian legalisms such as suggesting that the charge would not be "proven true"? Mrs. Clinton didn't have to answer that question.

Tim Russert wasn't the only bully the pro-Hillary pundits took on. Clinton supporters and news "analysts" vilified Rick Lazio because during a televised debate he denounced Hillary's blame-shifting and then "invaded her personal space" by crossing the stage and demanding she sign a no-soft-money pledge. Poor Hillary, the victim of the brutish Lazio! *Newsweek* suggested that Lazio had hurt himself with independents and women and that Russert had helped Hillary earn sympathy. The loaded *Time* headline declared, "No More Mr. Nice Candidate—In New York, Rick Lazio gets nasty with Hillary." In the *New York Times,* Gail Collins began by calling Lazio "Darth Vader with dimples" and "The Long Island Lex Luthor," which I presume made Hillary both Princess Leia and Supergirl. But Collins's colleague Maureen Dowd topped everyone by relaying one woman's claim that Lazio seemed like "her husband, waving a credit card receipt in her face, yelling at her that she had overcharged, his eyes bulging, his veins popping, screaming at her to return everything to the store."

The media's criticisms of Nasty Rick had their effect. In another case of the media's self-fulfilling prophecy, Lazio's ratings suffered dramatically, and come November, he crash-landed. Mrs. Clinton, the subject of so much favorable press, was elected as senator from New York.

Living History

After the victory over Lazio, Mrs. Clinton spent her final days in the White House basking in media adoration, and then came news of her book advance. Simon and Schuster announced it would pay Mrs. Clinton a staggering $8 million for a book not scheduled for release for another three years. The way the deal was reported was yet another illustration of the fact that the liberal media have different standards for different sides. Whereas Hillary was given a pass for her huge contract, back in 1994 the same national media had hammered Speaker of the House Newt Gingrich for accepting a seven-figure book advance.

As soon as Gingrich accepted a $4.5 million advance from Rupert Murdoch's HarperCollins in 1994, the deal became a scandal, as the media pummeled Gingrich for the appearance of impropriety. "We'll hear more about this one," CBS reporter Bob Schieffer promised. (True to his word, Schieffer was still hammering Gingrich about it six months later.) Pundits like CNN's Al Hunt quickly called for Gingrich to dump the advance or donate it to an orphanage. Media pressure was so great that within a few days Gingrich announced that he was giving up the advance. But that did nothing to end the controversy; emboldened, liberals wanted him to give up the book altogether. In the six weeks after the deal was announced, the network evening news shows aired twenty-seven news stories—seven each on ABC, CBS, and NBC, and six on CNN. CBS's Dan Rather suggested straight out that a businessman with interests before Congress could be bribing Gingrich: "More tonight about whether Australian-born and -centered communications billionaire Rupert Murdoch is trying to buy influence with politically connected authors." In the same story CBS reporter Eric Engberg attacked Gingrich, who had *already* surrendered the advance, for "standing fast" when the Speaker "could end the controversy by scuttling the book deal." Even the Clinton White House questioned the propriety of the book deal, with White House press secretary Dee Dee Myers saying that "it raises some very important questions. I think it needs to be looked at."

But when Hillary accepted her $8 million advance, there was no outrage, as a Nexis search covering the dates December 1, 2000, to January 31, 2001, revealed. NBC News mentioned the advance only a few times—on *Meet the Press* and Saturday *Today* but not on the *Nightly News*. ABC did two segments on *Good Morning America* and one on *World News Tonight*. CNN featured one prime-time debate in which moderator Greta Van Susteren (who is now with Fox News) suggested that conservative public relations expert Keith Appell was somehow a sexist for objecting to the Hillary/Gingrich double standard: "Some of the women in this country may think you have a huge double standard, because, you know, here's a woman who has obviously been able to go out in the marketplace and command a huge amount of money, and a lot of people are squawking."

And what about CBS? Hillary's publisher, Simon and Schuster, was an arm of Viacom, which also owned CBS. Did Dan Rather have the fortitude to repeat the charge of buying influence he had leveled at Rupert Murdoch and Newt Gingrich? Did reporter Eric Engberg call for Mrs. Clinton to "scuttle the book deal"? Did CBS's Schieffer hammer the deal for six months?

Of course not. Between December 1, 2000, and January 31, 2001, CBS News ran only one story on the new senator's book deal—and that was on a non-news Saturday.

And without any media-generated outrage, the U.S. Senate was happy to do nothing about Hillary's book deal. Whereas the Gingrich imbroglio had led to a House ban on book advances, the Senate had no such prohibition, as long as the arrangement for any book advance was "usual and customary." There was nothing usual or customary about Mrs. Clinton's deal, but that mattered not a bit to the Senate Ethics Committee. Indeed, when asked about the huge advance, the vice chair of the Ethics Committee, Democrat Harry Reid of Nevada, said he thought it was "wonderful." The Republican leadership was also content to let the deal slide, as Trent Lott, then the Senate majority leader, admitted on December 17, 2000, when he told Tim Russert that he thought "the abuse that Newt Gingrich took a couple of years ago was uncalled for. And, therefore, I'm a little bit hesitant to be critical here."

In some cases, the media have been so desperate to offer a favorable portrait of Senator Clinton that they have dramatically manipulated actual events. As John Stossel revealed on ABC's *20/20* in July 2002, the music video cable network VH1, a division of Viacom, went so far as to edit out boos that attended Hillary's speech at a New York City concert to benefit victims of September 11. Stossel played the original clip, in which people in the audience could be heard booing and heckling Senator Clinton. Then he played VH1's rerun of the same concert, which was also released on DVD; as Stossel noted, "The booing has been removed. Now and forever on the DVD the crowd applauds Senator Clinton."

As Mrs. Clinton's star rose in the Democratic Party, reporters gave her most favorable coverage, still portraying the senator as the victim when it helped her image. John Harris, a former *Washington Post* White House reporter, wrote a 7,400-word paean to New York's junior senator in the January 27, 2002, *Washington Post Magazine*. Even after quoting a Republican senator who said Hillary had had a successful first year in the Senate, Harris revealed that Hillary thought her enemies were still out to get her. "She does not believe her opponents have laid down their weapons, nor is she laying down her own," Harris wrote. "Perhaps, an interviewer ventured, now that her influence flows from voters rather than her husband, the political forces she described in the opening days of the Monica Lewinsky scandal as a 'vast right-wing conspiracy' may be ready for a truce." But Hillary Clinton would not concede that. "I don't know that it's a truce," she told Harris. "It doesn't ever seem to end. If a couple days go by and they haven't heard anything they can talk about, they make something up. It never ends." Of course, when Harris asked for examples of this torment, she didn't have any to offer. So the writer helpfully offered his own: "Perhaps she was talking about the criticism she got on talk radio and conservative Web sites for yawning and whispering to a colleague during President Bush's address to Congress after the September 11 attacks?"

As time went on and more and more people started discussing Mrs. Clinton's aspirations for the White House, the media dutifully bolstered her candidacy for national office. On July 28, 2002, the Associated Press ran an article under the headline "Hillary Clinton Emerges as Moderate." In the story, reporter Shannon McCaffrey argued that Clinton had "belied" predictions that she would be "a liberal's liberal." Her evidence: Clinton was scheduled to deliver the keynote address at a meeting of the Democratic Leadership Council, which, McCaffrey wrote, was a "centrist group." But Senator John Kerry belonged to the group and both Senator Tom Daschle and Congressman Dick

Gephardt spoke to the same gathering. Did that make them "moderates" as well? McCaffrey also contradicted herself later in the story when she stated, "Clinton now receives high marks from liberal groups," such as a 95 percent approval from the liberal Americans for Democratic Action for her 2001 Senate votes. But, as is so often the case, the truth is less important to the liberal media than the cause they are trying to serve—and in this case the cause was to portray Mrs. Clinton as a strong candidate for president.

The media, enamored with the idea of a woman president, actively participated in Hillary's image-building. Veteran journalist Barbara Walters provided the quintessential spin on Hillary on the ABC daytime show *The View* in May of 2002. "I went to a luncheon yesterday and Hillary Clinton was there," Walters said. "I don't get to see Hillary Clinton very much and she was talking about the problems of New York and the problems of safety. She was simply terrific. She was so well informed, she speaks without any written material, you know. We do a lot of kidding around, but boy, I was impressed."

When that $8 million memoir was finally published in the summer of 2003, the media were truly marveling at Hillary. *Living History's* biggest "revelation"—or at least the one the publisher selected to leak to the media first—was Hillary's claim that she did not know the truth about Monica Lewinsky until August 15, 1998, when, she said, her husband finally admitted to her that he had had a sexual relationship with the intern. Mrs. Clinton wrote that she was "dumbfounded" when her husband told her.

Most media accounts of the book treated this as the truth, subjecting the claim to no further scrutiny. Indeed, many reporters praised her for being so "candid" in the book. For example, Katie Couric of the *Today* show said, "She's very candid about a very personal matter," while her NBC colleague Sara James added, "Mrs. Clinton writes candidly about the moment her husband admitted he'd been unfaithful." On the *Nightly News,* Tom Brokaw said Mrs. Clinton was "a lot more candid about her personal life and feelings than many had expected." Meanwhile, CBS's *Early Show* simply read the relevant quotations from the book, offering no analysis. And on CNN, reporter Jonathan

Karl presented Hillary's tale as the truth: "Mrs. Clinton believed [President Clinton], and famously went on national television, unwittingly repeating his lies and denouncing the reports about Lewinsky as the product of a vast right-wing conspiracy." Note that Karl did not include in his report the phrase "Mrs. Clinton says" or "Mrs. Clinton claims," or any such qualifier that would typically be found in an objective news story.

This is important, for by no means should any news reporter have uncritically accepted Mrs. Clinton's account as the truth. To begin, many Americans were skeptical of the story Hillary offered in the book, given her husband's history of infidelity and the evidence of President Clinton's close connection with Monica Lewinsky that had emerged in the seven months between January and August 1998. More important, another book out at the same time as Mrs. Clinton's put forward a conflicting account—and this was a book by a Clinton loyalist. As Brit Hume of Fox News reported, Sidney Blumenthal, one of the Clintons' closest White House aides, wrote in *The Clinton Wars* that the first couple was getting along well—"still working as a team"— just hours after the president's grand jury appearance. That was only two days after Hillary claimed her husband had revealed the truth about Lewinsky. But in *Living History* she maintained that there was, in Hume's words, "a period of deep chill between the two of them" when she could "barely speak" to President Clinton. Moreover, a third book, *The Breach* by *Washington Post* reporter Peter Baker, also contradicted Mrs. Clinton's story, reporting that Clinton attorney David Kendall, not the president, had told the first lady the truth about the affair.

These conflicting accounts were certainly enough to justify at least a measure of skepticism from the news media. But expressions of skepticism were all too rare. While most of his colleagues were gushing about Mrs. Clinton's "candor," NBC's Lester Holt had this to say when he interviewed former Hillary aide Lisa Caputo: "A lot of folks have [a] hard time believing that that would be the first time she would know, given the evidence: the dress, the tape recordings, and the phone calls." And Barbara Walters, in a lengthy interview in which she lobbed softball questions to Mrs. Clinton, did at least press Hillary on her claim that she had not suspected the truth about Lewinsky even in the face of all the evidence linking her husband to the intern.

But that was about it. Otherwise, the media marveled at this woman, which prevented them from offering balanced news coverage. That's the way it is with the media when Hillary is involved. So much do they admire her that they never question the truth of her statements or why she says them.

Instead, they look ahead to how this great woman can achieve her next career goal. When *Living History* first made the news in the summer of 2003, Hannah Storm of CBS's *Early Show* skipped over any questions about Mrs. Clinton's veracity to get to the more important question: whether the book publicity could elect President Hillary. "Look," Storm said, "if she generates this goodwill and this enormous wave of popularity is it possible we could see her jump into the presidential race earlier than expected, maybe even in 2004?"

The liberal media certainly seemed to hope that was the case. One Clinton era might have been over, but they were eager to see another begin.

14

The War on the War on Terrorism

S EPTEMBER 11, LIKE December 7, is a date that will never need a
year attached to it. After the horrifying terrorist attacks that
claimed the lives of more than three thousand innocent men,
women, and children, the media that so often fail to do their duty per-
formed magnificently, and under the most difficult circumstances
imaginable. Even the most vocal critics of the national media had to
stand and applaud America's journalists for the way they reacted to the
attack on the nation.

Unfortunately, and all too predictably, the media quickly reverted to
old habits. But make no mistake about what we saw immediately after
September 11. The media's performance was remarkable. The emotion
was deep, the passion was fierce, the patriotism was sincere, and their
brief, shining moment in time needs to be captured.

On the corporate level, the networks and their affiliates sacrificed
hundreds of millions of dollars, if not billions, when they refused to run
commercials in the week after September 11.

On the professional level, journalists worked around the clock to
keep America informed of all developments, sometimes in the most
dangerous situations. There were many examples, but the most striking was Brit Hume of Fox, who at about 10 A.M. on September 11—
at a time when no one knew what might happen next—calmly
transmitted a report from the Capitol Hill police that an airplane had

just been sighted coming up the Potomac River at a high rate of speed. Had the threat been real, the target of that terrorist attack would have been the White House or the U.S. Capitol. The Capitol was right across the street from where Hume was reporting at that very moment. And he knew it.

On the personal level, reporters discarded the ridiculous notion that a journalist is a reporter first, an American second. Most journalists made known, loudly, unambiguously, unapologetically, *their* outrage, *their* sorrow, *their* love of country.

A typical case was NBC's John Palmer, a grizzled old veteran who had probably seen all there was to see in his thirty-plus years of experience. Still, Palmer suddenly couldn't find the words to describe to viewers what, exactly, had transpired during the memorial service at the Washington National Cathedral on Friday, September 14.

Fox's Tony Snow, the happy warrior who relishes political combat, put politics aside that Sunday to deliver an impassioned declaration of affection for his country, only to stop abruptly when the tears began to flow.

Seemingly the entire on-air staff at Fox proudly wore American flags on their lapels; Tim Russert donned red, white, and blue ribbons on *Meet the Press;* CNN ran graphics of a waving American flag in its broadcasts continuously.

Russert spoke movingly of his personal friend Father Mychal Judge, the chaplain of the New York City Fire Department, who had been killed in the World Trade Center. "Like all of you, I have spent this week wiping my eyes and grinding my teeth and wondering why," Russert said on Sunday, September 16. "I've drawn strength from a story about a man I knew, Father Mychal Judge. The chaplain of the New York City Fire Department, a Franciscan, he raced to the World Trade Center after the explosion to comfort the injured. While administering the last rites to a dying rescue worker, he himself was killed by flying debris.

"New York's bravest physically carried Father Mike away. They brought his body first to the altar of St. Peter's Church, where it would be safe, then to their firehouse on 31st Street, Hook and Ladder Company Number 24, directly across from the friary where he lived. They wrapped him in sheets and placed him in one of their own bunks. They asked his fellow Franciscans to cross the street and join them. Together—firemen, priests, and brothers—wept and sang the prayer of St. Francis, 'May the Lord bless and keep you and show his face to you and have mercy on you.' That is the way of New York. That is the spirit of America."

Tom Brokaw put his reporter's instincts aside when he tenderly invited Solicitor General Ted Olson *not* to answer questions about the murder of his wife, Barbara, who been a passenger on the plane that the terrorists crashed into the Pentagon.

The *San Francisco Examiner* raged with its September 12 headline: "Bastards." *Time* magazine defiantly proclaimed on its cover, "One Nation, Indivisible." *Newsweek* stated with wondrous simplicity, "God Bless America."

Dan Rather twice broke down on *The Late Show with David Letterman*, the second time unable to control his sobbing. Rather said, "George Bush is the president. He makes the decisions, and, you know, it's just one American, [but] wherever he wants me to line up, just tell me where." Then he asked, "Who can sing now, with the same meaning we had before, one stanza of ['America the Beautiful'] that goes, 'So beautiful, for patriot's dream, that sees beyond the years / Thine alabaster cities gleam, undimmed by human tears'? We can never say that song again, that way."

Of course, not everyone was pleased with the media's reaction to September 11. The always-irritable American radical Left were upset with the patriotic tone and the focus on the war on terror to which the United States immediately committed itself. This lunatic fringe believed that America had deserved the attacks.

The whiny complaints from the Far Left took many different forms. Dara Williams of the News Watch project at San Francisco State University used September 11 to argue for greater "diversity of commentary experts"—that is, for stricter quotas. "There are people who can put into context what's been going on in the Middle East who are not white men," she said. Apparently, Williams missed the news every time Colin Powell or Condoleezza Rice gave a press briefing.

Another San Franciscan, John McManus of GradeTheNews.org,

insisted that the American government must be relentlessly questioned and must never be cheered. "The press shouldn't say we're at war," McManus ordered. "It should say the administration says we're at war." Saying that America was at war "does the ideological dirty work of the administration," he claimed. Moreover, he complained, "There's still a dismissal on the part of the press that the Arab world has legitimate grievances against the United States. There's a tendency on the part of the media to look at this as if the United States is an innocent party set upon by people who have a grudge with each other, and it got hit with a stray punch."

Only someone who truly hated America could say to the families of innocent airline passengers and World Trade Center employees that their loved ones were just collateral damage, killed by innocents with "legitimate grievances."

Then there were the left-wing crackpots at Fairness and Accuracy in Reporting (FAIR), who worship Noam Chomsky, the man who regularly equates the United States with terrorist nations. They believed, like McManus, that the attacks were just "blowback" for supporting the mujahideen against the Soviets, propping up the shah of Iran, and running an embargo against Saddam Hussein's Iraq. FAIR's Steve Rendall, in the September 19, 2001, *San Francisco Chronicle*, called for anchors to bring on historians "to explain why resentment of the United States runs so deep among so many in the Middle East." Rendall also demanded that anchors highlight antiwar radicals during this time of national crisis—never mind that virtually all of America was united behind the president and the Congress. "Where are the experts who might take Martin Luther King or Mohandas Gandhi seriously?" he demanded. "The peace experts? You might think that's a joke, but there are people who study these things as seriously as war."

Once again we saw the real nature of the radical Left. They pleaded for "balance," which to them meant giving a platform to the Arab terrorists. The Blame America First crowd accused the press of "pandering to the public's appetite for revenge," but in the first days after September 11, the media didn't succumb to the outrageous demands of this fringe lobby. American journalists suffered with all of us, and they were welcomed into our saddened homes with gratitude.

It was particularly heartening to see how the media reacted to the September 11 attacks because their reaction was by no means to have been expected. Back in the late 1980s, during one of PBS's infamous "Ethics in America" debates, reporters were presented with a scenario wherein they are traveling with the armed forces of the enemy, the "North Kosanese," when they come upon American soldiers. Should the reporters set aside journalistic priorities to warn the Americans? "No, you don't have a higher duty," CBS's Mike Wallace said. "You're a reporter." After having initially said, "I think that I personally would do what I could to warn the Americans," ABC's Peter Jennings buckled and threw his support to Wallace: "I think he's right, too. I chickened out."

But September 11 blew away such theoretical pretense—for a while, anyway. In the *Wall Street Journal*'s *Weekend Journal* on October 19, 2001, Wallace admitted that he would like to interview Osama bin Laden but was quick to add that he wouldn't do anything to endanger Americans. "Look," he said, "if you have an opportunity to talk to someone the world would love to see up close and under genuine scrutiny by a mature reporter, you know your instincts will tell you, 'Let's go.' But you certainly don't want to do any harm to this country [or] to the war effort."

A Regrettable Return to Normalcy

Admirable as most journalists' early efforts were, it was only a matter of time before the media reverted to their tired ways of moral relativism. The first sign of a return to the media's standard approach came while crews were still clearing debris in New York and Washington. In mid-September, the Reuters wire service—the British news service headquartered in London—declared that its reporters and editors would not use the term "terrorist" to describe the attacks on the World Trade Center. A truly appalled Reuters employee sent the *Washington Post*'s Howard Kurtz an internal memo from Stephen Jukes, the wire service's global head of news. As Kurtz reported on September 24, Jukes wrote in his memo, "We all know that one man's terrorist is another man's freedom fighter and that Reuters upholds the principle that we do not use the word terrorist. To be frank, it adds little to call the attack on the World Trade Center a terrorist attack."

One suspects—hopes—that most Reuters journalists were as horrified by this callous posture as the other 99 percent of Americans who heard about it. Perhaps some of them lost friends or family in the attack, or had enough empathy to understand how Jukes sounded to the suffering: *I'm sorry your child, or your parent, or your spouse, or your college roommate was blown to smithereens, but however awful that may seem to you, their killers are people, too.*

The Jukes position went beyond the ridiculous. It was flat-out hypocritical. In 1995 Reuters had no qualms about labeling the Oklahoma City bombing a "terrorist" attack. Like many others from the Switzerland School of Media Neutrality, Jukes didn't have the moral sense God gives children. What if his news service's New York bureau had been located on the 104th floor of the World Trade Center? Would Jukes then have pledged not to take sides?

Reuters, at least, was a foreign news agency. Not so National Public Radio (NPR), our taxpayer-funded news service.

Loren Jenkins, a senior foreign editor of NPR, told the *Chicago Tribune* on October 12, 2001, that his job was to get a story, not worry about American lives. According to the article, Jenkins wanted his thirteen reporters in Afghanistan and the Middle East to find the American troops. "The game of reporting is to smoke 'em out," he said. Then, asked whether his reporters, at that early stage of the war on terror, would report the presence of an American commando unit in northern Pakistan, which presumably would mean putting those American lives at risk, Jenkins gave a cold-blooded answer: "You report it. I don't represent the government. I represent history, information, what happened."

Countless newspapers across the nation ran excerpts from the *Tribune* column, and soon NPR was hearing thousands of complaints. But NPR, which has a difficult time admitting it's wrong about anything, waited almost an entire month before issuing a "clarification." On November 6, Bruce Drake, vice president of NPR News and Information, suggested that Jenkins's comments were mysteriously taken out of context: "Loren Jenkins neither believes nor intended to suggest that NPR would engage in reporting that would put in peril the lives of U.S. military personnel. NPR reporters, producers and editors always take into account whether our reporting might put lives in danger, or pose an unacceptable security risk. NPR would never knowingly compromise the security or safety of American military or national security operations by reporting information that would endanger them."

NPR's bumbling, antimilitary comments and its inept "clarification" were almost expected, given the network's long history of left-wing promotion. But CNN, proudly displaying the American flag throughout its broadcast, should not have had the unsteady moments it did as America went to war in Afghanistan.

In mid-October, CNN announced that it wanted to present six questions to Osama bin Laden through the Al Jazeera television network. Apparently the cable network was unconcerned about providing an international forum for a terrorist madman to propagandize. The whole idea was preposterous. Had CNN existed sixty years earlier, would it have given an audience to Emperor Hirohito to let him explain the attack on Pearl Harbor? Would it have posed six questions to Adolf Hitler to allow him to justify the Holocaust?

In truth, however, such a stunt was not hard to imagine from CNN, which had a miserable track record of approaching America's enemies with a pose of moral neutrality. To CNN, there was no difference between the Soviet Union and America during the cold war, and no difference between Saddam Hussein and America during the Gulf War. For a while, it appeared that the same neutrality was going to apply to Osama bin Laden and America.

But after CNN announced its desire to interview bin Laden, the outrage against the network was fierce, and a couple of weeks later, CNN changed course. CNN chief executive Walter Isaacson issued an edict mandating that Taliban-manipulated reports from Afghanistan be balanced with the unsubtle reminder that these forces used civilians as shields and that their support for Al Qaeda terrorists helped kill more than three thousand Americans.

At least one prominent journalist immediately attacked the concept. "It's ill-advised," said former CNN correspondent Peter Arnett, who had moved on to NBC. Of course, this was the man whom CNN had fired in 1998 for his role in the "Tailwind" story, which dishonestly accused American soldiers of using nerve gas in Laos in 1970. Also, during the first Gulf War, when he was with CNN, Arnett had faithfully delivered Saddam Hussein's version of the truth, and later he had loudly proclaimed that he owed America nothing. On the one-year anniversary of Iraq's invasion of Kuwait, Arnett had said on CNN's *Crossfire* that he wouldn't have transmitted information that could have saved American lives in the Gulf War. "I would not have gotten that information in the first place, but I would not have transmitted it," he said. "I was in Baghdad because I was a correspondent for CNN, which has no political affiliations with the U.S. government, thank goodness." None of this was problematic for Arnett's new employer, NBC.

Not long after CNN announced its intentions to give Osama bin Laden a platform, ABC News president David Westin made a shocking announcement of his own. On October 23, speaking at the Columbia University Graduate School of Journalism, Westin made this unbelievable statement in response to a student's question about whether the Pentagon was a legitimate military target: "The Pentagon as a legitimate target? I actually don't have an opinion on that. And it's important I not have an opinion on that as I sit here in my capacity right now. . . . Our job is to determine what is, not what ought to be, and when we get into the job of what ought to be I think we're not doing a service to the American people." Westin finished with this: "I can say the Pentagon got hit, I can say this is what their position is, this is what our position is, but for me to take a position this was right or wrong, I mean, that's perhaps for me in my private life, perhaps it's for me dealing with my loved ones, perhaps it's for my minister at church. But as a journalist I feel strongly that's something that I should not be taking a position on. I'm supposed to figure out what is and what is not, not what ought to be."

After C-SPAN aired the event on October 27, Media Research Center vice president Brent Baker transcribed the tape and highlighted

Westin's comments in the center's *CyberAlert* Internet report, which is instantly zapped to the desks of thousands of opinion leaders. The *New York Post* and other newspapers immediately picked up the item, as did Rush Limbaugh and countless others on talk radio. Soon, Westin's phone was ringing off the hook. On October 31, less than forty-eight hours after the *CyberAlert* had highlighted the statement, the Media Research Center received an e-mail from Westin. "Like all Americans," he wrote, "I was horrified at the loss of life at the Pentagon, as well as in New York and Pennsylvania on September 11. When asked at an interview session at the Columbia Journalism School whether I believed that the Pentagon was a legitimate target for terrorists I responded that, as a journalist, I did not have an opinion. I was wrong. I gave an answer to journalism students to illustrate the broad, academic principle that all journalists should draw a firm line between what they know and what their personal opinion might be. Upon reflection, I realized that my answer did not address the specifics of September 11. Under any interpretation, the attack on the Pentagon was criminal and entirely without justification. I apologize for any harm that my misstatement may have caused."

Westin's statement at Columbia was hardly the only troubling development at ABC News. Peter Jennings began to inch toward that neutral-as-Switzerland standard on October 8, less than a month after the 9/11 slaughter. That night, speaking about the humanitarian aid the United States was giving to Afghan civilians as the U.S. military conducted its war against the Taliban, Jennings said, "One other item about these food and medicine drops: They're not popular with everyone. The international relief group Doctors Without Borders, which won the Nobel Peace Prize for relief work, described it today as military propaganda to justify the bombing." How nice of Jennings to bolster the group's credentials by mentioning the Nobel Peace Prize, the Nobel committee being a prime example of softheaded internationalists who make no distinctions between freedom and slavery, civility and savagery. A night later, ABC sent reporter Dan Harris to follow up on the internationalist argument. "Some humanitarian aid workers were saying this effort is little more than propaganda," Harris repeated.

"Some say the U.S. is actually doing more harm than good. . . . The attacks have significantly hampered a large humanitarian effort, and the U.S. food drops simply can't compensate for that."

This kind of reporting is infuriating. What other nation has ever been attacked and then proceeded to provide massive amounts of humanitarian aid to the country it is fighting? Yet ABC News found a way to condemn the United States for doing that very thing.

ABC was also quick to report unsubstantiated claims of civilian casualties at the hands of Americans. Indeed, the network was *obsessed* with it. The Media Research Center reviewed every story reporting civilian casualties on the evening broadcast news shows from October 8 through October 31. During the study period, ABC's *World News Tonight* devoted nearly four times as much of its programs (15 minutes and 44 seconds) to allegations of civilian casualties as did the *CBS Evening News* (4 minutes and 17 seconds) and almost twice as much as did NBC's *Nightly News* (8 minutes and 9 seconds). While all three newscasts showed pictures of structures identified as damaged civilian buildings—certainly part of the story and therefore newsworthy—ABC went overboard, repeatedly projecting grisly images of corpses and injured people, including children with facial wounds.

At the same time, ABC downplayed the American military's dedication to keeping such casualties low, ignoring the obvious benefits to the Taliban of exaggerating the number of deaths caused by U.S. bombs. The *CBS Evening News* spent twice as much airtime covering this point as did ABC's *World News Tonight*.

The various news reports from October 10, 2001, serve as piercing examples. CBS reporter Mark Phillips stated, "The navy talks about delivering a short, sharp shock to the Taliban, but its desire to limit civilian casualties has always been a restriction on what the pilots and the bombs can do." That same night, NBC's Charles Sabine similarly reported from an aircraft carrier that U.S. "planes returned with their bombs undelivered after airmen were instructed to abort missions where there was a risk of civilian casualties." But on ABC that night, reporter David Wright didn't even hint that U.S. pilots were trying to be careful. "The skies above Kabul have thundered for four nights now, four very long days and nights for those on the ground," he said. Wright found refugees to help him heap guilt on America: "Many who are leaving say it would be one thing if the Americans were only bombing the terrorist camps in Afghanistan, but they say the killing of innocents is not okay."

To be fair, not every ABC reporter followed this line. On October 25, ABC's Jim Wooten noted that bombing site visitors often found fewer casualties than the Taliban claimed, "but by then the story is already out: the Taliban version. It happens nearly every day." He noted that the Taliban's claims of American atrocities often came with "no pictures, no proof" (which was precisely why CNN's Walter Isaacson ordered that his reporters not transmit Taliban claims unquestioningly). But Wooten was clearly the odd man out at ABC News.

ABC also ignored civilian casualties if they weren't caused by American bombing. On Sunday, October 28, Islamic terrorists massacred sixteen Christians as they worshiped at a Catholic church in Pakistan. ABC's *World News Tonight* skipped this slaughter of innocents in its entirety. What did ABC run instead? A full story on how two people in Afghanistan were accidentally killed by U.S. bombs. "An old woman cried out to God in pain," David Wright relayed piously.

The Howling Mob

The military campaign in Afghanistan was just the first battle in a much broader war on terrorism, a war that President Bush said in no uncertain terms would take years to prosecute. But no matter how many times Bush, Secretary of Defense Donald Rumsfeld, Secretary of State Colin Powell, and countless other administration officials urged patience and reminded Americans that the war would be a long one, reporters, columnists, and pundits obsessed over the pace of the war. Was the U.S. military getting bogged down? Did we overestimate our military capabilities? Did we underestimate our enemy's? These questions came up again and again, first in Afghanistan, then in Iraq.

In Afghanistan, the leader of this howling mob was *New York Times* columnist Maureen Dowd, whose contemptuous and sarcastic columns are featured on the editorial page that Dan Rather has said he considers "middle of the road." Although Dowd is an opinion columnist, not a news reporter whose pieces are supposed to be objective, her columns should at least rise to a certain standard of truthfulness. On the subject of Afghanistan, unfortunately, Dowd's pieces did not do that. Her grasp of military matters was dismal. But she wrote anyway.

On November 4, 2001, Dowd ridiculed the CIA as "risibly incompetent" and similarly criticized our military efforts: "We spend $300 billion a year on planes and bombs and military marvels but still can't faze Taliban warriors who pop up out of the charred earth and mock us as ineffectual. . . . Our institutions are lumbering as they try to keep up with the simple, supple, clever paladins of Islam." On November 7 she mocked American military planners for backing Afghanistan's Northern Alliance in the war against the Taliban: Stories about "the lame rebel force with its wooden saddles and line of old Russian tanks get sillier and sillier, like scenes out of the Marx Brothers or Woody Allen's 'Bananas.' " Within days, of course, that "lame" Northern Alliance, backed by a U.S. air attack that was hardly "ineffectual," had captured the stronghold of Mazar-e-Sharif, causing the Taliban to collapse and opening the way for the rapid liberation of Kabul and the rest of Afghanistan. Was Dowd cowed? Not at all. In her next column, she suddenly purported to be appalled by the violence of the rebel force she had ridiculed just a week earlier: "We give the Northern Alliance an air force and they embarrass us with savage force."

Being a columnist at the *New York Times* apparently means you're never wrong.

Sadly, it wasn't only opinion columnists who were quick to jump on the story that the U.S. military campaign was somehow failing. On October 29, 2001, John McWethy of ABC News complained, "Two weeks after the Pentagon said Taliban forces had been 'eviscerated' by U.S. bombing, the Taliban still appear to be firmly in control." That same night, Jim Miklaszewski of NBC News stated, "Pentagon officials are now beginning to express some frustrations and doubts over the slow pace of the war. . . . Despite three weeks of air strikes, U.S.

military officials tell NBC News for now the war in Afghanistan has ground to a stalemate."

"Could Afghanistan become another Vietnam?" That's the question *New York Times* veteran correspondent R. W. Apple asked on October 30. "Is the United States facing another stalemate on the other side of the world? Premature the questions may be, three weeks after the fighting began. Unreasonable they are not, given the scars scoured into the national psyche by defeat in Southeast Asia. For all the differences between the two conflicts, and there are many, echoes of Vietnam are unavoidable."

Yes, all this came a mere *three weeks* into the fighting in Afghanistan. Secretary of Defense Rumsfeld reminded the press corps to be patient, but already the media were ready to proclaim a "stalemate." In fact, Peter Jennings would have nothing to do with Rumsfeld's plea. After reporting that the secretary of defense "said today that those people who are questioning the effectiveness of the U.S. bombing campaign in Afghanistan are too impatient," Jennings offered this kick to the groin: "The Pentagon is being pressed harder to be specific about what it has accomplished so far. The bombing campaign against the Taliban is now entering its fourth week and the Taliban are still standing."

Within just a couple of weeks the Taliban had collapsed. So much for a stalemate. Like Maureen Dowd, however, the supposedly objective news reporters acted as if they had never uttered their dire warnings about getting bogged down in Afghanistan.

We saw the same pattern repeated once the United States went to war in Iraq in 2003: Just a few weeks into the military campaign the press grew impatient and started talking about "setbacks" and "stalemates." On the April 4 edition of ABC's *World News Tonight*, John McWethy told Peter Jennings, "As the U.S. begins to really squeeze Baghdad, U.S. intelligence sources are saying that some of Saddam Hussein's toughest security forces are now apparently digging in, apparently willing to defend their city block by block. This could be, Peter, a long war." Jennings had the perfect rejoinder for emphasis: "As many people had anticipated."

In a March 30 analysis in the *New York Times*, R. W. Apple was again blasting the military as he had in the Afghanistan conflict. "With every passing day," he wrote, "it is more evident that the allies made two gross military misjudgments. . . . Already, the commander of American ground forces in the war zone has conceded that the war that they are fighting is not the one they and their officers had foreseen. 'Shock and awe' neither shocked nor awed." Then came the dramatic pronouncement: "Mr. Hussein seems to have decided that he can turn this war into Vietnam Redux."

In its April 7 "Conventional Wisdom" section, *Newsweek* gave President Bush a "down" arrow, explaining that he was "steadfast but his war cluelessly flings open the gates of hell, making any sort of victory Pyrrhic." Vice President Cheney also got a "down" arrow, with *Newsweek* commenting, "Tells *Meet the Press* just before the war, 'We will be greeted as liberators,' an arrogant blunder for the ages."

On the March 25 episode of CBS's *48 Hours,* Lesley Stahl posed this question to former secretary of the navy James Webb: "You fought in Vietnam. Are you getting any feelings of déjà vu?"

On CNN's *Larry King Live* on April 5, the History Channel's Arthur Kent, who had covered the first Gulf War for NBC, summed up the media's attitude: "There's too much civilian death going on here and the U.S. military flunked, flunked the test of devising a way to have an inside-out removal of this regime instead of setting up these almost medieval siege situations."

Most infamous were Peter Arnett's comments in an interview he gave to Iraq's state-controlled television network on March 30. The NBC Baghdad correspondent told his Iraqi interviewer, "Clearly, the American war planners misjudged the determination of the Iraq forces. . . . And I personally do not understand how that happened, because I've been here many times, and in my commentaries on television I would tell the Americans about the determination of the Iraqi forces, the determination of the government, and the willingness to fight for their country. But me, and others who felt the same way, were not listened to by the Bush administration." Arnett saved the best for last, saying that the American war plan had "failed."

"Baghdad Bob" could not have said it any better, and Saddam Hussein could not have been more pleased.

When the embarrassing Arnett was fired—again—he blamed the vast right-wing conspiracy for his ill fortune. "Right-wing media and politicians are looking for any opportunity to be critical of reporters who are here," he complained to Britain's *Daily Mirror*. "Some reporters have judgments, but that is not my style. I present both sides and report what I see with my own eyes."

It's too bad that what he reported was just plain wrong. A mere ten days after he made his statement to Iraqi TV, Arnett's willing, determined Iraqi forces had been annihilated courtesy of a dazzling American military plan. Peter Arnett's claim, like Arthur Kent's—and like Maureen Dowd's about Afghanistan—was incredibly stupid. By April 9, U.S. forces had seized Baghdad, jubilant Iraqi crowds had toppled a huge statue of Saddam Hussein, and the murderous dictator was looking for holes in which to hide, literally.

Really, though, a Republican administration just can't win with the liberal media. Although a host of reporters announced the failure of American policy at the first hint of struggle, as if any war is a simple enterprise, some journalists attacked the U.S.-led coalition for being *too* successful in Iraq. At a Pentagon press briefing on March 21, just a day into the war, a reporter actually saw the substantial accomplishments the coalition forces had made as a potential setback for the United States. Addressing Defense Secretary Donald Rumsfeld and General Richard Myers, the chairman of the Joint Chiefs of Staff, the reporter acknowledged that U.S.-led forces were already a hundred miles inside Iraq's borders, that there had been mass surrenders, and that we had degraded Saddam's communication capabilities. But this was what he wanted to know: "Are you concerned at all that we will be seen as a bully?" That same evening, David Gergen, editor-at-large for *U.S. News & World Report,* echoed the sentiment on ABC: "One danger the administration may face in the next few days is . . . when we win, will it appear that we have been a bully?" Not surprisingly, *Newsweek's* Eleanor Clift also criticized the American bully, telling Fox News on April 3, "I know we want to call it a war of liberation, but I think this looks more like a war of conquest than a war of liberation."

On the Attack

The media's negative spin on the Bush administration's Iraq policy, had, in fact, begun long before the military operations started. The news media often gave voice to the most virulent critics of U.S. foreign policy. On September 29, 2002, ABC's *This Week* featured a live-from-Baghdad interview with Democratic congressman, Jim McDermott of Washington, who sounded more like leftist actor Martin Sheen than a U.S. congressman. *This Week* host George Stephanopoulos asked McDermott if he still believed, as he had previously suggested, that President Bush was lying about Iraq in order to get the United States into a war. The Washington Democrat replied that, yes, "I think he would mislead the American people."

Stephanopoulos did not challenge McDermott on this point; he simply thanked the congressman for appearing. But the in-studio guest, Senator Don Nickles, Republican of Oklahoma, was outraged, suggesting that McDermott had sounded like a spokesman for the Iraqi government. Stephanopoulos turned on Nickles, claiming, "That's a pretty harsh charge." But a U.S. congressman had just stood in the middle of enemy territory and called his president a liar, coming perilously close to treason. Why was it so "harsh" to challenge him? Later in the show, conservative panelist George Will pointed out why McDermott's statement was so significant, and why Stephanopoulos was wrong not to press the congressman further: "Let's note that in what I consider the most disgraceful performance abroad by an American official in my lifetime, something not exampled since Jane Fonda sat on the antiaircraft gun in Hanoi to be photographed, Mr. McDermott said in effect—not in effect, he said it—we should take Saddam Hussein at his word and not take the president at his word."

McDermott's statement revealed toxic anti-Americanism, but to the liberal media, such appalling claims don't merit examination, at least if Democrats make them. In December 2002, the other senator from Washington State, Patty Murray, made an outrageous statement of her own, saying in a speech that Osama bin Laden had been widely supported in the Middle East because he was some sort of . . . humanitarian. Bin Laden had been building schools, roads, day-care facilities, and infrastructure, Senator Murray said, and "the people are extremely grateful." In fact, Murray placed bin Laden on a higher moral plane than the United States, stating, "We have not done that. How would they look at us today if we had been there helping them with some of that rather than just being the people who are going to bomb in Iraq and go to Afghanistan?" Apparently Senator Murray forgot that the United States sends billions of dollars annually to the undemocratic Middle East.

Much of what Murray had to say was demonstrably untrue. Worse, it was insulting, particularly to the memory of every innocent man, woman, and child massacred on September 11 and to the hundreds of thousands of military personnel risking their lives to conduct the war on terrorism, which this wretched butcher bin Laden had begun.

So how did the news media treat Senator Murray after her unquestionably un-American screed? Was there a feeding frenzy like the one we saw that same month when Senator Trent Lott made what were perceived to be racist comments at a birthday party for Strom Thurmond? Quite the contrary: The mainstream media ignored the comments. There was nothing in the *New York Times,* the *Los Angeles Times,* or *USA Today.* Or in *Time, Newsweek,* or *U.S. News & World Report.* Or on ABC, CBS, or NBC.

This approach—burying negative or unflattering news about liberals or liberal causes—is an old media trick, and it's one that has been used throughout the war on terrorism.

The mainstream media were particularly kind to the "peace" protesters who in the winter of 2003 opposed America's entry into the Iraq war. The "peace movement" was driven by anti-American radicals, but the press gave no indication of this radicalism in its glowing reports. Consider the news coverage of a major antiwar protest held in Washington, D.C., on January 18, 2003. Though the media made the protest a major story, the public was never informed of what really happened in Washington that day.

The "peace" marchers weren't radicals, the media told us. They were real Americans—Republicans, grandparents, honor students, and soccer moms—all upset about a possible war with Iraq. ABC's Lisa Sylvester reported, "Braving frigid temperatures they traveled across the country—black and white, Democrat and Republican, young and old." A second ABC story from Geoff Morrell reinforced that notion, as he told of a doctor and his "honor student" daughter who "rode a bus all night from Asheville, North Carolina. On board were businessmen, soccer moms, military veterans—all members of the same church." MSNBC's Jeannie Ohm echoed the everyman line: "A growing number of people are speaking out against a war with Iraq. Students, grandparents, businessmen, politicians, teachers, actors, and activists, standing shoulder to shoulder in protest." CBS's Joie Chen agreed: "Young, old, veterans and veteran activists united in the effort to stop the war before it starts." The print media took the same approach, with the *Washington Post* reporting, "The marchers . . . represented a cross-section of the nation, from World War II to Gulf War veterans, baby boomers and their children, teenagers and many older citizens."

What nonsense. The media knew, but refused to report, that a Far Left group with a radical agenda had organized the protest. The rally organizer, ANSWER (Act Now to Stop War and End Racism), was a fringe left-wing coalition that included such leftists as America hater Ramsey Clark, the former attorney general; conservative hater Cynthia McKinney, the former congresswoman; Bush hater Jessica Lange, the actress; Fox News Channel hater Janeane Garofalo, the actress and comedienne; and self-hater Michael Moore, the bloviating filmmaker and author. ANSWER, according to its website, classified possible military action against Iraq as "Bush's criminal war for oil" and denounced the "nuclear threat posed by the United States." The site also demanded the "immediate elimination of the U.S. non-conventional weapons systems" and called for a "people's inspection team" to have unfettered access to those weapons. Some "cross-section of the nation."

Nor did the media reveal the radical, inflammatory rhetoric spewed at the rally. Ramsey Clark called for President Bush to be impeached while others made speeches on Muslim causes and Palestinian liberation. But these didn't make the news. Instead, ABC gave us only a small sound bite of actress Jessica Lange deploring the "immoral war." The major newspapers were even worse. A thousand-word article in the *New York Times* failed to quote a single speaker, and a fifteen-hundred-word article in the *Washington Post* contained only one, nine-word quote from Jesse Jackson, who told the crowd that "the world is cold but our hearts are warm." Nor did these papers make much of the fact that the oh-so-mainstream protesters were holding placards saying things like "Bush Is the Real Terrorist" and "USA Is #1 Terrorist."

No, the media wouldn't highlight any of this in their reports, because they wanted to promote the "antiwar" movement and make it appear to be part of the mainstream, full of regular people. What no one wanted to discuss was just how radical, how fringe, the protesters were. Telling the real story were the polling data from the very same news outlets that made it seem as if the great mass of the American people were antiwar. On January 17—a day before the antiwar rally in Washington—a CBS survey found that 64 percent of the American people supported the war, and on January 16 a Fox News/Opinion Dynamics poll had pegged the number at 67 percent. And polls showed that support for the war only increased over the next two months. On March 3 an ABC News/*Washington Post* survey showed support for war against Iraq was up to 72 percent, and by March 27 support for military action had reached 78 percent, according to a Fox News/Opinion Dynamics poll. Armed with these data, journalists could have exposed the radical fringe for what it was. No one was in the mood to do that.

Ignoring the Truth

The fact that the mainstream media have continually offered dire but unfounded warnings about the war on terrorism provides one more example of the media's pervasive liberal bias. But in the case of the media's Iraq reporting, it seems that something even more troubling was at work. The first insight into this problem came just days after the fall of Baghdad.

On April 11, 2003, the *New York Times* ran a remarkable op-ed by CNN's chief news executive, Eason Jordan. Jordan revealed that he had made thirteen visits to Baghdad over a dozen years to convince the Iraqi government to keep the CNN bureau there open. "Each time I visited," he wrote, "I became more distressed by what I saw and heard—awful things that could not be reported because doing so would have jeopardized the lives of Iraqis, particularly on our Baghdad staff." Jordan proceeded to document some of the unimaginable atrocities that Saddam Hussein and his sons had orchestrated but that CNN kept from the American people, including murder and horrific torture.

If Jordan's piece was intended to elicit sympathy, it failed. Here was a CNN executive admitting that his news organization had known about atrocities but buried the stories. The article only validated what CNN's critics had maintained all along about that network and its relationship with the Iraqi dictatorship going back to the first Gulf War. In response to the CNN executive's piece, the *New Republic*'s Franklin Foer wrote a *Wall Street Journal* opinion piece in which he revealed that in October 2002, "Mr. Jordan told me flatly that his network gave 'a full picture of the regime.'" Said Foer, "In our conversation, he challenged me to find instances of CNN neglecting stories about Saddam's horrors. If only I'd had his *Times* op-ed."

CNN was not the only problem. In the months and years before the war, many American journalists had given Saddam's tyrannical regime embarrassingly favorable coverage. *New York Times* and CBS reporter John Burns, whose dispatches from Baghdad merited particular praise in a special report that the Media Research Center issued on the media's Iraq war coverage in late April 2003, said explicitly what Eason Jordan had only hinted at: Too many journalists in Baghdad had kowtowed to Saddam's government and refused to tell Americans the whole story about that horrific regime. It was, Burns revealed, a shameful episode in the history of American journalism.

Burns told his story to Bill Katovsky and Timothy Carlson for their 2003 book *Embedded: The Media at War in Iraq, An Oral History.* "I was the most closely watched and unfavored of all the correspondents [in Baghdad] because of what I wrote about terror whilst Saddam Hussein was still in power," he recounted. "Terror, totalitarian states, and their ways are nothing new to me, but I felt from the start that this was in a category by itself. . . . I felt that was the central truth that had to be told about this place. It was also the essential truth that was untold by the vast majority of correspondents here. Why? Because they judged that the only way they could keep themselves in play here was to pretend that it was okay."

Burns told of how some correspondents wined and dined Iraqi officials, especially members of the Ministry of Information, and plied them with expensive gifts. Some journalists resorted to bribes, he revealed. "Senior members of the information ministry took hundreds of thousands of dollars of bribes from these television correspondents who then behaved as if they were in Belgium." Reporters would do almost anything to show that they were obedient servants, he maintained. Burns spoke of one correspondent who "printed copies of his and other people's stories—mine included—specifically in order to be able to show the difference between himself and the others. He wanted to show what a good boy he was compared to this enemy of the state." According to Burns, this reporter was with a major American newspaper.

John Burns's account of how journalists operated in Baghdad provided one possible explanation for why American reporters could have been so wrong about Iraqi opinion in the months leading up to war. The footage of Iraqis celebrating the news of the downfall of Saddam Hussein's murderous regime by tearing down Saddam statues revealed the truth about how the Iraqis had yearned to escape from under the yoke of the Butcher of Baghdad. Yet many Baghdad-based correspondents had painted a far different picture as they reported from behind enemy lines.

On September 17, 2002, for example, NBC's Ron Allen reported, "Many Iraqis believe America's true motive is to remove Saddam Hussein from power, to install a puppet government and seize Iraq's vast oil wealth. On the streets, many see Hussein's offer to allow the inspectors back as a wise, brave decision showing strength." In mid-October, when the dictator called a sham election known as a "referendum," journalists in Baghdad treated this as a real exercise in giving the Iraqi people a voice in their government. On October 14, CNN's Nic Robertson said, "Iraqi reverence for President Saddam Hussein is rarely more expressive than when their leader calls a referendum. . . . Amid even bolder demonstrations of devotion to the Iraqi leader, students at Baghdad's fine arts school, too young to vote in the last referendum in 1995, appear eager now." When Saddam was "reelected" with, yes, a full 100 percent of the vote, NBC's Keith Miller told *Today* show viewers said that the "celebrations were genuine." By March 2003, on the eve of war, when *Good Morning America*'s Diane Sawyer asked reporter Dan Harris about the "love that the Iraqis have for" Saddam Hussein, the Baghdad correspondent remarked that Saddam "is one to point out quite frequently that he is part of a historical trend in this country of restoring Iraq to its greatness, its historical greatness. He points out frequently that he was elected with a 100 percent margin recently." Harris, in parroting the Iraqi propaganda, did not question the validity of that vote.

All in all, the news media's handling of Iraq was, in John Burns's words, "an absolutely disgraceful performance." The Baghdad correspondents ignored their "obligation of telling the truth about these places," he said.

"There is corruption in our business," Burns concluded. "We need to get back to basics. This war should be studied and talked about. In the run up to this war, to my mind, there was a gross abdication of responsibility."

Negative Spin on Positive Stories

To be fair, the Iraq war brought out the best in many reporters. Embedded reporters were our eyes and ears in Iraq, and by and large their reporting was masterful. The Media Research Center's special report on the hard war coverage revealed that both reporters and anchors had done fine work. In fact, all but one of the network and cable anchors received a grade of B-minus or higher for their war coverage. (The only anchor who did not acquit himself well was Peter Jennings, who was awarded an F.)

Sadly, though, the media's performance fell off once the major combat operations ended. With the battlefield conquered, the United States and its allies began the arduous, hugely expensive, and utterly thankless work of rebuilding a nation devastated by decades of totalitarian excess, self-destructive sectarian strife, and three major wars—all the while suffering almost daily terrorist attacks. There was a story of real heroism to be told, of the altruistic American spirit at her finest, but that apparently was too boring. Instead we got negative spin even on positive stories. All along, the Bush administration had made clear that bringing democracy to Iraq would be a long and difficult process, taking years, not months. (President Bush reiterated this important point in a September 2003 address to the nation: "Two years ago, I told the Congress and the country that the war on terror would be a lengthy war, a different kind of war, fought on many fronts in many places.") Still, many journalists rushed to proclaim—again—that America was getting bogged down.

The old adage "If it bleeds, it leads" could not have been more fitting. Rather than celebrating the removal of a murderous dictatorship, the new freedoms for an enslaved people, the schools, hospitals, and roads rebuilt and reopened, and the emerging democratic process amid the turmoil of Islamic oppression, the news media instead focused—and continue to this day to focus—on the headline America's enemies created almost daily: "Another American Soldier Killed."

Some in the press were so intent on finding fault with the U.S.-led military operation that they actually invented problems that didn't exist and then blamed the Americans. Take, for example, the story of 170,000 priceless items allegedly looted from the Baghdad Museum. On the April 17 *World News Tonight* broadcast, a somber Peter Jennings announced, "Two of the Bush administration's cultural advisers in Iraq have now resigned. They were frustrated by the failure of the U.S. forces to prevent the pillage of Iraq's national museum," which, he said, was just one of "a variety of places the U.S. has not been protecting." Over on CNN, Aaron Brown picked up the story, too: "There has been intense focus on one question: Did the United States do enough to prevent the theft?" His colleague Jim Bitterman claimed that the "antiquities had been plundered under the very noses of U.S. troops," adding that "critics" (and who might they be?) had charged that the U.S. priority was "protecting hundreds of oil wells scattered across Iraq and the Oil Ministry building in Baghdad, ahead of protecting the Baghdad Museum and other cultural sites."

That same night, ABC's *Nightline* devoted an entire show to the museum looting, and the next morning, *Good Morning America* had yet another report. On April 18, Jennings was back with another story on *World News Tonight,* this time delivering both a history lesson and a scolding. "The country has been a living archive of man's earliest history," he said, "which is why the Pentagon is being so widely criticized for not protecting the history when it captured the capital city." He concluded his report by dismissing the Pentagon's defense as inadequate: "The Pentagon has said, in reply, 'Look, this is war, and stuff happens, the U.S. was fired on from the museum grounds.' Not a satisfactory answer for people who say that if the U.S. managed to protect the Ministry of Oil, why not this repository of civilization? Why, they ask, is neglect forgivable?"

Those were pretty tough accusations. There was only one problem. They weren't true.

As London's *Telegraph* reported, the National Museum of Iraq declared that the reason so many items were missing was that they had been removed from the museum for safekeeping before the war. Donny George, the museum's research director, explained: "There was a mistake. Someone asked us, 'What is the number of pieces in the whole collection?' We said over 170,000, and they took that as the number lost. Reporters came in and saw empty shelves and reached the conclusion that all was gone."

On May 1, Jennings offered a correction—sort of. "The looting at the national museum may not have been as extensive as some people first reported. . . . Twenty-seven so-called 'significant pieces' were stolen, some of them priceless, but those who said that more than 150,000 items were looted appear to be wrong." What Jennings should have added was: "Given that the 'some people' included this network, and given the manner in which we erroneously and repeatedly blamed the U.S. military, we apologize." That, however, would have required a certain degree of humility, a trait in short supply at ABC News.

Fast-forward now to the summer of 2003, to July 23, the day American forces found, fought, and killed Uday and Qusay, Saddam Hussein's sadistic sons. These two butchers engaged in a fierce firefight with coalition forces who attempted to arrest them, and finally a well-aimed TOW missile claimed the lives of the brothers. This was most welcome news both at home and in Iraq. Unbelievably, however, some in the American media had to denounce this triumph, too.

What possibly could be the problem? Well, if you watched NBC's *Nightly News* that evening, you heard Jim Miklaszewski gripe, "There are questions today why the U.S. military used such heavy firepower to take down a few lightly armed men." Never mind that those "lightly armed men" had managed to injure three soldiers before they were finally overcome by superior firepower. Over on CNN, Aaron Brown couldn't understand why the American forces attacked at all. "Why not wait 'em out, starve them out?" he demanded to know. "Try and take 'em alive opposed to engaging in this gun battle? Once they had 'em surrounded and cornered, they weren't going anywhere."

When military forces displayed photographs of the dead sons to confirm to the world that it was true that they'd been killed (since previous speculation had proven incorrect), ABC correspondent Terry Moran took offense. "Article 17 of the Geneva Conventions requires countries at war to 'ensure that the dead are honorably interred, if possible, according to the rites of the religion to which they belong,'" he said to White House press secretary Scott McClellan. "Does the president, as commander in chief, believe that the United States is bound by that, when it comes to the bodies of Uday and Qusay Hussein?"

But those pictures of the bullet-riddled corpses with the bearded, disfigured faces did not look like Hussein's sons, and in an attempt to satisfy a skeptical Iraqi community, the military had its morticians clean and shave the faces, presenting them a day later looking far more familiar. And wouldn't you know it, the American media complained.

NBC's Tom Brokaw asked reporter Richard Engel in Baghdad, "Richard, as you well know, there's a fresh video tonight as well of the bodies of Saddam's two sons after they were cleaned up by Army morticians. . . . Are those new images any more persuasive to the Iraqi people?" That question was sensible, but Engel's answer was an outrage. "They are not really more persuasive," he huffed, wholly inaccurately. "But they certainly are more controversial. Those bodies are quite radically altered. First, the men were shaved, then putty was used to remodel their faces. Makeup was also applied to make them look more lifelike. . . . All of this has been quite offensive to Islamic sensibilities here. Muslims are generally buried in a simple white shroud without any embalming process at all, Tom."

As if all that wasn't bad enough, the Associated Press ran a national story suggesting that the United States had broken the law by putting an end to these two men. "Odai, Qusai Deaths Go Against U.S. Ban," the headline screamed. The story began, "In theory, pursuing with intent to kill violates a long-standing policy banning political assassination. It was the misfortune of Saddam Hussein's sons, Odai and Qusai, that the Bush administration has not bothered to enforce the prohibition. . . . The ban on assassinations, spelled out in an executive order signed by President Ford in 1976 and reinforced by Presidents Carter and Reagan, made no distinction between wartime and peacetime. There are no loop holes; no matter how awful the leader, he could not be a U.S. target either directly or by hired hand." The Associated Press conceded in its report that, according to U.S. officials, people inside the villa where Uday and Qusay were holed up had opened fire against U.S. troops. Still, to highlight the anti-American angle, the article played down this fact, as well as the fact that the attack on Uday and Qusay was not a "political assassination" but rather part of the hostilities.

It seemed that the American liberal media could always find a negative angle on good news. The most shocking example of this came several months later, on the morning of December 14. At 7 A.M., Ambassador Paul Bremer, the presidential envoy to Iraq, held a live press conference in Baghdad, where he uttered this simple but memorable phrase: "Ladies and gentlemen, we got him!" Saddam Hussein had been captured, hiding in a hole, like a rat. One can only imagine that in living rooms all over America people pumped their fists in triumph and let out a collective whoop of national joy. All over Iraq, citizens took to the streets to dance in celebration.

Surely *this* news was something the leftist American media wouldn't try to spin, right? Wrong.

ABC News stooped to new lows of ridiculousness with waves of yes-buts, so-whats, and blatant omissions. It took Terry Moran less than an hour to find a negative slant. A Saddam Hussein trial, he intoned, could embarrass the United States, which "had an interesting relationship, to say the least, with the Iraqi government. . . . There are allegations that the United States provided weapons to Saddam Hussein's regime during the Iran-Iraq war. And all that could spill out in a big show trial." A few minutes later, Moran added another twist. The Nuremberg trial of the Nazis was "not considered to be a model of legal niceties. They railroaded, in some respects, those defendants through, in the eyes of many jurists today." Later that day Moran would send an e-mail to National Review Online conceding that saying the Nazis had been "railroaded" was "foolish and wrong," but, as usual, ABC did not see fit to relay this admission to its own viewers.

Later on that evening, Peter Jennings was equally dour and self-delusional. After showing footage of Iraqi citizens in the streets cheering and waving banners, Jennings declared, "There's not a good deal for Iraqis to be happy about at the moment. Life is still chaotic, beset by violence in many cases. Huge shortages. In some respects, Iraqis keep telling us, life is not as stable for them as it was when Saddam Hussein was in power."

The following morning, Monday, December 15, ABC was still at it. On *Good Morning America,* anchor Charles Gibson picked up the Moran line that a trial for Saddam Hussein could prove "embarrassing for the United States" because "we supported him for so long" and "gave him some of the instruments that he used to terrorize his own people." A day later, on *Nightline,* ABC was still harping on the issue. Anchor Chris Bury introduced the show by declaring, "Saddam Hussein has not always been America's enemy, and as *Nightline* correspondent Deborah Amos reports, that might prove embarrassing in any trial."

ABC wasn't alone, however. CBS's Lesley Stahl demanded assurances from Secretary of Defense Donald Rumsfeld that the captured Saddam was being treated humanely. Even after Rumsfeld assured her that Hussein's treatment would be governed by the protocols of the Geneva Convention, Stahl remained worried about the murderous tyrant: "Let me raise the whole question, for lack of a better term: torture. Let's say he's not forthcoming. Would we deprive him of sleep, would we make it very cold where he is, or very hot?" Rumsfeld didn't hold back in his answer: "You know, to even raise the word 'torture' in terms of how the United States military would treat this person, it seems to me, is very unfortunate. We don't torture people, and here's a man who has tortured to death tens of thousands of people, conducted rape and brutality the likes of which it would be difficult to find a more vicious and brutal dictator in our adult lifetimes. . . . To suggest that anyone would be engaged in torture or conduct inconsistent with the Geneva Conventions seems to me isn't on the mark at all."

But perhaps the most bizarre statement came from Kimberly Dozier on the December 16 *CBS Evening News,* an analysis for the ages: "A tyrant has fallen. But for some, he's a fallen hero. . . . Even many who suffered under Saddam have mixed feelings. . . . Iraqis are like abused children scarred by the man who was both father figure and enforcer. His rules were simple. Obey, and he would provide jobs, food rations, electricity, and security. Rebel, and punishment was merciless. But Saddam Hussein also gave Iraqis dignity and pride."

One has to wonder: Had these CBS reporters been around in 1945, how would they have reported the fall of Adolf Hitler?

The Ongoing Story

As this is written, the Iraq story is far from finished. There will be many developments—political, economic, social, and military—to cover in the months and years ahead. Many legitimate questions remain unanswered. The media should examine important questions about the Iraq situation and U.S. foreign policy. But simply attacking the U.S. government at every turn does not amount to a serious examination of important foreign policy issues. The record shows that the news media have repeatedly been wrong when issuing dire warnings about what would happen during the war on terrorism. Rarely have they corrected themselves, however.

The relentless negative coverage of America's foreign policy can have profound consequences, for the news media still play an essential role in shaping public opinion. The ongoing war on terrorism is, many would concede, the single biggest issue facing the United States today. Sadly, the news media's coverage of this vital issue has not always been strong. In a number of cases, in fact, it has been abysmal.

If the media has seen fit to hammer, hammer, hammer the Bush administration on its record, isn't it fair that they be held accountable for their own performance as well?

Conclusion

The Coming Meltdown of the Liberal Media

THE POLITICAL DISCOURSE in this country is spirited, and on many issues—the economy, the proper role of government, foreign policy, national security, social issues, and much more—conservatives can enjoy an energetic debate with liberals.

Unfortunately, media bias is not one of those issues on which conservatives and liberals can engage in intelligent debate. Liberals continue to do what they have always done in the face of conservative critiques of the media: They simply refuse to acknowledge that any bias exists. No matter how many times the obvious is proven, and no matter how many ways evidence is documented, liberal elites offer denials and prevarications.

A case in point is NBC's Tom Brokaw, who in a January 2004 interview with the *Columbia Journalism Review* was asked about the Media Research Center's criticisms of the liberal media. Brokaw's answer was as illuminating as it was undiplomatic: "It is a little wearying, but you've got to rise above it and take it case by case. Most of the cases are pretty flimsily made. . . . What I get tired of is Brent Bozell trying to make these fine legal points everywhere every day. A lot of it just doesn't hold up. So much of it is that bias—like beauty—is in the eye of the beholder."

Ouch. After reading that attack I had to respond, cognizant that I risked exhausting Mr. Brokaw even further. So I offered Mr. Brokaw a simple challenge: We would assemble a mutually acceptable panel of media experts and have it review the Media Research Center's evidence of liberal bias. If the panel deemed our case to be "flimsily made" and agreed with Mr. Brokaw that the argument "just doesn't hold up," the Media Research Center would make a $1 million gift to the charity of his choice. If, on the other hand, the panel agreed with us, then Mr. Brokaw would make a $1 million gift to the Media Research Center (it's tax-deductible). And to sweeten the pot, I offered to limit our evidence of media bias only to NBC and Tom Brokaw.

Brokaw may be biased, but he is also wise: He didn't accept the challenge.

Some journalists might concede, under extreme pressure, that some *other* reporters are politically liberal, though they'll *never* concede that *they* are biased. Still, they are quick to deny that this political philosophy affects the media's performance.

But how can the overwhelming bias in favor of liberals *not* affect the work product? Each day editors in news organizations are presented with a range of critical questions. *What is news? What is the top news story? Who should cover it, and how should it be covered?* The journalists who report to those editors face their own questions. *What is the proper lead for a story? Who is to be cited? What ought to be the conclusion?* Every single one of these questions demands a subjective response— that is, a biased response. "Objective news" always was, always will be, a myth.

Yet most journalists, and many of their liberal defenders, continue to deny the obvious. And the mainstream media continue to provide a leftward slant to the news. This is a huge problem, and it is no longer just a problem for the American people who have to endure biased news coverage. No, the liberal media are beginning to suffer the consequences. Their credibility is in doubt, and as a result the era of complete liberal dominance over the media is coming to an end.

Polls reveal that the American people now recognize the extensive bias in the mainstream media. According to a poll conducted by the

Pew Research Center for the People and the Press in 1997, only 27 percent of Americans feel the news media "deal fairly" with political and social issues, while 67 percent—two out of three respondents—believe the media "tend to favor one side." A Pew survey in October 2000 found that 89 percent of the public believe the media "often or sometimes let personal politics influence their coverage." Yet another poll, this one published by *Brill's Content* magazine in 2000 (and cited in Bernard Goldberg's *Bias*), noted that a sizable plurality of Americans, regardless of political affiliation, believes the media have a liberal bias. It is no surprise that some three-quarters of Republicans (74 percent) find most journalists to be more liberal than they are, but it *is* shocking that nearly *half* the Democrats (47 percent) also feel that most journalists are to their left politically.

The evidence mounted in 2003 with two new surveys. A Pew Center report in July found that "most Americans (53%) believe that news organizations are politically biased, while just 29% say they are careful to remove bias from their reports." What kind of bias? According to the survey, "twice as many say news organizations are 'liberal' (51%) than 'conservative.' "

In September, a Gallup poll found that 45 percent of Americans believe that the news media are too liberal, while only 14 percent say that the press is too conservative. The report made clear that this was not an aberration: "These perceptions of liberal inclination have not changed over the last three years." The Gallup report also stated, "About 4 in 10 Americans today identify themselves as conservatives and about the same number identify as moderates, while less than 20% identify as liberals. Given all of this, the overall conclusion is that Americans, on average, are more likely to see the news media as too liberal than too conservative."

And yet the elites in the media somehow believe that their liberalism represents the mainstream in this country.

Does bias affect Americans' confidence in the media? Most assuredly. The September 2003 Gallup survey sums up the public's mood: When asked how much trust they have in the news media, nearly half of all Americans (46 percent) say "not very much" or "none at all."

And will Americans who have lost faith in the mainstream media try to find other news outlets in which they have more confidence? You bet.

In fact, the signs are everywhere that the liberal media are headed for a meltdown.

The Liberal Media Ignore the Warning Signs

A meltdown? How could this be true? After all, earlier in this book I acknowledged that Eric Alterman—he of the Far Left magazine *The Nation*—is right to say in *What Liberal Media?* that mainstream news outlets still dominate. Fox News may be leading the pack on cable, but its 1.3 million nightly viewers (as of this writing) still pale in comparison to CBS's 6.5 million, ABC's 8.2 million, and NBC's 8.9 million. The conservative *Washington Times* has a tiny circulation (about 105,000 readers) compared with that of the liberal *Washington Post* (796,000). The conservative *New York Post* has a circulation of 620,000 while the ultraliberal *New York Times*'s circulation is nearly double that, at 1.1 million; even the *New York Post*'s fellow tabloid, the liberal *Daily News*, has a circulation nearly 20 percent larger (737,000). If that's not enough, throw in *USA Today*, the *Los Angeles Times*, the *Chicago Tribune*, and God-knows-how-many others. And if you still need more, add *Time*, *Newsweek*, and *U.S. News* and their nine million subscribers.

Moreover, the same liberal networks and newspapers that dominate traditional news markets are making real inroads on the Internet, which more Americans are turning to for news. The Pew Research Center released a report in January 2003 that detailed the use of Internet news sites during the previous congressional campaign. While noting that a respectable 11 percent of news consumers get their news online—the vast majority still favor television—the survey found that the "sites of major national and local news organizations continue to be the leading sources of online campaign information. . . . Roughly half of the online election news consumers (52 percent) said they went most often to the sites of major national media organizations such as CNN and the *New York Times,* while 18 percent cite websites of local news organizations."

Given all that, how could the liberal media be in trouble? Well, consider the significant drops in viewership and readership they have experienced. The Big Three evening newscasts are losing the most, as Paul Farhi documented in the June 2001 *American Journalism Review.* Farhi showed that from 1981 to 2001 CBS lost half its viewership while ABC's numbers dropped 35 percent and NBC's fell 30 percent. And the numbers have only gotten worse since Farhi ran his article. The 6.5 million viewers that Dan Rather's *CBS Evening News* drew in July 2003 were, as noted, the fewest the show had had in at least a decade, and perhaps ever.

The print media are not immune to this drain, either. According to surveys conducted for the Newspaper Association of America, the percentage of adults who consider themselves to be weekday readers of newspapers dropped from 77.6 percent in 1970 to 55.4 percent in 2002.

Ask journalists to explain these developments and the reasons pour out. They point to the rise of cable television and the change in viewing habits created by the twenty-four-hour news channels. They cite the Internet, which can provide news whenever a person wants it. They talk about the growing apathy for news and the lack of interest in reading. It's everything, according to the media elite, except the public's rejection of their liberal bias.

Eric Alterman takes precisely this approach in his book. He posits that "quite obviously" the only reason for the "significant decline in [the networks'] ratings for their news programs" is "the enormous rise in viewer choice." The fact that many Americans now have hundreds of channels to choose from is undoubtedly a factor in the viewership drain—but the *only* factor? Surely there are other reasons. But Alterman doesn't want to entertain other arguments. Indeed, he scoffs at Bernard Goldberg's perfectly reasonable suggestion in *Bias* that someone like Bill O'Reilly of Fox News has seen his ratings shoot upward because of Americans' frustration with mainstream news leaders.

Alterman calls Goldberg's logic "genuinely difficult to fathom" and "entirely nonsensical," and then launches this broadside against Goldberg: "Had he, or anyone related to the book, had enough respect for readers to bother with even ten minutes of research, this claim would have never made it into print."

Seems a little extreme, doesn't it? What is so "nonsensical" about Bernard Goldberg's claim? After all, doing the research that Alterman calls for—looking at polling data, Nielsen ratings, circulation statistics, and much else—leads to an unmistakable conclusion: Americans are dissatisfied with the mainstream media, which they consider to have a pronounced liberal bias. But Alterman, like the rest of the liberal media deniers, blithely dismisses the evidence proving Americans' lack of confidence in the mainstream media—and shoots spitballs at Goldberg. Incidentally, Tom Brokaw took much the same approach when he was interviewed by the *Columbia Journalism Review*. Brokaw proclaimed, "The simple test is that if people thought I had a bias, they wouldn't watch me." Well, the fact is, many Americans *do* think he and his brethren are biased, and as a result the mainstream news divisions are losing viewers.

That dismissive attitude is why the liberal bias in the mainstream media continues unchecked, and why more and more Americans, disgusted by the arrogance, are turning to alternative news outlets that collectively present a challenge to the hegemony of the broadcast networks and major newspapers. The most visible of these outlets is the Fox News Channel, which was launched in October 1996 (much to the amusement of the old television establishment). Fox News was the brainchild of Australian media magnate Rupert Murdoch and the creative product of its president, former Republican media strategist Roger Ailes. Right off the bat, Fox News was brazen, uppity, challenging—different. It rolled out a prime-time conservative lineup to go alongside liberals like Mara Liasson and Juan Williams, thus putting meat on the "fair and balanced" bone. It confidently proclaimed its slogan of "We Report, You Decide"—and America quickly decided. In January 2002—after only five years—Fox overtook CNN as the number one cable news network. By February 2004 Fox News was thoroughly trouncing CNN, registering some 1.3 million prime-time viewers compared with CNN's 715,000; lowly MSNBC was managing a meager 312,000.

Hysterical Attacks

While Fox News still has quite a bit to go to rival the networks' numbers, it has made truly remarkable progress in just a few years. And this has the political Left in a panic. Instead of taking a closer look at why Americans have grown fed up with the mainstream media, liberals have gone on the attack against Fox News and the "right-wing media." Their reaction has been nothing short of hysterical.

For example, after Republicans won the Senate and increased their majority in the House of Representatives in the November 2002 elections, the so-called conservative media became piñatas for liberal pundits and politicians who simply could not accept the fact that voters had once again rejected a liberal vision for America. Unable to blame the Supreme Court for invalidating the Constitution this time, they blamed the vast right-wing conspiracy, led by Fox News, the *Washington Times,* the *New York Post,* the *Wall Street Journal*'s editorial page, and, of course, talk-radio hosts like Rush Limbaugh, Sean Hannity, Bill O'Reilly, and Michael Reagan. It was this partisan coverage, this fifth column, that was most responsible for the Republican victory, according to the theorists.

A typical liberal response came just three days after the election, in a *New York Times* op-ed piece by Paul Krugman, who has never hidden his contempt for conservatives. "When it comes to free publicity," sniffed the liberal Princeton economist, "some of the major broadcast media are simply biased in favor of the Republicans. . . . Talk radio and Fox News let the hard right get its message out to its supporters, while those who oppose the juggernaut stay home because they don't get the sense that the Democrats offer a real alternative."

Three weeks later, former vice president Al Gore attacked Fox News in the *New York Observer,* telling his interviewer that the network was nothing more than an extension of the GOP. "There are some major institutional voices that are, truthfully speaking, part and parcel of the Republican Party," he said. "Fox News Network, the *Washington Times*, Rush Limbaugh—there's a bunch of them, and some of them are financed by wealthy ultra-conservative billionaires who make political deals with Republican administrations and the rest of the media." Gore added that this nefarious enterprise gets its signals directly from Republican headquarters: "Something will start at the Republican National Committee inside the building. . . . It will explode the next day on the right-wing talk show networks, on Fox News and in the newspapers that play this game."

Gore's former boss, Bill Clinton, weighed in on the subject in February 2003, telling the *Today* show's Katie Couric that the Republicans won the midterm elections in large part because "they have a much better media machine than we do. They worked on it for thirty years and they've got it. They've got everything from the Heritage Foundation to sympathetic newspapers to sympathetic cable programs that are heavily weighted in their favor."

To be sure, op-ed columnists like Krugman and politicians like Gore and Clinton are in the business of pushing their own ideas, and one is not too surprised to hear their crackpot theories about conservative media bias. But what about "news" reporters? Incredibly, some of these supposedly objective journalists are following the Democrats' party line that this was a conservative conspiracy. In the November 18, 2002, issue of *Time* magazine, for instance, Josh Tyrangiel wrote, "Even if Democrats pull together on some big issues, they'll still have to overcome G.O.P. bully pulpits in the White House and Congress—and a new reality: conservative bias in the media." What was Tyrangiel's evidence to prove that this "conservative bias" was a "reality"? He quoted a "senior elected Democrat"—note: no name—complaining about Fox News: "They're No. 1 in the ratings," the Democrat whined, "and they follow everything the President does all the time. How do you get around that?" That was it—but that one statement from a member of the party that had just lost the election was apparently enough for America's leading newsweekly to conclude that conservative bias in the media was a "reality." In actuality, though, the Democrats had plenty to help them "get around" Fox News—ABC, CBS, NBC, CNN, PBS, the *New York Times*, and so on. Remember, too, that the same liberal news organizations that dominated television coverage also were Americans' main source of Internet news coverage during the 2002 campaign.

Liberals hyperventilate over not just the "Fox Factor" but also Rush Limbaugh. Of course, Limbaugh was on the scene long before Fox News; he was a pioneer in the world of talk radio, particularly as someone unapologetic about his strongly held conservative beliefs. His national audience grew quickly in the early 1990s, and liberals, aghast that so many Americans would embrace a conservative message that ran counter to their leftist thinking, began attacking Limbaugh. In a fit of signature self-pity, Bill Clinton used the president's bully pulpit to slam the radio host in June 1994. Clinton complained to a St. Louis radio station that as soon as he finished his interview, Limbaugh would have "three hours to say whatever he wants. And I won't have the opportunity to respond." Other comments were more harsh. That same summer, leftist poet Allen Ginsberg, writing in the liberal magazine *The Progressive*, claimed quite seriously that if Limbaugh and fellow conservatives "ever got real power, there would be concentration camps and mass death." Meanwhile, former NBC News president Michael Gartner griped in a *USA Today* column that Limbaugh "has but a passing acquaintance with [the truth]. He's toying with you, folks, getting you all riled up with a stew of half-truths and nontruths. . . . He's making fools of you, feeding you swill—and you're taking it in." All this came from the man who had left NBC News the previous year after it was discovered that *Dateline NBC* had rigged pickup trucks to explode for a "news" story.

As we have seen, the anti-Limbaugh rhetoric became even more pronounced after the 1995 Oklahoma City bombing, when President Clinton, without mentioning Rush by name, claimed that Limbaugh and other talk radio hosts who "spread hate" "leave the impression that . . . violence is acceptable." Bryant Gumbel, then on NBC, made Clinton's point even more forcefully, characterizing "right-wing talk show hosts like Rush Limbaugh" as those who "embolden and encourage some extremists." Others piled on. Wrote the *Washington Post*'s David Broder, the dean of Washington political correspondents, "The bombing shows how dangerous it really is to inflame twisted minds with statements that suggest political opponents are enemies. For two years, Rush Limbaugh described this nation as 'America Held Hostage' to the policies of the liberal Democrats, as if the duly elected President and Congress were equivalent to the regime in Tehran. I think there will be less tolerance and fewer cheers for that kind of rhetoric."

The anti-Limbaugh vitriol has kept up over the years, and it became particularly severe in the fall of 2003, when many liberals in the press saw the opportunity to pounce on Rush. First, working as a football commentator for ESPN, Limbaugh claimed that some liberals in the sports community were praising Philadelphia Eagles quarterback Donovan McNabb because of his race (McNabb is black), not because of his performance on the field. The outcry from the liberal establishment was immediate and sustained, and it cost Rush his ESPN gig. Never mind that some respected sportswriters agreed with Limbaugh that McNabb was overrated as a quarterback. To take just one example, Allen Barra, who writes a sports column for the *Wall Street Journal* and *Slate,* carefully analyzed McNabb's statistics and concluded, "Limbaugh pretty much spoke the truth. Limbaugh lost his job for saying in public what many football fans and analysts have been saying privately for the past couple of seasons." Ignoring such commentary, and refusing even to consider whether Limbaugh was making a defensible point, politically correct liberals went on the attack. "What must it be like to live in Rush Limbaugh's world?" asked CBS *Sunday Morning* contributor Nancy Giles on October 5. "A world where, when anyone other than conservative, white men attempts to do anything or enter any profession, be it business, politics, art, or sports, the only reason they're allowed entry or incredibly attain excellence is because the standard was lowered. Be they liberals, people of color, women, the poor, or anyone with an accent. What a way to shake up intelligent sports commentary. Hitler would have killed in talk radio. He was edgy, too." Such was the ugly, over-the-top rhetoric from liberals.

Shortly after the ESPN incident, Limbaugh admitted to his twenty million listeners that he had become addicted to prescription painkillers, and many liberals couldn't contain their sheer *happiness* at Rush's misfortune. (And liberals are supposed to be the compassionate ones?) On October 10, the day Limbaugh made his announcement, CNN anchor Aaron Brown introduced a discussion by saying, "Rush Limbaugh has been more than a bit unkind to me more than once. He's also been unkind to Al Franken, who in turn has been unkind to him. He's taken shots at Michael Wolff, *New York* magazine's media critic, and Michael is hardly the retiring sort. So here we all are, Al, Michael, and me, and the subject is Rush—made worse, no doubt, by the permanent smirk that seems to be attached to my face." This came just seconds after Brown assured his viewers that they would see "no gloating or joy" from the CNN anchor.

Some spewed poison. In his October 20 *Newsweek* cover story, Evan Thomas proclaimed, "The man behind the curtain is not the God of Family Values but a childless, twice-divorced, thrice-married schlub whose idea of a good time is to lie on his couch and watch football endlessly. . . . Granted, Limbaugh has won over, or fooled, a lot of people. With his heartland pieties and scorn for 'feminazis' and 'commie-symps' like *West Wing* president Martin Sheen, he is the darling of Red State, Fly-Over America." The next time Thomas preaches against "mean-spirited conservatives," I hope someone slugs him.

And then there was *Newsday* columnist Jimmy Breslin, who was in a category all his own. On October 12, using the news of Limbaugh's addiction as a perfect opportunity to insult Rush's audience, Breslin proclaimed, "His people are hopelessly, embarrassingly dumb. Or— sudden revelation!—they're all out there whacked out on 'hillbilly heroin' just like Rush. Only they can understand his babble."

Of course, with the rise of Fox News and other conservative personalities like Sean Hannity, liberals see more and more targets out there besides Rush Limbaugh. The silly complaints about the "conservative media bias" grow louder and more fevered, all as a direct extension of the Left's panic over the coming meltdown of the liberal media.

And panic it is, because the liberal media's near monopoly on information has been contested for the first time. For decades the liberal media went completely unchallenged, save for the occasional *National Review,* George Will, or Paul Harvey. As a result, the American Left enjoyed a cherished power: the ability to determine who and what is considered news in this country. More important, the liberal media could not only influence but could actually *set* the political agenda in this country. That gave extraordinary power to unelected editors, reporters, and producers to direct policy, affect culture, and make the occasional politician or government official—or destroy him.

But those heady days are ending for the Left.

Meltdown

The liberal media may dominate at the moment, but the media landscape is changing rapidly. Remember, Fox News needed a mere five years to overtake CNN, which was a firmly established, respected cable news outlet that had been on the air for more than sixteen years by the time Fox debuted. So what will happen after another five years? Where are the media headed? These are crucial questions for our society, for as we have seen, the news media have extraordinary influence over how we see the world and also how our world is shaped. For that reason I will venture forward with a few predictions about the future of the media, although I recognize that with the world of communications evolving at such a mind-numbing pace, one ought to have a certain trepidation about predicting what will happen next month, let alone in a few years.

To begin, it is clear that the Fox News Channel's meteoric rise is just beginning. Fox News is, compared with the Big Three news programs, just a small player at this point, but its viewership will continue to grow. For example, it is possible that the Fox News morning show *Fox and Friends* will surpass CBS's *The Early Show* in the ratings by the end of 2005; in fact, in the spring of 2003 it *did* outdraw *The Early Show* for a short time. By the end of 2006, *Fox News Sunday* could reach par with ABC's *This Week* (at which point George Stephanopoulos would be long gone from the host's chair). And in prime time, where Fox News has made its most visible gains in recent years, the success could be even more dramatic: Fox News prime-time offerings could pass at least the *CBS Evening News* in the ratings by the end of 2006. In short, the cable network that was the laughingstock of the industry when it launched in 1996 will have broken the Big Three broadcast networks' stranglehold on ratings by 2006. Not a bad way to celebrate its tenth anniversary.

Having been left in the dust, Fox News's cable competitors will have three options: compete for the conservative audience, consolidate from weakness, or collapse. MSNBC has shown the most willingness to go the competition route, bringing on conservative former congressman Joe Scarborough and, in an embarrassing and ill-advised move, radio host Michael Savage (who was quickly fired). And it will continue to try to compete with Fox News—look for a raid on Fox talent—but the liberal culture at NBC will prevent its cable enterprise from making the serious institutional changes necessary to make a conservative viewership comfortable. CNN's overtures to the conservative audience have been more rhetorical than substantial, but I suspect that this will change as the gap widens between this proud former leader and archrival Fox News. CNN will probably move further away from the hard news field, shifting its resources toward popular culture and covering real news only when major events warrant.

The Big Three networks will continue to deny that any liberal bias exists, and they could suffer the most. If Fox News is the *Monitor* of the industry—fast, racy, and daring—the networks are the *Merrimack*—big, slow, and unable to turn quickly. The Big Three news bureaus not only lack the entrepreneurial savvy necessary to meet the Fox News challenge, but more fundamentally, the liberal perspective is so institutionalized in network newsrooms that no concession will be given to the conservative charge—not, perhaps, until it is too late. At least one network could consolidate its losses by merging its operations with CNN.

Of course, if the major networks do not seize the opportunity to compete with Fox News, others will. By the end of the decade, there could be plans in the works for another network to go after the 80 percent of Americans who identify themselves as conservatives or moderates but aren't represented by ABC, CBS, NBC, CNN, and so forth.

Will liberals respond to the gains that Fox News and conservative talk radio have made (that is, will they respond in ways besides smearing these ventures)? They will try. In fact, some liberals are already trying. In early 2003 it was reported that Al Gore and others were exploring the possibility of forming a new liberal cable network, which would require an investment of hundreds of millions of dollars. And in February of 2003 AnShell Media, headed by venture capitalists Anita and Sheldon Drobny, announced that it would invest some $10 million to launch a national network of liberal talk-radio stations—a liberal response to Rush Limbaugh and Company.

But after months of "attaboy" press coverage, with liberals eagerly anticipating this historic venture, which was supposed to be akin to Ferdinand and Isabella's investment in Columbus . . . nothing. In fact, in November 2003 the Drobnys backed out, selling a majority of their shares to a group of investors led by former America Online executive Mark Walsh. As the Drobnys removed themselves from the company's management, the Associated Press revealed that they hadn't followed through on any of their grand plans: They hadn't spent $10 million, hadn't hired any talent, hadn't purchased any stations, and hadn't signed any distribution contracts. So Walsh, formerly the chief technology adviser to the Democratic National Committee, became the new liberal savior. But it was clear that Walsh had learned the Left's politics of disingenuousness. Asked to describe the program content, he called it "centrist, with a hint of liberalism," a definition which I suspect he'd find equally applicable to the Reverend Al Sharpton. Walsh claimed that the backers of "Air America" were prepared to pour some $30 million into the radio venture.

Conservatives should hope that these liberal groups invest as much as possible in these schemes, for the millions of dollars that go into them will be millions of dollars that can't be spent on other liberal ventures. Besides, if a liberal is going to do something this stupid, he doesn't deserve to have that money.

While the mainstream media breathlessly reported the liberal talk-radio plan as some kind of revolutionary venture, the concept was hardly new. Liberals have tried making inroads into talk radio for years—and have failed miserably. Former New York governor Mario Cuomo, former Virginia governor Doug Wilder, and former Texas congressman Jim Hightower were all given national radio programs, and all were disasters. True, some liberal talk-show hosts have been successful on the local level, but in plenty of local markets liberal shows have not worked. Radio station managers all over the country have bowed to pressure from local liberal organizations and hired liberal talk-show hosts, only to cancel the shows in short order. Talk radio is entirely market driven. San Francisco, Boston, or Washington, D.C., may embrace a local liberal talk-show host, but America will continue to reject national ones.

If you doubt the lack of market interest in the liberal political conversation, explain the monumental business failure also known as National Public Radio (NPR). NPR was launched in 1970. Hundreds of stations and billions of dollars in federal, state, and private funding later, it should have established itself firmly, right? But if it is so successful, why does it come back to Congress every year begging for millions upon millions of dollars in federal handouts to prevent it from going under?

There are those who reject the NPR model as instructive of a viable liberal radio alternative to Rush and Company. The secret to Limbaugh's success, they point out, is his focus on entertainment, not polemics. A successful liberal response to Rush, they say, will come from those who emulate his style, not that of dour NPR.

And therein lies the conundrum. Liberalism *is* dour NPR. Liberalism looks at America and shakes its head in despair. It studies the culture of free enterprise and finds Enron in every successful business, with Ken Lay as the poster child for entrepreneurship. In liberalism's world, the free enterprise system is, for lack of a better word, greed. Liberalism sees America as not just flawed in its institutions, but faulty in its behavior. Liberalism has not forgiven America for leading the Free World against world socialism in the twentieth century. Even now, as the world continues to free itself from the yoke of totalitarianism, liberalism lurches forward, chasing not a dream but a disaster. The New Deal and the Great Society were experiments designed to bring social utopia; their programs were faithfully executed—and trillions of dollars later they are documented failures. World socialism would also lead us to the Promised Land but left in its wake nothing but poverty, oppression, and millions of dead. To be a liberal is to embrace a philosophical cadaver.

The right-thinking conservative has every reason to brim with confidence. He sees his philosophy—championing the freedoms bestowed by a Creator in pursuit of the virtue demanded for salvation—and knows it is the essence of the American miracle. The conservative would preserve the culture of free enterprise and the moral authority of the Judeo-Christian tradition, knowing they are what built and made America the most successful nation in the history of man. Oh, America is not flawless. The conservative will find flaws and will fight to correct them because he must, rejecting all temptation toward fatalism, for to surrender hope is to sin against God. He is patient but understands Burke's admonition that "there is, however, a limit at which forbearance ceases to be a virtue." The conservative sees challenges and finds in them opportunities. He throws himself with brio into the arena with the wind of success at his back and with golden horizons ahead, cognizant of his duty to his progeny, to his forefathers, and to his God. The conservative will tell you, as the poet told us a century past, that "the world's as ugly, ay, as Sin / And almost as delightful."

Acknowledgments

THERE ARE APPROXIMATELY 66 studies and 607 quotations cited in this book to prove the leftist influence dominating the American media. I did not document this bias; that is the work product of the research staff at the Media Research Center, the brightest group of media analysts in the business. Headed by Brent Baker, and with a healthy assist from Rich Noyes, this team today includes Geoff Dickens, Jessica Anderson, Brian Boyd, Brad Wilmouth, Ken Shepherd, Patrick Gregory, Clay Waters, and Amanda Monson, with Kristina Sewell serving as research associate extraordinaire. But in order for this state-of-the-art research operation to be in place there is the need for the funding, always the funding. So I thank the benefactors of the Media Research Center, past and present, for making this work possible.

Tim Jones spent the better part of a year slogging through the data, culling and sharpening the book's presentation: This book would not have been possible without his help. Tim Graham, meanwhile, has been doing that for me for a decade; only God knows how many times I've turned to him for assistance. I offer my gratitude to them both profusely, as I do to Darlene Nelson and Helen Fullinwider, who learned to roll their eyes in disbelief *after* I turned away from them, promising that *this*, the eleventh draft, was the *very last rewrite* they were being asked to prepare for the publishers.

One of the benefits of working on a book like this is the opportunity to work with some of the best in the business. I recognize, and thank, Alex Hoyt, the agent who arranged my marriage to Crown Forum for this work. I recognize, and love, my mother, Patricia Bozell, who has now edited virtually every important author in the Western world—and me. I recognize, and can't thank enough, Crown Forum editor Jed Donahue, who just dazzles with his critiques. I also thank Steve Ross, Crown's publisher, for his faith in my book. And what a staff he has at Crown: production editor Jim Walsh, production manager Leta Evanthes, editorial assistant Mario Rojas, copy editor Laurie McGee, and publicists Brian Belfiglio and Teresa Brady—all excel at making the author appear far more learned than he deserves.

I thank my five children—David, Brent IV, Joey, Caitlin, and Reid—for their patience, especially when everyone was asked to "Keep it down!" because their father was working and never mind that we were on vacation at the beach. In equal measure I thank their mother and my wife, Norma, for all her encouragement and for the patience of an angel throughout.

Finally, I thank Peter, Dan, Tom, Aaron, and Co.; the folks at *Time, Newsweek*, and *U.S. News & World Report*; the *New York Times*, the *Washington Post, USA Today*, and so on; and let's not forget PBS and NPR.

Without you I'd be unemployed.

Index

About the Author

L. BRENT BOZELL III is the founder and president of the Media Research Center, the largest media watchdog organization in America. He is regularly invited to provide media expertise for all of the major television networks, the cable news channels, and hundreds of radio programs, including NPR's *Morning Edition*, the *Sean Hannity Show*, and the *Rush Limbaugh Show*. Bozell is also a nationally syndicated writer whose work appears in publications such as the *Wall Street Journal*, the *Washington Post*, the *Washington Times*, the *New York Post*, the *Los Angeles Times*, and *National Review*. His frequent speaking appearances take him to college campuses and civic and political organizations around the country. As the founder and president of the Parents Television Council, he leads the only Hollywood-based organization dedicated to restoring responsibility to the entertainment industry. Bozell lives with his wife and five children near Washington, D.C.